N. ELDON TANNER
His Life and Service

G. HOMER DURHAM

With the collaboration of
Glen M. Leonard, Steven L. Olsen, Dale F. Beecher,
Donald L. Enders, William Hale Kehr, James L. Kimball, Jr.,
Gordon I. Irving, and Associates

Deseret Book Company
Salt Lake City, Utah

©1982 Deseret Book Company
All rights reserved
Printed in the United States of America
First printing July 1982

Library of Congress Cataloging in Publication Data
Durham, G. Homer (George Homer), 1911-
  N. Eldon Tanner, his life and service.

  Bibliography: p.
  Includes index.
  1. Tanner, N. Eldon (Nathan Eldon), 1898-
2. Mormons—Utah—Salt Lake City—Biography. 3. Salt
Lake City (Utah)—Biography. 4. Statesmen—Alberta—
Biography. 5. Alberta—Biography. 6. Executives—
Canada—Biography. I. Title.
BX8695.T284D87   1982   289.3'3 [B]   82-9681
ISBN 0-87747-913-5

Contents

APPENDICES

Preface

This volume is an effort to outline some of the clearly visible events and related circumstances in the life of Nathan Eldon Tanner. It will be clear that the texture, color, and character of the life require larger canvas, finer pigments, more skilled artists than could be supplied by the undersigned and those who collaborated in the effort. Nevertheless, the effort had to be made in order that there could develop wider and greater understanding of President Tanner than was previously available for a growing audience beyond his family and intimate associates.

That something more extensive be done than existed in available sketches was urged on President Tanner by his family. Finally, his diffidence gave way and his consent was given. Accordingly, after two conferences with him, I convened a group of collaborators on January 23, 1981, presented an outline and sample materials to them, and invited their assistance. The response was willing and enthusiastic. I then requested and secured encouraging suggestions from President Gordon B. Hinckley, then of the Council of the Twelve, and Elder Boyd K. Packer of that council. With their concurrence I then sought and obtained the hearty consent of President Spencer W. Kimball. At the same time it must be strictly understood that this was not undertaken as a Church-sponsored or authorized book, and that these leaders bear no responsibility for its contents.

Preface

We are indebted to President Tanner, his wife, Sara M. Tanner, and his five daughters for making available life sketches prepared at various times, chiefly since 1962, as well as pictures, photograph albums, scrapbooks, memorabilia, and family mementos. President Tanner kindly provided access to available copies of his diary. His secretary, LaRue Sneff, provided unusual help, especially her 1973 compilation of his addresses, *Seek Ye First the Kingdom of God,* and a valuable oral history. Some oral histories were available and others were requested and enthusiastically recorded, reviewed by interviewee, transcribed, and have found place in the Church Archives. Among them are contributions from James Saks, assistant to President Tanner in the oil business and Trans-Canada Pipeline; B. Z. Kastler, chairman of the board of Mountain Fuel Supply Company; Douglas H. Smith, president of Beneficial Life; Irwin Tanner, President Tanner's brother; Charles Ursenbach, counselor to President Tanner in the Calgary Stake; J. Howard Dunn of Zion's Securities Corporation; J. Alan Blodgett of the Church Financial Department; Wilford W. Kirton, Jr., general Church counsel; Isabelle Tanner Jensen; and the Honorable Ernest C. Manning, former Prime Minister of Alberta, Canada. Mary C. Livingstone, President Tanner's secretary during his years as Cabinet Minister and as oil company and pipeline executive, contributed a valuable life sketch. Dr. McCown E. Hunt of Salt Lake City provided an insightful interview, several conversations, and the descriptive essay that appears as an appendix. Many others responded to correspondence and assisted in a number of ways.

The chief collaborators are recognized in footnote entries that appear on the chapters to which they contributed. Much of the work would have been impossible without the help of Gordon Irving, director of the James Moyle Oral History Program of the Church Historical Department. Ronald D. Watt and Dean C. Jessee contributed memoranda in the initial stages. Isabelle Tanner Jensen and Ruth Tanner Walker made available important materials and also suggested a number of clarifying details in reading drafts of the manuscript. Eudora Widtsoe Durham read and corrected typograpical errors in the final draft and helped clarify meanings not immediately apparent to the general reader. Mrs. Beth S. Rasmussen typed various drafts of the manuscript. Finally, the help provided by Lowell M. Durham, Jr., Eleanor Knowles, Ralph Reynolds, and other members of the staff of Deseret Book was indispensable.

I assume personal responsibility for errors, omissions, shortcomings, and all failures short of a worthy result. All who have participated have said many times how much they have been enriched by reviewing President Tanner's life. This book has been an effort to bring together in one place the story of a remarkable man's life. Others are invited to enlarge the work, as free enterprise, where this falls short.

G. HOMER DURHAM
May 1982

N. ELDON TANNER
His Life and Service

CANADA

ALBERTA
PROVINCE

•EDMONTON

•CALGARY

•LETHBRIDGE

HILL SPRING
•
•CARDSTON

BRITISH COLUMBIA
WASHINGTON

IDAHO

SASKATCHEWAN
MONTANA

THE UNITED STATES

1

The Beginnings

In 1970 Professor William Kilbourne of Canada's York University published a 222-page volume entitled *Pipeline: Trans-Canada and the Great Debate, A History of Business and Politics.*[1] Holder of a B.A. in history at Toronto, an M.A. from Oxford, and a Ph.D. from Harvard, he titled Chapter 5 of the book "A Strange Story." The first paragraph of that strange story begins as follows:

> Let us begin with a skill-testing question. What Canadian born in humble circumstances, a teacher by profession who rose to be a Bishop, became head of one of the most important organizations in the country, then retired from his position to become a foreign missionary, and finally was chosen to be operating head of a world-wide church? Conceivably, one answer to this question might be Paul-Emile Cardinal Léger. He left his teaching post in Rome to run the great archdiocese of Montreal, which he in turn gave up for an African leper colony. He could become the first Canadian Pope. But if he does, he will not be the first but rather the second man to answer the description. The correct reply to the question is in fact Nathan Eldon Tanner of the Church of Jesus Christ of Latter-day Saints, an Alberta schoolteacher and Mormon bishop who became first chief executive of Trans-Canada Pipe Lines, left in his prime to become a Mormon missionary full time, and in 1965 became Counsellor to the ninety-five-year-old formal head of the Mormon Church, President David O. McKay, Prophet, Seer, Revelator and Trustee-in-Trust, lineal successor to Brigham Young, and in Mormon belief capable of receiving direct revelations from God.

On Sunday, July 27, 1980, a special "Business Portrait" feature of the Salt Lake *Tribune* appeared under the headline "At 82, President Tanner Looks Back Over an Eventful Lifetime of Service to Church and Nation." The article covered nearly a full page of that edition. It began with reporting the judgment that over the years, there had been mutterings that the Mormon Church was against industrial development. Then, "In the late 1960's President Nathan Eldon Tanner, counselor in the First Presidency of the Church of Jesus Christ of Latter-day Saints, stated the Church's view."

"Industrial development," he said, "even development originating from out of the state is welcome. The only concern would be that it would be qualitative development and that the immigrants would also be good fiber." The feature then went on to describe how in the years since that statement, Utah had gone through "explosive industrial growth and diversification," including the 1974-1975 recession when "Utah fared far better than the nation as a whole." It predicted that despite the double-digit inflation threat of the 1980s, Utah would probably ride out such a problem in like manner.

In 1978 President Tanner was honored by a large banquet in the Grand Ballroom of the Hotel Utah, organized by the Salt Lake Area Chamber of Commerce. He received the Chamber's "Giant in Our City" award. With modesty and characteristic diffidence, but warmly appreciative, he accepted the award with a few well-chosen words at the climax of the evening.

The Salt Lake *Tribune* feature concluded by noting that President Tanner had lived for more than half of the 150-year history of the Church; that he was born before men flew; that he had flown over the oceans many, many times. Then the writer asked: "What does it all mean?" His response came in two short, concluding paragraphs:

"President Tanner reverts to the majestic King Jamesian syntax: 'Seek ye first the Kingdom of God and His righteousness.'

"Then back to the 20th Century: 'Do the best you can in whatever you do.' "

4

These words represent guidelines that have marked the life of a man whose character was formed on a Canadian homestead in Alberta, a man of whom Dr. McCown E. Hunt, past member of the Salt Palace board of directors in Salt Lake City, said: "If we had forty men like Eldon Tanner spread around the globe, the problems of this world would be reduced by about fifty per cent."[2]

The background for settlement of Alberta, Canada, by Europeans was laid by French explorers in the eighteenth century. Others appeared in the same century to extend the fur trade. Hudson's Bay Company and the North West Company built trading posts after 1775. In 1821 the two companies merged. Hudson's Bay Company, the successor, controlled and governed the area from 1821 until 1870. Following the passage of the British North America Act of 1867 by the British Parliament, the region became part of the then Dominion of Canada. Settlements in the ranching economy of southern Alberta began after 1870. The Indian tribes had been placed on reservations. In 1874, the North West Royal Mounted Police established Fort Macleod. The following year Calgary was established one hundred miles north as a Mounted Police outpost. The railroad reached Calgary in 1883, leading to an influx of settlers from eastern Canada, the United States, and Europe to secure cheap or free land. By the time Eldon Tanner was born in 1898, the population was about seventy thousand. A wheat-based economy was developing and expanding; particularly was this true after 1904, when agricultural science produced an early ripening wheat that made production less hazardous in those latitudes.

In the spring of 1886 Charles Ora Card, president of the Cache Stake of The Church of Jesus Christ of Latter-day Saints, was settled comfortably in Logan, Utah. The Territory of Utah, created in 1850 by the Congress of the United States, was subject to federal control from Washington, D.C. Particularly onerous to Latter-day Saint settlers of Utah Territory was the Edmunds Act of 1882, which was aimed at the practice of plural marriage, and which extended unusual political controls, with subsequent tensions. John Taylor, who had succeeded Brigham Young as President of the Church following the latter's death in 1877, called Charles Ora Card in 1886 "to explore British Columbia with a view of founding a settlement of the Saints as a place of refuge for certain families who were driven into exile by the Edmunds law."[3]

From that exploration mission developed the Mormon settlements of Southern Alberta and the setting of the scene for the birth of Eldon Tanner. Accompanied by James W. Hendrix and Isaac E. D. Zundell, President Card found that accessible lands in British Columbia were unavailable. In October 1886 they met a mountaineer named McDonald who described empty "grass-covered plains to the east of the continental divide." The Mormon "scouts" took the train east to Calgary. By team and wagon a site was eventually located at Lee's Creek. On October 25, 1886, prayer was offered to confirm their selection. Following the prayer, Charles O. Card announced to his companions, "Brethren, this is the place."[4]

Returning to Utah, President Card was instructed by President Taylor to select forty families "and lead them there as soon as possible."[5] The first small group left March 23, 1887, and established what by October 1888 became known as Cardston. In 1890 Charles O. Card was released as Cache Stake president and was designated president of the Canadian Mission. On April 10, 1895, he was set apart as president of the Alberta Stake by Wilford Woodruff, who had succeeded to the leadership of the Church following the death of John Taylor in 1877, and President Woodruff's counselors, with George Q. Cannon being mouth. The membership of the new Canadian stake was less than seven hundred. John A. Woolf and Stirling Williams became counselors in the stake presidency at a conference held May 27, 1895.

Word of the productive land of Canada reached Salt Lake

City and a young man named Nathan William Tanner. Born October 19, 1870, in Wanship, Summit County, Utah, he and his twin brother, George, were sons of John W. and Lucy Snyder Tanner in a family of ten children. John W. Tanner was a grandson of John Tanner, the first Tanner to affiliate with the Latter-day Saints.

On July 14, 1896, Nathan William Tanner began his first journey to Cardston, Alberta. Impressed by what he found, he bought shares in the Alberta Land and Livestock Company, then returned to Salt Lake City for the winter. There, on April 28, 1897, he married his childhood sweetheart, Sarah Edna Brown, in the Salt Lake Temple. Sarah Edna was a granddaughter of Captain James Brown, member of the Mormon Battalion and, like John Tanner, a great pioneer.[6] The young couple left for Canada June 2, 1897, to establish their first home—a log shelter built into the side of a hill. A one-room affair, it had to accommodate the needs of the young couple and an uncle, Henry Tanner, who had accompanied them. The hill provided one wall of the shelter. Its slopes contributed to log-supported sides and a log front. While Nathan William sought a living by breaking horses and developing the land, Sarah Edna prepared for her firstborn through the winter and spring of 1897-98. It was anything but an attractive place for a young woman to bring forth her firstborn child. The homestead was three miles from the tiny settlement of Aetna, with Cardston seven miles to the south. And neither Uncle Henry nor Nathan William was prepared for the requirements of such an experience. As Sarah Edna's time drew near, the decision was made that she should return to Salt Lake City to give birth to the child at her mother's comfortable home. She was taken from the ranch to Lethbridge by team, and from there she took the train to Salt Lake City for the blessed event.

So it was that Nathan Eldon Tanner came to be born in Salt Lake City, Utah, on May 9, 1898, in his grandfather's home, the Homer Manley Brown house on Second South and Redwood Road. And thus he was born in the United States of America. The fact that Canadian citizenship would bring him into later

Sara Edna Brown Tanner with her firstborn son, Nathan Eldon, who was born May 9, 1898, in Salt Lake City

prominence, and that his life and service would be shared with the two nations and much of the world, was not foreseen in those early years when the homestead was only a few miles north of the Montana border.

The Salt Lake City *Deseret Evening News* for Monday, May 9, 1898, proclaimed the motto "Truth and Liberty" on its front-page masthead. It also appealed to readers with the assertion "The evening paper is the paper of today. The morning paper is the paper of yesterday."

Page one featured items from the Spanish-American War: "Dewey Asks for Order." "Plan of the Campaign: Admiral Sampson Is Under Orders to Attack and Capture Porto Rico." "To Resist to the Death" headlined a dispatch describing an order of the Spanish government to its Governor-General in the Philippines.

The flavor of life in Salt Lake City was far different from the log hut in the Canadian hillside. A half-page, seven-column notice of Madsen's Furniture Store, at 51, 53, 55 East First South Street, stated the store would offer "Every Day This Week Bargains Which Cannot Be Approached in This Market." "Carpets and *great* wallpaper," but no sod roofs, were advertised. Religious services had been held in the Tabernacle at two o'clock the day preceding Eldon Tanner's birth. Sunday Schools had convened in the various Salt Lake City ward buildings at 10:00 A.M. Sacrament meetings in the same twenty-four wards of the city, as well as in the Center, Farmers, Cannon, and Forest Dale wards, were at 6:30 P.M. There was an East Brighton Branch and a Twenty-Second Branch, the latter in Sugarhouse. German and Scandinavian meetings were being held in the Assembly Hall. All were part of one stake, the Salt Lake Stake.

Money was available at 2.5 to 3 percent interest in New York. The British pound stood at $4.845. Fresh butter sold for 15 cents a pound, cheese for nine cents. R. K. Thomas's Dry Goods Store offered "ladies' waists" at 25 cents each. "Dress skirts" were listed at "prices to suit all purses." Kid gloves were 35 cents a pair. The Oliver R. Meredith Company at 29 East First South offered missionary discounts on valises and handbags. At Thomas's, men's elegant black calf shoes in three styles sold at $2.50 a pair plus a "written guarantee with each pair."

Such were the times when Sarah Edna Brown Tanner, wife of Nathan William Tanner of Aetna, Alberta, Canada, gave birth to her black-haired baby boy. He was destined to emerge as a truly significant administrative and financial genius, serving the government of Alberta, presiding over Merrill Petroleums and the Trans-Canada Pipeline, and later a counselor in the First

Presidency to four Presidents of The Church of Jesus Christ of Latter-day Saints: David O. McKay, Joseph Fielding Smith, Harold B. Lee, and Spencer W. Kimball. No awkward, untrained male hands, but assisting at the birth of N. Eldon Tanner was the excellent Latter-day Saint midwife, Dr. Ellis Shipp. And standing by to help, had the doctor not arrived, was the newborn child's fourteen-year-old uncle, Hugh B. Brown. Their paths were to intertwine for subsequent decades in marvelous ways. Hugh later wrote, "My first recollection of Eldon was his birth cry, as I waited to help if needed. Ever since that time there has been a bond between us, as I instinctively recognized a child of promise."[7]

When he was about six weeks old, Eldon was taken to the Canadian land of promise with his mother. They traveled by train to Lethbridge, by wagon to the ranch. En route the train was robbed. "The robbers took everything valuable except the baby," recalled Edna. Delays occurred. But they arrived during the long Canadian June days, which brought sunlight and reunion with Nathan William. When the new father met them, he looked at the babe and said, with some of the humor for which he was well-known in the family, "Is that the best you can do?" In retrospect, it was to turn out to be a most remarkable production.

While Eldon's parents were both native Utahns, his grandfather, John William Tanner, had been born November 6, 1841, in the Mormon settlement of Montrose, Lee County, Iowa. His grandmother, Lucy Rhona Snyder, was born August 28, 1848, in St. Joseph, Hancock County, Missouri. On the maternal side, grandfather Homer Manley Brown was a native of Salt Lake City, born in the early pioneer days, June 10, 1854. He married another Brown, Lydia Jane Brown. She was born in Ogden, Weber County, Utah, August 10, 1855.

Eldon never knew his Grandfather Tanner, who died in Montpelier, Idaho, January 13, 1893. His other three grandparents, Lucy Snyder Tanner, Homer Manley Brown, and Lydia Jane Brown, lived until 1917, 1936, and 1935, respectively, adding dimension to his ancestral understanding. And the stirring examples of great-great-grandfather John Tanner and great-grandfather James S. Brown of the Mormon Battalion were part of his cultural inheritance. One of his ancestors twelve generations back, Francis Cooke, came to America on the *Mayflower*. Based on the documentary verification submitted, Nathan Eldon Tanner was officially enrolled March 31, 1966, on the Plymouth, Massachusetts, Register of the Mayflower Society as Number 29,706, and on the Utah Register as Number 139.

Other distinguished names in Eldon's ancestry include Stewart, Smith, Snyder, Comstock, Hatch, Barker, Mumford, Cook, Warren, Woolf, Devoe, and Stephens. As a member of the First Presidency he recorded, "I have always been so thankful that John Tanner remained true to the Church and that his grandson William and his son Nathan William, who is my father, all remained true to the Church. As a result, I feel I am here where I am today."[8]

In his mature years President Tanner described his father as a most faithful, devoted, honest man. Said he, "I don't think I ever met a man who was liked by everybody and disliked by nobody more than my father." He recalled his father's description of the original homestead in Canada as a place "where the government bet` a quarter section of land against $10 that you couldn't make a go of it." His sister-in-law Ida Capson Tanner recalled from the upbringing of Nathan William, her father-in-law, "One thing of this childhood home is certain: It instilled religious training and deep-rooted desire to search for truth." This quality descended to Nathan Eldon, eldest of the eight children born to Nathan William and Sarah Edna Brown Tanner, whom Ida described as "a splendid woman."[9]

The other seven children, following Eldon, were William Irwin, Leroy B., Hugh Henry, Lucy Lydia, Evelyn Edna, James Lynn, and Beth. A mother and father tend to place great reliance on the eldest child in large families. Such reliance was not misplaced in the firstborn of the Tanners.

The Prophet Joseph Smith proclaimed the glory of God to be intelligence, or light and truth, providing an inspiring, far-

11

reaching, and challenging basis for religious faith. The Tanner source of this religious impulse in Eldon's inheritance deserves brief telling.

John Tanner, born at Hopkinton, Rhode Island, August 15, 1778, was the first of a long line of Tanners in The Church of Jesus Christ of Latter-day Saints. He was eleven years old when George Washington became the new nation's first president in 1789. In 1791 the family moved to Greenwich, New York, forty miles north of Albany. New York State then had a population of 340,000; the Union had reached a population of about four million. In Greenwich John married Lydia Stewart in the fall of 1801. Seventeen years later, with a family of six, he moved to the Lake George area of New York.[10]

Thirty miles long by three miles wide, Lake George was a favorite waterway for Indians, trappers, and combatants of the French and Indian War. The novels of Kenneth Roberts portray much of life in those days, including Fort William Henry. The one-hundred-mile waterway formed by Lake Champlain and Lake George was used by the English and French in their attacks upon each other during the power struggle for control of the continent. This finally resulted in the defeat of France and her withdrawal from North America, establishing influences for the federal-provincial issues faced by N. Eldon Tanner, John's great-great-grandson.

Mormon missionaries came into the Lake George area in 1832. Their message provided a new spiritual life and a miraculous restoration for the physically impaired body of John Tanner. The testimony he gained has borne fruit. In 1981 Eldon noted that his Mormon pioneer ancestor had more than twenty thousand descendants. Many gained prominence in Arizona, Utah, Idaho, Canada, and other parts of North America. The conversion of John Tanner, a devout Baptist, has been described by a son:

My father, through hardship and exposure, had contracted a disease that broke out in sores on his leg, similar to fever sores.

This had troubled him for years, and finally became so bad that he was deprived of the use of it, and for months had not put it to the floor. He had a couple of doctors examine it, but they decided that the leg could not be saved, and must be amputated or it would prove his death. To this he could not consent, but said he and the leg would go together. At this he set out making arrangements to settle up his business affairs. He heard that a strange people called Mormons, who were going about turning the world upside down, were going to preach about seven miles from where he lived. Fearing that they might get away with some of the Baptist brethren, of whom he had the watch care, he had his horse and cart made ready; and he had to have his foot bolstered as high as his seat to keep the swelling from going into the foot. When he heard the Mormons, he found they had the truth, and he told his Baptist friends they had better not fight against it, lest haply find themselves fighting against God.

He bought a Book of Mormon and took it home with him. He heard Elders Simeon and Jared Carter preach. Elder Carter told him if he read the book and believed it, he should see an alteration in his leg. He read the book over and over again and compared it with the Bible. When he had decided that it was the work of the Lord, he set his foot on the floor and ordered his horse and cart, and went to notify the people of a meeting at his house the next day. He was out five hours. Then the Elders came, and when they learned that father had made up his mind that the book was what it represented to be, Elder Jared Carter asked him if he had seen any change in his leg. Father then remembered that when he decided that it was the work of the Lord, he put his foot down for the first time in months. Elder Carter then asked father if he would be afraid to put his foot down if he (Carter) commanded him in the name of the Lord to rise and walk. Father did not reply, and the Elder said, "In the name of Jesus Christ I command you to arise and walk," at the same time clasping his hand on father's shoulder. At this, father arose to his feet. Said the Elder, "You need not be afraid to put down your foot. Remember, you do it in the name of the Lord." Father laid aside his crutch and walked back and forth from the front porch through a long hall and into the long kitchen. All this time he wept and praised God for his mercy in bringing the gospel and its attending blessings. The next day my father, mother and myself were baptized.[11]

Following John Tanner's conversion, he and his family participated in the trials of Kirtland, Ohio; Zion's Camp and Far West, Missouri; Nauvoo, Illinois; Winter Quarters, Iowa; the crossing of the plains; and the settlement of the West. The Tanner legacy was one of hard work, generosity, and integrity. John sold most of his land holdings in Bolton, New York, to gather with the Saints in Kirtland. It had been said that he sold his possessions and traveled to Kirtland in response to a dream that he was needed by the Church in the West. On Christmas Day 1834 he commenced his journey. It was some five hundred miles to Kirtland, and he arrived in midwinter, January 20, 1835.

John was impressed to go immediately to the place where the Prophet Joseph Smith and some of the brethren were meeting. In prayer they had asked the Lord to send them someone with means to assist in lifting the mortgage on the farm upon which the temple was to be built. The next day, John and his son Sidney met with the high council. The mortgage was about to be foreclosed. John loaned the Prophet two thousand dollars and the farm was redeemed. Later, he loaned the temple committee, headed by Hyrum Smith, Reynolds Cahoon, and Jared Carter, thirteen thousand dollars in merchandise, taking their note for security. In addition, he made liberal donations to the building of the temple.[12]

There is no evidence that any of these loans were repaid. Later, when John moved his family to Missouri to build up Zion there, he had a "borrowed team, one old broken down stage horse, an old turnpike cart, a keg of powder, and $7.50 in cash," according to his son Nathan. But these sacrifices brought blessings to numbers of his posterity, who were independent, hardworking individuals, for in Nauvoo, the Prophet Joseph Smith laid his hand upon John Tanner's shoulder and said: "God bless you, Father Tanner, your children shall never beg bread."[13] Such were the forebears of the son of Nathan William and Sarah Brown Tanner.

After their beginnings in the log hut, Nathan William Tanner moved his little family to nearby Aetna. Life in the hillside log shelter near Aetna, a hamlet of about one hundred inhabit-

N. Eldon Tanner, right, and his younger brother Irwin

ants, was primitive. According to Irwin Tanner, there may have been (with generous count) two or three hundred people within a five-mile radius. He remembered the village itself as having a dozen homes, a two-room school, a church house, and a store.[14] There was no plumbing or electricity. The only source of hot water was in a boiler on the stove. There were no newspapers, telephones, or library.

Eldon's early life was filled with the numerous responsibilities and labors attendant upon dry-farming wheat and oats in the frontier setting that developed with his pioneering parents. In times of drought, prayers for rain were frequent, for in time his father operated five or six sections of land in addition to his own farm. Horses and horsemanship were vital to such a life. Almost as soon as Eldon could walk, he was put on a horse. He remembers, as a boy of twelve, being sent by his father to haul grain seven and a half miles to the grain elevators. At fourteen he drove the route with two wagons and four head of horses. He learned the meaning and value of long days, hard work, and the use of time. His best teacher in his early life, he has said, was his father, who was also his bishop.

> Faithful always in his church duties, my father tried to instill this same desire in me to attend my meetings and perform my assignments. When I was a deacon we had to travel eight miles to attend priesthood meeting and the general stake priesthood meeting, which was held once a month on Saturday. We had no cars or trucks, but only wagons and buggies.
>
> Father used to make those trips pay both ways. For instance, he would drive a team and wagon full of wheat, and I would follow him with a team and wagon full of wheat, taking a little more than two hours to go eight miles. We went early enough to unload the wheat and load our wagons with coal to take home after the meeting. But we never missed the priesthood meeting.[15]

There were other lessons learned in the home of Nathan William and Edna that, although based in Latter-day Saint doctrine, could sometimes be set aside or conveniently forgotten by some fellow members. That lesson involved the basic doctrine that all mankind are the children of God, brothers and sisters. This lesson was to play a vital role in Eldon's service in the First Presidency. Ruth Tanner Walker described it as follows:

> At one time my grandparents had a Chinese cook in their home. This was very unusual in Cardston and of great interest to everyone. They marveled that there was no race prejudice in the Tanner family. They loved this Chinese helper and treated him as one of the family.
>
> This is possibly the reason my family is so unprejudiced. We were never taught to hate people because of the color of their skin or a difference in their customs and beliefs.[16]

As the eldest of eight, Eldon was expected to set a proper example for the younger members of the family. On one occasion, when his father was about to leave for the afternoon on Church business, he outlined several tasks for the boys to do during his absence. After he departed, the boys decided it would be great sport to ride some of the calves in the corral. They had so much fun that they did not notice the passage of time until their father stood before them. Seeing that they had not done their work, he merely walked over to Eldon and, instead of scolding or spanking him, said, "My boy, I thought I could depend on you." Eldon recalled, "I made up my mind at that moment that Father would never have reason to say that to me again as long as I lived and as long as he lived."[17]

In his youth he assumed responsibility beyond his years. As a young teenager, he contracted smallpox. Then after he recovered, the entire family became ill with the disease and neighbors refused to come near the home, for fear of the dreaded disease. For two nights and three days Eldon went without sleep, as he was the only one available to care for the family. On another occasion, when a younger sister suffered from spinal meningitis and was very ill, the importance of prayer was deeply impressed upon him when, as the family knelt by the sick one, his father said, "My boy, you are a deacon. We would like you to lead in prayer tonight and remember Lillie." Although the girl did not recover immediately, she began to improve and was eventually restored to her health, which Eldon felt was an answer to his prayer.

Eldon learned to ride early in life. He loved horses. Riding was recreation as well as a necessity. Boylike, he responded to a newspaper advertisement and bought a kit on how to train horses. He trained a mare to lie down, permit a person to mount, and then rise. According to his brother Irwin, this stunt was, on occasions, used to entertain a girl friend.

While herding cattle one day, at age fifteen, Eldon was thrown from his horse. When he got up, he found that three fingers of his left hand were broken. One was fractured so badly that the bone was protruding through the flesh. The fingers bent back against his hand. He straightened the fingers as best he

17

could, remounted his horse, and rode to a doctor, who admired his grit and marveled that the bones were correctly in place.

His schooling was often interrupted by harvesting and other farm work. Eldon completed his first nine grades in the little town of Aetna, some of it under the tutelage of Oswald A. Steele, Mattie Allred, and Miss Eastwood. His education in Aetna was in a two-room schoolhouse with no furnace or central heating, but a stove in each room. In the summer most children went barefoot out of choice or because they couldn't afford shoes. In the winter "German socks" one-half-inch thick were worn over four-buckle overshoes for working outside. Eldon's parents were not any better off financially, but they would not let him go barefoot to school. To the youngster this was a source of disappointment.

When Nathan William Tanner moved from Aetna to Cardston, it was to secure better schooling opportunities for his children. There, in addition to farming, he formed a partnership with Joe Low to sell McLaughlin cars. (The same line in the United States was Buick.) His son Irwin said that nobody had any money to buy cars, so the partners probably escaped riches in the venture.[18]

Although opportunities were limited, Eldon sought every chance for education. He described it:

> In our little town, they taught only through grade eight so when I completed that, I said to Dad, "I would like to go to grade nine." We went to talk to the principal of that two-room school, and he said, "If you can get five kids to take grade nine, I'll teach it."
>
> As fall approached, my father, though he was on the school board, said, "I need you to work on the farm." That was a little disappointing, but I went to the school principal and said, "If we come in after Christmas, will you teach us?" We had found four others who would be able to go also, and he said, "Yes."
>
> So I took my grade nine after Christmas, and later grade ten. While I went to grade eleven, I worked in a butcher shop, in the slaughter yards, building fences, or doing anything I could get to do, for twenty-five cents an hour. But I enjoyed it, and it did get me through my high school.[19]

Following these eleven grades, Eldon wanted to attend Normal School to qualify himself to teach. He had finished grade eleven at a Church school, the Knight Academy in Raymond, where he "batched" part of the time with his brother Irwin and Heber Jensen. Once at a school ball Eldon, a graceful dancer, won a waltz contest with Irwin's girl friend. Irwin seemed not to mind, for he considered himself a poor dancer anyway.

At other times Eldon worked for his board for Fred Piepgrass, helping at a butcher shop and at a slaughter yard, and as a general "roustabout." He had no money to continue his studies at Calgary Normal, nor did his father have any to give him. His experience in obtaining funds for this schooling taught him a valuable lesson:

> I couldn't save money at twenty-five cents an hour, not very much of it anyway. Father said, "If you can borrow the money, I'll spare you from the farm so you may go to Normal School." I went to the bank to see if I could borrow the money, and here I learned another great lesson.
>
> I trembled as I sat in the manager's office, waiting to see if I could borrow $400 to go to Normal School. Although I think he knew who I was, I told him my name was Tanner.
>
> He said, "Oh, are you so-and-so's boy?"
>
> "No, I am N. W. Tanner's boy."
>
> "N. W. Tanner's boy?"
>
> "Yes."
>
> "When can you pay this money back?"
>
> "I would pay it out of my first earnings when I start teaching school," I said.
>
> "Very well. If you are N. W. Tanner's boy, we'll let you have the money." . . . After that I wouldn't let my Dad's name down for anything.[20]

Significant consequences were to grow from that bank loan, the manager's trust, and the additional schooling. Eldon was able to attend Normal School in the fall of 1918. Irwin went also to study automobile engineering. Heber Jensen went with them, and again the three stayed together. The influenza epidemic caught them here. School was closed "for two or three weeks," according to Eldon, so the Normal School short course in which he was enrolled had to continue into January 1919.

Footnotes

[1]William Kilbourne, *Pipeline: Trans-Canada and the Great Debate, A History of Business and Politics* (Toronto and Vancouver: Clarke, Irwin and Co., Ltd., 1970).

[2]McCown E. Hunt to G. Homer Durham, June 17, 1981.

[3]See Melvin S. Tagg, "A History of The Church of Jesus Christ of Latter-day Saints in Canada, 1830-1963" (Ph.D. diss., Brigham Young University, May 1963), pp. 88ff.

[4]Ibid., pp. 95-96.

[5]Ibid.

[6]James S. Brown, *Giant of the Lord, Life of a Pioneer* (Salt Lake City: Bookcraft, 1960). James Brown was at Sutter's Fort January 24, 1848, when gold was discovered. He served a mission to Tahiti, 1850-52, and to Great Britain, 1860-62. He was born in Davidson County, North Carolina, July 4, 1828, and died in Salt Lake City March 25, 1902.

[7]Hugh B. Brown, "President N. Eldon Tanner, a Man of Integrity," *Ensign* 2 (November 1972): 13-14.

[8]N. Eldon Tanner, interview by Charles Ursenbach, 1973. James Moyle Oral History Program, Archives, Historical Department of The Church of Jesus Christ of Latter-day Saints. Hereafter cited as N. Eldon Tanner, Ursenbach interview.

[9]Ida Capson Tanner, "Life Sketch of Nathan W. Tanner," paper read for the seventieth birthday anniversary of N. W. Tanner, October 19, 1940.

[10]George S. Tanner, *John Tanner and His Family* (Salt Lake City: John Tanner Family Association, 1974), pp. 22-23.

[11]Ibid., pp. 51-52.

[12]Ibid.

[13]Ibid., p. 103.

[14]Gordon Irving, interview with Irwin Tanner, Salt Lake City, Utah, 1981.

[15]N. Eldon Tanner, *Seek Ye First the Kingdom of God*, comp. LaRue Sneff (Salt Lake City: Deseret Book, 1973), pp. 1-2. Hereafter referred to as *Seek Ye First.*

[16]Ruth Tanner Walker, "My Father" (talk delivered at Brigham Young University, June 12, 1980), pp. 10-11.

[17]Ibid., p. 2.

[18]Gordon Irving, interview with Irwin Tanner.

[19]N. Eldon Tanner, *Seek Ye First*, p. 12.

[20]Ibid., pp. 12-13.

2

Schoolteaching and Marriage, 1919-1927

Before he enrolled in Knight Academy, the Church school in Raymond, Eldon had gone to Cardston to register for grade eleven there. Romantically speaking, fate or his lucky stars may have taken him first to Cardston. Providentially speaking, it brought him his first recognizable glimpse of Sara ("Sally") Merrill. He has described that fateful visit to Cardston.

"While I was waiting to register I saw in the far corner of the room two girls talking. I asked my friend Ken Woolf who the beautiful girl was. He said it was Sally Merrill. I said, 'Someday I'm going to marry her.'"

Later that day his father called and told him he wanted him to go to Knight Academy in Raymond for grade eleven instead of to Cardston. Thus ended that first, never-to-be forgotten sight of Eldon's beloved Sally.

They both vividly recall the next time they met. In June the following year Sara went into Eldon's uncle's grocery store, the Cardston Trading Company, to buy some groceries. Eldon was working there during vacation time and waited on her. She is the only customer he remembers serving, and she doesn't remember anything else of that day. It is quite significant that although they didn't acknowledge each other, they both remember the meeting vividly.[1] But other forces were astir, for after Knight Academy, Calgary Normal School beckoned Eldon.

Sara Merrill had attended the same school, entering in the autumn of 1917. The Normal School prepared elementary teachers for Alberta.

After he graduated from the Normal School, Eldon was offered two jobs. One was at Hill Spring, the other at Rocky Ford, Alberta. Rocky Ford offered the higher salary, but there was no branch of the Church there. Accordingly, he accepted the position at Hill Spring, and at age twenty he became principal of the three-room school. It was to be a fateful year. He and Sara would both find themselves and each other in Hill Spring.

Sara Merrill was born in Lehi, Utah, October 8, 1899, a daughter of John Booth and Isabelle Elizabeth Gibb Merrill. In the summer of 1899 her parents moved to Magrath, Alberta, pursuant to a call from President Wilford Woodruff to go and help build houses for Church members who were settling in that area. Sara remembers living in a two-room house on two and a half acres in Magrath. As the family grew, a lean-to would be added, and eventually the house had two front rooms, a lean-to across the entire back, and a smaller lean-to for a bedroom that extended about one-third of the way of the first lean-to. Her father made his living as a carpenter. He was not always paid in cash, but sometimes received nursery stock, which he planted. Accordingly, their lot featured trees of all kinds as well as shrubs and flowers. On the floor were hand-woven rag rugs. Straw ticks were used for mattresses, with the straw being replaced each autumn. Coal oil lamps provided them with light. Sara remembers that the family always seemed to be running out of coal oil or breaking a lamp chimney.

Their family life included the hearty celebration of Dominion Day on July 1 and Christmas. Sara always had a new dress for Dominion Day. One of her favorite dresses received for one celebration was a pale blue voile. Christmas Eve was usually spent with the entire family at Aunt Jehzell Merkley's home. These get-togethers were complete with Christmas trees, visits by Santa Claus, and the exchanging of gifts. However, as the children became old enough to know about Santa Claus, they received no more presents. As Sara remembers, "Christmas was for children."[2]

In 1907 John Booth Merrill was called on a mission to his native England. He left behind his wife and six small children: Jehzell, aged 13; Gwen, 11; Sara, 9; Magrath, 8; Booth, 6; and Don, 4. Florence was born one month after his departure. Another daughter, Emma, had died earlier of pneumonia at eight months; her place in the family was between Don and Florence. As is often the case, John Merrill returned from England with gifts and new perspective. He brought Nottingham lace curtains and an Axminster rug for the house. And Magrath no longer seemed the best arena for his ambitions and the welfare of his family. Soon after his return, he traded his property in Magrath for a building site in Hill Spring. The Hill Spring property was part of the 66,000-acre Cochran Ranch purchased by the Church to encourage members to secure land for farming on easy terms. In Hill Spring he began a nursery business.

Sara learned early the power of prayer. When she was ten, she was asked to babysit some younger cousins while their parents attended a church conference in nearby Raymond. According to her report, "All went well till it began to get dusk. I was afraid to light the coal oil lamp, and I was also afraid to go the six or seven blocks home if it got any darker; so I gathered the children together and we prayed for [our parents] to get home. When we arose from our knees, there the parents were at the gate."[3]

The reality of spiritual powers was again impressed upon her on an occasion when her sister Gwen's eyes had become so sensitive to light that she preferred to sit in a darkened corner than suffer the pain inflicted by even indirect sunlight. The entire family fasted for her health, and that night she emerged from her corner for the first time in days. Her eyes were completely healed, and she did not need to wear glasses to correct her vision until much later in life.

There were no girl friends of Sara's age in Hill Spring. As a result, she devoted a great deal of time to reading "anything I could get hold of." On one occasion she read a French novel borrowed from an adult in town. Her father was so shocked that he burned it. In her own words, she "got a Scotch blessing."[4] Despite this indiscretion, she numbered books among her dearest and most frequent companions while growing up.

Only eight grades were available in Hill Spring. Completing these, she went to Cardston, where, skipping grade nine, she took grades ten and eleven. She had Lila Little and Jennie Beazer as close friends, and roomed with them the first year. She also developed a close companionship with Fannie Duce, young wife of Will Duce, whose first wife had died, leaving him with three small boys. She and her two roommates paid five dollars a month for their room in the Duce home.

Sara was sixteen when she went to Cardston. Most boys she knew at the time seemed to be "a nuisance or too old."[5] But this did not last long. In company with others in their late teens, she had many dates with many fine young male friends by the time she left in September 1917 for Normal School in Calgary.

Except for Salt Lake City, which she had visited eight years earlier, Calgary was the first large city she had ever seen. Here she experienced for the first time railroad trains, hotels, electric lights, and indoor plumbing. She arrived in Calgary with two hundred dollars from her father. This amount was designed to last for four months. But she confessed buying a new coat for forty dollars (a ridiculously high price for the day) and a new hat. She further confessed that she generally acted as though she had never had any money before—which, she added, "I hadn't." The result was that she was without funds after two months. Her father sent another hundred dollars with the firm instruction that it was to last for the rest of the term. It did, though she did have to borrow money to return home. The loan was repaid out of the first paycheck she received from her first teaching post.

At the Normal School Sara had boyfriends who took her to the Pantages or Orpheum theaters or for rides in their new cars. In particular she remembers Reed and Lucien Kenny. "They used to take turns coming into town from their ranch every weekend, and as their father had a beautiful McLaughlin Buick Special car, I was thrilled to go out each weekend with whichever one was in town. . . . As the elder Kennys liked me, the boys could always have the car to take me out, so I was quite the envy of the other girls at the Normal School."[6]

After graduation she received her first teaching post, in Mountain View. Life in that rural community was in sharp contrast to life in bustling Calgary. The new schoolmarm boarded at the home of Albert Henderson and made friends with Chauncey Snow, a grandson of President Lorenzo Snow. He, however, was soon called into the Canadian Air Force for duty in World War I.

From Mountain View, Sara received an offer to teach in Hill Spring, at the same school where Eldon Tanner had recently been made principal. She was to replace a teacher who had become ill and had to leave the profession. Eldon later wrote: "That's where I fell in love with Sara and actually tried to get her to marry me." He added, in a biographical memorandum to his daughter Ruth years later, "I was not a good enough salesman."[7] The romance did not have time to blossom. At the end of the school year Eldon went to work on a local haying project, which kept him traveling most of the summer. In the fall, Sara went to Magrath to teach, while Eldon remained at the Hill Spring school. "We found it just a little difficult to do our courting while she was in Magrath and I was in Hill Spring," he later noted.[8]

Sara remembers that her courtship with Eldon was dull, "judging from the standards of today."[9] She was not particularly anxious to marry, since she did not consider many of the marriages happy that she observed. She also needed time to think about this new man who had burst into her life. She followed the counsel of her patriarchal blessing to pray about any contemplated marriage. She came to realize the blessing's promise that she would know the correctness of her decision to marry. She has written: "I have been so much more fortunate in my marriage than nearly anyone I know that I feel very thankful. I have had many evidences of God's goodness to me in other ways. It seems that all my prayers have been answered."[10]

25

The courtship was continued intermittently during that year. Eldon went to Magrath twice, once en route to a teachers convention in Lethbridge and once expressly to see Sally, as he affectionately called her.

In November 1919 they arranged to meet in Cardston. Eldon had borrowed a horse from a man named Harker and rode to Cardston in the company of his brother Roy and a friend, Morgan Coombs. It was at Cardston that Eldon and Sara decided to marry, setting the date for December 20, a little more than a month away. Thus it was important that he and his two companions made the trip.

For the return trip to Hill Spring, on a bitter, cold night, the three men decided to rent a cutter rather than ride horses. Eldon let his own horse go, to return to Hill Spring by itself. While crossing the Blood Indian Reserve, the three men were trapped in a sudden blizzard. Eldon later described the experience:

> After we got out about eight or nine miles on the reservation we were entirely lost in a blizzard and traveled around all night. After about one o'clock, we gave up and turned the cutter up on one side and tied the horses to it and then Roy and I walked all night to keep from freezing. Morgan Coombs wouldn't walk, so we put him on the lea side of the cutter and covered him up with what blankets we had. When daylight came, we found we were only a few hundred yards from a haystack. We didn't get back to town that morning until about ten o'clock. That means we were out on the reservation from seven o'clock that night until ten o'clock in the morning in a blizzard and not too well dressed. In fact, we were very cold and suffered something that none of us will ever forget.[11]

Eldon's comments here contain at least one impressive understatement: "In fact, we were very cold." Despite spending the night in a blizzard on the plains of Southern Alberta, the three young men were in remarkable shape. The only lasting consequence was a vivid memory of this brush with death. And despite such difficult circumstances, Eldon managed to continue successfully his long-distance courtship and to plan with Sara their wedding.

On December 19, 1919, when school closed for the Christmas holidays, Eldon traveled alone to Magrath, where he picked up Sara, her mother, and her sister Gwen. They took the train to Lethbridge, where they were married the next day, December 20, by Bishop George W. Green, with Sara's mother and sister as witnesses. The newlyweds took the train to Calgary, where they stayed for three days in the Palliser Hotel. While there they met several friends who also were on honeymoons. Of the experience Eldon remembers, "I was glad that we had a little more money than we absolutely needed, because one of the couples ran out of money and I had to pay the hotel bill."[12] Upon their return to Hill Spring, they gave a big reception and dance, which the entire community attended in honor of the newlyweds. Their marriage was later solemnized by Elder Joseph Fielding Smith in the Cardston Temple, when that privilege became available at the time of the temple dedication, August 26-29, 1923.

The young couple's first living quarters after their marriage were in the home of Sara's parents in Hill Spring, where they stayed until the end of the school year. In the summer of 1920 they purchased a two-room house measuring twelve by twenty-two feet, located on eighty acres of land half a mile south of Hill Spring. Their first two daughters were born while they lived here, Ruth on October 7, 1920, and Isabelle on January 3, 1922. In order to obtain better medical care, Sara traveled to Cardston to deliver her babies. After Isabelle was born, Eldon moved their cottage to Hill Spring across from the three-room school where he taught and was principal.

During the winter of 1922-23 Eldon decided to complete grade twelve and thereby qualify to introduce high school courses into the Hill Spring curriculum. He moved his family temporarily to Cardston and rented his childhood home, which had earlier been sold to J. F. Gibb when his parents moved permanently to Salt Lake City.

While Eldon attended school, Sara taught school in Cardston that year. Eldon also taught his grade nine English class. To sup-

Eldon Tanner with his firstborn daughter, Ruth, outside the Tanners' two-room home in Hill Spring, about 1921

plement their meager income he milked the cows and delivered milk to many local customers, including the Cardston Municipal Hospital. The family's "survival system" included providing room and board for Sara's brother Don, who was attending grade twelve along with Eldon. During the days when Sara was teaching, Hazel Marsden was hired to care for Ruth and Isabelle.

The Tanners returned to Hill Spring in September 1923 and rented the home of D. H. Grow. Eldon and Sara both taught during that school year while Aunt Florence Merrill tended Ruth and Isabelle. They also took as boarders two fellow teachers, a Miss Meldrum and Harold Merkley. In the spring of 1924, the family moved back to their Hill Spring cottage, and Eldon began to beautify the yard with trees and shrubs.

With a grade twelve certificate in hand, Eldon introduced the grade nine curriculum to the school in Hill Spring so that those who so desired could begin their high school education. In subsequent years he added grades ten and eleven to the curriculum. To accommodate the added teaching load, he hired another teacher for grades seven and eight. To pass the high school grades, the students had to take the governmental examinations. These tests were prepared in Edmonton and administered with considerable formality in all provincial high schools. Of all the students who prepared for this examination under Eldon's tutelage, he recalls that only one failed.

Punctuality was one of Eldon Tanner's standards for good performance in school, together with the ideals of achievement and hard work. One of the childhood memories of his eldest daughter, Ruth, is of Gordon Low, a grade one pupil, getting the "strap" for being late for school, despite his excuse that there was heavy mud on the road.

One of his students was Heber Wolsey, who later became assistant to the president of Brigham Young University and then managing director of the Public Communications Department of the Church at its Salt Lake City headquarters. Heber remembers fighting an eighth-grade classmate named Hugh Sloan during an entire noon hour. The fight was a draw, he writes, "but the tragedy was that we fought so long we didn't have time to eat lunch." To Eldon Tanner, their teacher and principal, fighting was against the rules. He sent Hugh to his room but slapped a gym suspension on Heber. Later, the two boys compared notes regarding the discipline each had received. Heber, showing skill in communicating ideas under pressure, approached Principal Tanner with indignation. The principal listened carefully and kindly, then granted the point of inequity and suspended the suspension.

Heber Wolsey says it was the same Eldon Tanner who taught him literature "with such love and enthusiasm that I couldn't wait for his classes." As a consequence, he read everything within reach and kept his test scores secret for fear his friends would think he was a sissy for enjoying literature so much. He was also motivated through years to come by words that this same teacher wrote in his autograph album:

> *The heights by great men reached and kept*
> *Were not attained by sudden flight,*
> *But they, while their companions slept,*
> *Were toiling upward in the night.*[13]

The young eighth grader figured that the teacher was trying to tell him something. His thoughtful repetition and reexamination of that concept came to bless his life.

Heber also describes a classroom situation. The first day, Eldon Tanner walked into the room promptly at nine o'clock, welcomed all to a new year of school, and then said, "You and I are going to be together six or seven hours a day for the next year. I am your teacher, the only teacher you have, and I want to teach you only one thing this entire year." This puzzled young Heber Wolsey. He thought to himself, "This guy is going to be a pushover. I can learn *one* thing easily if I have a whole year to do it in."

Then the teacher continued: "That one thing, the only thing I really care if you learn this year, the only thing that really matters is how to think—how to think for yourself, how to reason out a solution to a problem—above all, how to think."

The young teacher then turned to the blackboard and wrote in letters two feet high, "THINK! THINK! THINK!"

One day he told Heber he was going to "remunerate" him. "What does 'remunerate' mean?" Heber asked. Principal Tanner pointed a stern finger and said, "I'm not going to tell you until *you* find out." That was his style of teaching—not to make it easy, but to make it challenging. Heber Wolsey and his fellow students came to know that their teacher was no pushover. He always held to exacting, high standards.

His students revere him as one of the best, fairest, and kindest men they have ever known. To this day Heber Wolsey writes: "Yet every time I have occasion to be with him now, I still imagine he sees a fatherless, depression kid hollering for recognition." Recognition he got. Learning to think became his goal and remains his constant companion. Characters were built at Hill Spring. Struggling country kids in a simple school they may have been, but many have joined in Heber Wolsey's evaluation that N. Eldon Tanner "ruined me for ever settling for less than my best."[14]

In addition to the demanding curriculum Eldon introduced into the school at Hill Spring, he fostered an ambitious sports program. He was coach of the basketball, track, baseball, and wrestling teams. This untrained but enthusiastic coaching was sufficient to produce several provincial championship wrestling teams from Hill Spring.

Eldon Tanner's involvement with his students paid off in other ways besides trophies. Hill Spring was known for its rough-and-tumble male adolescents. Nevertheless, while Eldon was teaching, the behavior of these former rowdies improved dramatically. He credits his philosophy for this success. "Children will do what you expect them to do. Congratulate them and compliment them on what they are doing and good things that they do. Now with the boys and girls that I had in school . . . I participated with them in sports in every way. . . . I tried to show them that I had confidence in them and expected them to progress and amount to something."

In addition to his involvement with the Hill Spring school, Eldon served the community as health officer, Scoutmaster, and constable and "took as active a part as he could in a little community in public affairs." One of his former students, in fact, remembers that Mr. Tanner was at one time his schoolteacher, Scoutmaster, cadet instructor, and coach of boxing, wrestling, basketball, baseball, and dramatics. Of his former mentor this man declares, "He became my ideal of manhood. He was an influential teacher and outstanding coach in Alberta and had a very positive influence on his students to achieve scholastically and to be upright citizens."

Nevertheless, community service, however willingly given, did not put bread on the table and clothes on the backs of Eldon's growing family. The teaching profession was also occasionally inadequate to meet their modest material needs. There were times when notes of credit were issued instead of salary for Eldon's teaching. During one six-month period, Eldon received no compensation at all for his teaching. Seeing that the municipality was able to pay the salaries of other civil servants, he investigated why teachers' contracts were being ignored. He recalls: "I went to the secretary-treasurer of the school board and asked him how it was. And he said, 'Well, they [other municipal workers] would sue us [the municipal government] if we didn't pay them.' I said, 'So, I'm going to sue you for money.' He didn't think I would dare do that because I was teaching. So I started a suit through a lawyer in Lethbridge and they came to me and said, 'You'll never teach here again as long as we live.' I said 'That's all right.' But they came and settled and paid me in full, rather than go to court about it. And they wanted me to go on teaching with them the next year."

Although he continued to teach, Eldon sought other means of support for his family during those difficult times. In the summer of 1924, he gave his new Model T Ford as a down payment on a general store owned by Henry Gibb. In accordance with his agreement with Mr. Gibb, Eldon continued to make payments on the car with profits from the store. He supported his family from his teaching salary. He also moved his family into the store's four-room second-story apartment. There the Tanners lived during the school year 1924-25 while Eldon taught and Aunt Florence Merrill managed the store. He has described the way in which he got into the store business as follows:

When I found that I couldn't make a living at teaching, I decided to buy a store—a general store in the little town of Hill Spring. Well, I didn't have any money, so how could I buy a store? I made a down payment on a lovely Ford car; then I took the car to the man who owned the store and said, "I would like to put this car as a down payment on the store." He accepted it. Then I went to a wholesaler, because now I had a store, and said, "I would like to have credit here for $500." And he gave me the credit. I went to another wholesaler who dealt in dry goods and hardware and he said, "Yes, I'll give you $500 credit."

This is the way we got into business. I did my own trucking and freighting. I couldn't give credit because I didn't have any money to carry on if I did; I had to take cash for everything that I sold."[15]

The strain of teaching, rearing a young family and being pregnant with their third child, moving frequently, caring for boarders, and living only slightly above subsistence level took its toll on Sara's health. Emotionally and physically weak, she took her children to Salt Lake City in October 1924 to recuperate at the home of Eldon's parents. Grandma and Grandpa Tanner took care of Ruth and Isabelle while Sara prepared to deliver her third daughter. Zola, a beautiful baby with dark hair and eyes, was born May 16, 1925. Although the trip was not as restful as she might have hoped, Sara returned to frontier Alberta and her husband shortly thereafter.

Eldon's store was general in the true sense of the term. It sold everything from domestic supplies to tools to groceries and meat. In order to keep his costs down, Eldon performed many of the store's functions himself. He hauled the supplies, kept the books, and manned the store when he was not teaching. Wishing to avoid a credit operation, he accepted neither credit nor futures in livestock and crops. He did, however, trade in kind when the goods were delivered and at a fair market price. As a result, he found himself feeding hogs and cattle and marketing grain. To expand to a growing feedlot business, he purchased an eighty-acre farm to raise additional feed for his livestock. He did his own freighting from the back of an old Dodge car that he had converted into a small truck. Operating in the center of the business district in Hill Spring, he also became the postmaster and the payee for the local grain elevators.

The increasing complexity of his business operations required that Eldon leave his teaching post at the end of the 1925-26 school year to devote full attention to the store. He expanded his already diversified operations to include a gas station, a butcher shop, and a farm implement business, affiliated with Massey-Harris. A separate building was constructed near the store to house the inventory of farm machinery. During this time, Eldon had a corner on the business in Hill Spring because the population was insufficiently mobile to shop regularly at the larger markets in Lethbridge and Cardston and because no one seemed willing to compete with him in Hill Spring. He had to hire an assistant, Glen Fisher, to help him manage these various operations. He later remarked, "I didn't have very many hours of sleep those nights."

Although he was becoming a very successful small-town businessman, Eldon had always wanted to study law. Feeling that his assets were finally adequate, he sold his store to A. L. Wood of Taber, Alberta, in September 1927. At the same time he sold his implement business to Dewey Smith and the farm to Orin Fisher. The family hoped then to move to Salt Lake City to begin law school at the University of Utah. But, according to Eldon's record, "I had to take the business back from Dewey Smith, and Orin Fisher never did pay for the farm. It was not possible, with the money I got from the store and with the debts I had, for me to go to school."[17] Meantime, a fourth daughter, Beth, had arrived March 16, 1927. Disappointed that his law school ambitions would have to return to the shelf, Eldon remained in Hill Spring. That winter he was asked to assume the role of teacher again, but this time at the high school in Cardston, a larger school in a larger community, with enlarged opportunities.

Footnotes

[1]Ruth Tanner Walker, memorandum to G. Homer Durham, August 10, 1981.

[2]Sara M. Tanner, Life Story, Leatherhead, Surrey, England, 1962.

[3]Ibid.

[4]Ibid.

[5]Ibid.

[6]Ibid.

[7]N. Eldon Tanner, Life Story, dictated to Ruth T. Walker, Leatherhead, Surrey, England, 1962.

[8]Ibid.

[9]Sara M. Tanner, Life Story

[10]Ibid.

[11]N. Eldon Tanner, Life Story.

[12]Ibid.

[13]Henry Wadsworth Longfellow, "The Ladder of St. Augustine," stanza 10.

[14]Heber Wolsey, memorandum to G. Homer Durham, March 1981.

[15]N. Eldon Tanner, *Seek Ye First,* pp. 14-15.

[16]N. Eldon Tanner, Life Story.

3

The Cardston Years,
1928-1935

Cardston lies seventeen miles north of the Montana border between the United States and Canada. It was settled in 1887 by Mormon colonists seeking refuge from enforcement in Utah of the Edmunds-Tucker bill enacted by Congress that year. Dominating the rural community of straight streets and large residential lots is the Alberta Temple of The Church of Jesus Christ of Latter-day Saints, completed in 1923. By the end of 1927, the population of Cardston had grown to around fifteen hundred.

Late in 1927 the Tanner family moved the second time from Hill Spring to Cardston. Eldon had been invited to fill the principalship at the Cardston High School, a position being vacated in midyear by J. W. Low, who had been appointed a police magistrate. In addition to serving as principal, Eldon would also teach senior class courses in mathematics.

The Tanners rented at first, then purchased a home from John Peterson for five thousand dollars. According to Sara, that was their "first nice home."[1] A bungalow, the home had a kitchen, living room, dining room, bathroom, and three small bedrooms. Outside was sufficient land for a garden and for cows and chickens. To help make ends meet, the family took in board-

Note: This chapter is based on an original draft by William Hale Kehr.

ers; they also canned fruits and vegetables for their year's supply. They worked hard and had few holidays from chores.

Eldon Tanner's own education extended only to a six-week teaching course beyond the twelfth grade. In the four years since his graduation he had never taught senior math courses. Now he was thrust into a midterm class schedule that included instruction in trigonometry and analytical geometry. This often required hours of nightly preparation to understand problems to be taught his students the following day. But he was used to discipline, and such hard work resulted in a successful return to teaching.

At the end of that school year yet another challenge presented itself. The school board decided to make a change in the principalship of the grade school, and their search for a replacement led them to N. Eldon Tanner, a man who already had half a dozen years as principal of the school in nearby Hill Spring.

The change was unwelcome to the incumbent and his friends, so a decision like this in a small community was not without its repercussions. The small Mormon settlement was liberally sprinkled with names of extended families like Brown, Card, Low, and, recently, Tanner. In the two wards, aunts, uncles, nephews, nieces, in-laws, and cousins abounded. For some time the former principal and kin regarded Eldon as an interloper, although the new principal had no hand in his predecessor's termination.

As principal in Cardston, Eldon continued his discipline with the always high expectations of the best from each of his charges. Everyone clearly understood what was expected. He accepted no excuse for nonperformance or for disregard of the rules. Good citizenship and its discipline were expected. Each day the children lined up in the schoolyard and went to their classes in single file. From his office, Eldon could oversee the formations. Anyone observed "horsing around" could expect a summons to the principal's office, a far cry from today's permissiveness in many public schools.

Another area that received considerable attention was tardiness. With the first offense, the teacher issued a verbal warning. If a second occurred, the offender was ushered into the principal's office, where a sterner warning was issued along with a pointed display of the strap. A third offense brought an application of the strap to the front of the offender's hands. As Eldon was adept and impressive at step two, step three was seldom necessary.

Eldon lived by similar standards himself. His daughter Beth tells of a time they were home for lunch. Eldon suddenly realized he should be at school in only a minute or two to ring the bell ending the lunch period. Grabbing Beth's hand, he was out the door on a dead run in an instant. To the young Beth, it seemed that she was actually flying behind her father, rarely touching the ground.

Eldest daughter Ruth also remembers home discipline. She and her sister Isabelle were carefully informed not to get into a certain drawer. Returning from school one day, their father found the drawer's contents on the floor. Queried, the girls denied involvement. He knew otherwise. The results, as noted by Ruth, comprised "a sound spanking." Thus, respect for parental status and wisdom grew and young lives were stabilized.[2]

The four oldest daughters all attended schools in which Eldon was principal. They were treated as was any other child—with one exception. It was made very clear to them that because their father was principal, they were expected to be on good behavior. If they required classroom discipline, they could expect additional discipline at home. Since they were being reared in a home of order and respect, they rarely needed such action. An exception occurred when Ruth was about thirteen. She sassed her mother while sitting at the dinner table one day. "That," she wrote, "my father would not tolerate. He adored my mother and treated her like a queen and expected his children to do the same. I'll tell you, I never talked back to my mother after that."[3]

Eldon Tanner was an innovative and enthusiastic teacher. In the classroom he could get students genuinely interested in literature, agriculture, grammar, or mathematics, all of which he

Sara and Eldon Tanner with four daughters, about 1927 (their fifth daughter, Helen, was born in 1931)

taught. He involved the students in choral readings, and instituted an accelerated program for students of greater mental capacity. This group was not permitted to skip any grades; rather, they compressed three years of classwork into two school years.

These were hard times for nearly everyone. The year following his appointment as principal, the Great Depression began. His contract called for fifteen hundred dollars a year with raises to two thousand. But no raises were possible. One year the school board found it necessary to issue notes as part of teachers' salaries. Without ingenuity and Eldon's love of hard work, the family would have found things much more difficult. To maintain his family and supplement his income, he launched several enterprises. He sold insurance and custom-made suits. He did this work on Saturdays, and would not permit these jobs to interfere with other responsibilities. But the largest project of all, and the most demanding on each one's ability to cooperate, was a family venture.

The Tanners had cows that produced sufficient milk for a small milk route. Milk brought the handsome depression price of ten cents a quart or three quarts for a quarter. The Tanner daughters made deliveries in the morning and the evening, blizzard, rain, or shine. They carried the bottles in their arms and in a big heavy bag similar to a newsboy's over-the-shoulder bag. Ruth remembers that on occasion the snow was waist deep, for no pathways had been cleared in those early morning hours. Eldon would never permit the girls to milk the cows. This task he reserved for himself, occasionally hiring a boy to do it when emergencies arose. But the girls were responsible for cleaning the milk separator, though they would have preferred just about anything else, even herding the cows, which was also their work.

Cow herding was not without its adventures. The small Cardston community had long since found it best to keep privately owned livestock in one central place during the day. Accordingly, a central grazing pasture had been set aside for the "town herd," and leading the cows to pasture and back was frequently the lot of Zola and Beth, the younger daughters.

The cowpath to the summer pasture brought the girls close to the border of the Indian reservation. Beth was a blue-eyed, self-assured blonde who never imagined that any self-respecting

Indian would bother her. But for Zola, who had beautiful dark hair and striking eyes, there were fantasies, stimulated by pioneer legends and playmates' myths, that an Indian would steal her away. Whenever they approached the reservation, she would try to hide behind the younger, smaller Beth.

Actually, Indians were frequent visitors to Cardston. An Indian hospital was near the Tanner home. It was not unusual for Indians to come to their house seeking food, and, respecting Mormon pioneer tradition, Sara never sent them away. Despite the depression, there was always a little something to share.

In Cardston the family also maintained a large garden. One or two of the girls regularly helped their father care for the garden while the others helped their mother with the housework. They also continued the Hill Spring experience of keeping chickens and pigs. While recognizing that they grew up during hard times, the children never experienced a feeling of deprivation. To them it seemed natural to exchange an egg for some candy or pay for a visit to the movies with some milk. Sara made all their clothes. They felt well cared for.

Days began at five A.M. in the Tanner household. Before the family owned a house with central heating, Eldon, who was usually whistling, was up first, to make the fire, light the stove, and begin breakfast preparations. The girls frequently piled into bed with their mother, and, while the house heated up, mother and daughters sang songs together. Eldon loved to hear the sweet voices ring through the house.

After mother and daughters arose, there was breakfast to be served, the cows to tend, the milk route to complete. Morning chores done, the girls were off to school. No matter what other things were done in the morning, their arrival at school was on time.

Because Cardston was small enough that a person could walk practically anywhere in minutes, the family usually ate lunch at home. If their father was available, they also enjoyed evenings together, usually playing games. To win a game against Eldon Tanner, you had to beat him fair and square, no matter what

41

your age. If he was away, which was often, there were many playmates for the daughters among the Atkins girls next door and other Cardston friends.

The Tanner girls had rich associations with their father. For example, while selling tailored suits and insurance during the Depression, he invariably took one of his daughters with him across the prairie to the farms. As father and daughter rode along, they played many games. Isabelle said she never realized that she was learning—and enjoying the learning all the while. "We would see who could name the crop in the next field first— hay, alfalfa, barley, or oats; who could spot and name an animal first—a Leghorn or Rhode Island chicken; Percheron, Belgian, or Clydesdale work horse; Hereford, Holstein, Jersey, or Guernsey cattle. Then we would see who could recognize the kind of car we passed; there weren't too many! It was all fun. The time went quickly, and we learned."[4]

One of the things that set Eldon Tanner apart from other fathers was his deep sense of obligation to get up in the night if one or more of his children cried out. He brought nursing babies to their mother and returned them to their cribs when finished. This was an enormous boon for his wife, and one that she was ever thankful for. Throughout their lives, the Tanner children didn't know whom else to cry for in the night but "Daddy," be it for a drink of water or a reassuring word. Ruth believes it must have been his childhood experience of nursing his family through smallpox that helped make him a dependable and gentle night nurse to his children.

In Cardston, Eldon acquired a horse and went riding daily. Each year he tried to fit in a week-long pack trip into a remote area of the province with some of his men friends in town. The role of organizer and leader always fell to him. One year, as the men slept in their camp for the night, their horses scattered to seek greener pastures. The next morning the men split up to search for the animals. Eldon found them, but they were unbridled, and he had no rope with which to tie them together and lead them back to camp. What a sight they presented as he led them back into camp with tethers made of his bootlaces, shirt, and trousers! Necessity was indeed the mother of invention that morning.

Summers for the family were neither lazy nor relaxed. Days began as early as usual and brought a full load of activities. Each summer usually included time spent at Waterton National Park, located at the Canadian end of the beautiful area that terminates as Glacier National Park in Montana. In earlier years, visits to Waterton were spent camping out in tents. When more prosperous times came later, the Tanners purchased a cabin for summer use. Waterton Lake was a marvelous fishing spot. If the girls or Sara wanted to go fishing with Eldon to help catch breakfast in the morning, they were expected to do their share of the rowing. Each one also baited her own hook and retrieved it from any fish caught. Stern stuff for little girls, but surprisingly popular just the same!

Soon after the Tanners arrived in Cardston in late 1927, local church leaders were not long in discovering their talents. Within weeks, in January 1928, Sara was called as first counselor in the Young Women's Mutual Improvement Association of the Cardston First Ward. At year's end she was called as president. In August of the same year, Eldon was called into the bishopric as second counselor to Bishop Gustave Nielson.

Cardston First Ward was the ward in which Eldon's father had served with Gustave Nielson under Bishop C. W. Burt. In 1922, when Eldon's father moved back to Salt Lake City, Brother Nielson became first counselor, and in 1928 he was called as bishop. The circle came full turn when Bishop Nielson called as his second counselor the son of the man who had been first counselor when he himself had begun his service in the bishopric ten years before. Thus, Eldon Tanner was no stranger to Bishop Nielson.

As second counselor, Eldon was directly responsible for the deacons. Beginning in November 1928, he served as one of three Scout leaders in the ward. When he began, many of the boys were not attending priesthood meetings. Cardston was not a community known for its material riches; its citizens were hard-working people wresting a living from small farms and ranches. As Eldon visited the homes of his deacons, he found that some had no clothes to wear but overalls or coveralls, and some had only one pair of those. Few had "Sunday clothes." It was a situation that required diplomacy and some skill in human relations. On one hand, Eldon had a group of boys who felt they did not have proper attire to wear to church; on the other, he knew of the sensitive pride that characterizes teenagers and their peers. He was aware also of the need of young men to grow up with the positive influence of the Church in their lives. For a man to whom principle was absolute but fashion was negotiable, the answer became clear. Going to each of the boys, he offered a deal. If they would come to priesthood meeting, he too would wear coveralls. A boy could hardly be the object of derision if his file leader was so attired. The result was one hundred percent activity among the three quorums of deacons in the First Ward.

One thing many old-timers remember about Eldon Tanner occurred shortly after the family moved to Cardston. Eldon was asked to give the Christmas sermon, and he addressed the subject "The Reasons We Have for Celebrating Christmas," speaking on the blessings to mankind of the coming of the Savior. The message was beautifully and impressively delivered, and Eldon continued to be in demand as a speaker. In 1929, asked again to give the Christmas message, he spoke on "The Visit of the Angels to the Shepherds in the Fields." A few months later he addressed the ward on the centennial anniversary of the Church, April 6, 1930.

The centennial observance was a notable one. The program had been outlined by Church headquarters in Salt Lake City, with a special centennial address from President Heber J. Grant to be read by a selected speaker from the stake. The service was held at 10:00 A.M. in the stake tabernacle. Part of the program included the sacred Hosannah Shout, and the choir rendered the "Hallelujah Chorus" from Handel's *Messiah*. Regular services were held in each ward following this special meeting. At the ward meeting April 6, 1930, there was a change in the bishopric, effected at ward conference. Sylvester W. Low, first counselor in the bishopric, was called to the stake high council, and N. Eldon Tanner was sustained as first counselor to Bishop Nielson. Eugene Robinson, who had been superintendent of the Sunday School, became second counselor. Other changes occurred that summer. In July Sara was released as YWMIA president, and Eldon was released from the Old Folks Committee and was called as principal of the junior seminary.

On August 12, 1931, the last child and fifth daughter of the Tanners arrived. It is reported that as the little baby emerged and its gender became apparent, the attending physician said, "Hel'n! Another girl!" Evidently the physician, if not others, was hoping for a boy. Humor has it that Sara and Eldon took this cue and named the baby Helen. Eldon blessed her with that name on Sunday, October 31, in the Cardston First Ward.

Eldon felt the need to press ahead with his own education. During the summers of 1932 and 1933 he enrolled in courses at the University of Utah. One child went to Salt Lake City with him each summer and spent those weeks with Grandma and Grandpa Tanner, who had returned to Utah in 1922.

In November 1933 Eldon was called as bishop of the Cardston First Ward. He was ordained to that office by Elder George F. Richards of the Council of the Twelve. Thereafter, bishop's duties preempted summer school. Selected to serve as Eldon's counselors in the bishopric were William Burt and Heber Matkin, both older than he. Both agreed without hesitation to serve.

At year's end, presiding at his first monthly ward fast meeting, the new bishop bore his testimony. He endeavored to set an encouraging tone for the ward despite depression and drought. He reminded the Saints that they enjoyed many blessings despite their economic difficulties, then invited them to bear testimony of the Lord's goodness. He concluded his own witness of something that President Joseph F. Smith had said during a visit to Alberta years before: "Some of the finest young people the world

has ever seen will rise from the plains of Canada." An uncon-
querable man, Eldon Tanner was sharing his spirit with a group
that was being sorely tested and from whose number that
prophecy would be fulfilled.

Eldon was a fairly young bishop with a flock of both young
and old. Within the ward boundaries was the Alberta Temple.
Over the years the ward membership had seen a gradual increase in the numbers of older members seeking to live close to
the temple, and their participation in temple assignments always
represented the ward well in that phase of church activity.
Bishop Tanner was therefore able to focus on reactivation of
other ward members. He worked constantly with the ward's
youth. Over time the ward attendance slowly increased. The
hard times also brought the fruits of humility, namely greater
recognition of man's dependence on the Lord.

One principle Bishop Tanner was not prepared to compromise was personal worthiness. Whether it was a priesthood
advancement or a temple recommend, a person, though judged
with kindness, always had to measure up. A challenging situation
greeted him in this area.

As bishop, he was president of and directly responsible for
the priests quorum, which had six members. Five were what
neighbors could describe as "good, solid members." One of the
six, however, was careless not only in church attendance, but in
other duties as well. As the time approached for these young
men to be recommended to receive the Melchizedek Priesthood
and be ordained elders, Bishop Tanner initiated frequent interviews with each. It became increasingly evident that the one
young man would not qualify for advancement with the other
five. Concerned family members, including a former bishop of
the ward, warned Bishop Tanner that not to recommend the
young man would destroy his activity. They placed complete responsibility for the young man's future on the bishop and church
for the act of advancement, rather than on the individual's qualifications and conduct. Eldon, while kindly disposed toward the
young man, did not flinch and would not budge, despite the

pressures. Reception of the higher priesthood was too important a matter to be trifled with. Accordingly the five were advanced; the one was not. Bishop Tanner continued to labor with him, and later, the young man would credit this action with impressing upon him the importance of the priesthood, and leading him into full church activity. He would later have many callings in leadership positions.

Civic service acquired a new dimension in 1933 when Eldon Tanner was elected to a term on the Cardston City Council. He was now in a unique position. He was at one and the same time principal of the grade school, bishop of the First Ward, and member of the City Council. His assigned responsibilities were the critical areas of health and welfare relief. This gave him an even more comprehensive view of his community and of human needs and social conditions. These were the days before extensive state, province, national, or highly organized church welfare programs. The care and feeding of the needy fell heavily on bishops, city government, and local resources.

When Eldon took over the health-care program, the city had contracted with the local hospital to care for needy families for a lump sum payment of twenty-five dollars per family per year. As families needed hospitalization, the city had to come up with the money to fund the contract. The amount was unpredictable and created a hardship on the city's financial planning, so Eldon did some analytical thinking and then went to the hospital and proposed a modified program. Under his plan, the city would make a payment of two hundred and fifty dollars at the beginning of the year. When a member of one of the needy families needed hospital care, the patient would be admitted to the hospital and assigned the benefits from the fund. This relieved the city council of having to come up with funds on a random, unplanned basis. The plan was accepted and worked very smoothly.

During this time of deep distress in the community and nation, William Aberhart of Calgary began to propose a radically new approach to the economic woes of the time. The principal of a school in Calgary, he had developed a remarkable weekly religious radio program. From his personality and his radio broadcasts was to come a marked political change in Alberta. That change was to bring about an unexpected turn in the lives of Eldon and Sara Tanner and eventually take them away from Cardston.

One day in 1935 it was advertised that two representatives of Aberhart's new Social Credit party would be in Cardston to hold a public meeting. As the appointed hour approached, the place they planned to hold their meeting suddenly was unavailable. Bishop Tanner offered to make available the basement of the stake tabernacle for the meetings. They gratefully accepted this service. When Eldon arrived at the building, he was asked to chair the meeting. Demurring at first, he was prevailed upon to serve in the traditional spirit of English-Canadian impartial chairmanship. During the presentation, he became mildly interested in the program. As it was explained in detail, a glimmer of thought occurred to him that it might affect the economic future of Alberta.

Near the end of the meeting, the two representatives asked those attending to set up a study group to further examine Social Credit. Eldon was asked to serve as chairman of the group. "After much argument and protestation," he recalls, he finally accepted. "I had advised them that I was not a Social Creditor, but I always felt that it was an opportunity to study and to find out whether they had anything or not. My mind was definitely of the opinion that I would disapprove of what they were teaching. The result was that Grant Woolley, Heber Jenson, George Low, and a group of us carried on a study group, each giving reasons and discussing thoroughly the theory of Social Credit. The result—I became converted as did Heber."

The decision to accept opened unexpected and unanticipated doors to the future. It was a future of which the boy from log hut beginnings in Aetna had hardly dreamed.

The Cardston Years

Footnotes

[1]Sara M. Tanner, Life Story.
[2]Ruth T. Walker, "My Father."
[3]Isabelle T. Jensen, memorandum to G. Homer Durham, August 3, 1981.
[4]N. Eldon Tanner, Life Story.

4

Speaker of the Assembly

In order to understand better Eldon Tanner's involvement with Alberta's provincial government, the political history of Alberta needs a brief retelling. Alberta, as part of the North West Territories of Canada, entered the Canadian confederation in 1867. The North West Territories Act went into effect in 1875, establishing a government for the area, and in 1882, Alberta was made a district. In 1897, the year after Nathan William Tanner's first trip north, a legislative assembly was elected. The boundaries of Alberta were enlarged to their present composition in 1905, and the area became a province of Canada.

The Liberal party formed the first cabinet, with Edmonton, a former trading post of Hudson's Bay Company, as the capital city. Oil was discovered at Turner Valley near Calgary in 1914, and that influenced the city's future development. Agricultural and coal production had previously brought the railway.

World War I saw the beginning of the end of the Liberal domination. Wheat prices dipped after the war, and this led to the formation of a new political party, the United Farmers of Alberta (UFA), which took control of the government in 1921. The party retained control until 1935, when the Social Credit party,

Note: This chapter is based on extensive research and interviews by Steven L. Olsen, supplementing initial drafts by Paul L. Anderson.

led first by William Aberhart, followed by Ernest C. Manning, captured the government. That party retained power for the next thirty-six years, until 1971.

In October 1929 the value of stocks in North American stock exchanges tumbled. Earlier that year Alberta wheat production had brought farmers as much as $1.14 per bushel, for a total of approximately $103 million. By 1931 the price of wheat had fallen to incredible lows, reaching 32 cents a bushel in the early 1930s. Meanwhile, interest on farm debt was running only slightly behind the value of the entire wheat crop. Alberta farmers carried debts totaling $318 million in 1931, at interest rates ranging from 7 to 10 percent. In 1934 the value of the entire Alberta wheat production fell to $46 million, which could not possibly sustain the debt load, taxes, and subsistence living for most farm families.[1] It was this depression situation that led to the Social Credit party's rise to power.

During the prosperous pre-depression years of the 1920s, radio broadcasting came into prominence, and nearly every Alberta wheat farmer acquired a radio set. In 1925, only three years after the first radio broadcast in Calgary, William Aberhart, founder, principal, and dean of the Calgary Prophetic Bible Institute, began a series of Sunday afternoon radio broadcasts. By 1927 he was broadcasting for two hours every Sunday afternoon, and study groups were being formed throughout Calgary. The influence of the institute continued to expand, and by 1935 Preacher Aberhart was broadcasting five hours every Sunday to an audience estimated at 350,000 listeners. S. D. Clark wrote: "Long before they had seen the man, thousands of people throughout the farm and urban areas of Alberta had become his devoted followers, prepared to accept his every word and to support him in whatever he proposed to do."[2] His broadcasts had become what W. E. Mann described as "a provincial institution."[3]

William Aberhart was born in Huron County, Ontario, in 1878. Educated at Queens University, he went west to Alberta, where he became principal of Crescent Heights School in Calgary in 1915. In 1918 he organized the Calgary Prophetic Bible

Conference under the auspices of the Westbourne Baptist Church, where he was also preacher and discussion leader of a weekly study class. The increasing popularity of the conference led to the founding of the Calgary Prophetic Bible Institute in 1925. In addition to Sunday Bible sessions, the curriculum of the institute included English, music, domestic science, shorthand, typing, and auto mechanics, a three-year course. In his broadcasts, Mr. Aberhart emphasized literal interpretation of the Bible with particular interest in its prophetic and millennial passages.

Tall, heavy, a commanding figure with seemingly inexhaustible energy, William Aberhart had unquestioned oratorical ability, which brought him great popularity. The devotion of his radio followers is reflected in the story of the druggist in Saskatchewan whose son had become addicted to drugs. The man took his son to Calgary to have Mr. Aberhart pray for him. He was so impressed by the preacher that upon his return home he set aside five acres of his small farm, with the income to go to the "Back to the Bible" hour. The radio preacher was as adept at fund-raising as he was at broadcasting, and by 1930 he had been able to construct a building in downtown Calgary for his new church, the Bible Institute Baptist Church. Among the features of the building were a thousand-seat auditorium and flexible classrooms to accommodate study classes.

During the years William Aberhart was building his Bible Institute and expanding his radio program, the theory of social credit was beginning to have impact in Alberta. The movement began in the 1920s through prominent members of the United Farmers of Alberta. Primary developer of the theory was Major Clifford Hagen Douglas, a Scottish mechanical engineer who was impressed with the possibilities for almost unlimited production afforded by modern technology. While Karl Marx had expressed the view that one could reach the "classless society" through the production process, finally arriving at what he called the "second stage of Socialism," Major Douglas felt that prosperity could be obtained through social credit and without the Marxist "dictatorship of the proletariat." Socialism, he felt, was not the answer to industrial society's ills. "Monetary Reform was the answer because it could destroy the mechanism by which economic power was being increased, and by which the material well-being and the freedom of the individual were being diminished."[4] Thus, simplified, ran Major Douglas's argument. ("Technocracy" had comparable vogue in the United States in those same years, but with different methodology.) Major Douglas wrote and published in England three books on his theory: *Economic Democracy* (1920), *Credit-Power and Democracy* (1921), and *Social Credit* (1924).

In Alberta, the United Farmers began to publicize the work of Major Douglas beginning in 1922. Poverty, depression, and the insecurity of wheat farmers were the seedbeds for the panaceas the doctrine seemed to offer. Whereas Major Douglas would have the people practice and exert broad influence, the development and technical direction of the social credit system would remain with experts.

In July 1932, Mr. Aberhart went to Edmonton to mark departmental examinations for the provincial educational system. On the train he marveled at the abundance of grain and livestock on the plains of Alberta, in contrast to the poverty and idleness of inhabitants of cities and towns. One of his fellow instructors had previously tried to interest him in the philosophy of social credit, but the apolitical Mr. Aberhart was not interested. This time, however, he listened. He not only listened, but he began to devour everything he could find on the subject. He found himself introducing social credit ideas into his radio sermons. What he may have lacked in analytical understanding, he made up in organizational ability and leadership.

The Alberta Social Credit party as led by William Aberhart evolved from his broadcast-inspired study groups. Ernest Charles Manning, the first graduate of the three-year Bible Institute program, became the party secretary. He described the development as stemming from Mr. Aberhart's deep concern for young people, which led him to "active interest" in economics.

This led him to the theories of Major Douglas. "As a result," Mr. Manning recalls, "Mr. Aberhart started giving lectures on these economic theories, at first in Calgary, and as a result . . . a number of groups sprang up which were really economic study groups. He then initiated in the summer of '32, I believe, during the school holiday, a lecture tour around Southern Alberta, on which I accompanied him. . . . There was a tremendous response . . . and usually we left behind a nucleus which organized an economic study group in the community."[5]

Social credit doctrine of a "just price" for farmers found a counterpart concern in the United States, where farmers were clamoring for "parity" farm prices, and Franklin D. Roosevelt's administration brought forth the Agricultural Adjustment Administration with crop controls and subsidies. While Major Douglas's scheme seemed to prefer qualified technicians to guide political leadership, William Aberhart's Social Credit party evolved from province-wide economic study groups and made its own adaptation and application of the Douglas theory without the technical guides.[6]

As the depression deepened in Alberta, William Aberhart was increasingly disturbed by the inequalities around him, especially the plight of high school graduates in an economy with few jobs. The Douglas theory attacked "the foolishness" of governments that paid people to destroy food and other goods, or of merchants who kept their stock unsold on the shelves while people were in desperate need of these commodities but lacked the money to buy. Production and consumption were out of balance, but they could be corrected, ran the argument, by replacing private credit institutions with government programs administered for the benefit of the people. Credit would be extended to all bona fide citizens in the form of dividends on the wealth of the province. They would use this credit to purchase what they needed, thus stimulating business, creating more jobs, and restoring prosperity. Mr. Aberhart's system as to how this might work has been described by author John S. Barr. Each citizen would be issued a passbook, he writes, in which a $25 entry would be made each month at a State Credit House. The citizen could write $25 of nonnegotiable certificates for goods, but the amount was never redeemable in money. This would be "social credit," a supplement to cash. Such prospects were irresistible to debt-ridden people.[7]

During the election campaign, Mr. Aberhart preached a greatly simplified version of social credit theory. He believed that his election was based mostly on his reputation as an able and honest man, aided by the widespread dissatisfaction of voters with the ruling United Farmers of Alberta (UFA) and the other national parties. To many voters, social credit seemed a relatively safe alternative to the status quo, particularly when compared to the competing philosophies of socialism and fascism that were circulating at the time.

William Aberhart now began to feel increasing pressure from his broad-based following to create a political party to challenge the existing government. Hesitant at first to enter the political arena, he later recognized the inevitability of his candidacy. As a political philosophy, social credit confronted concerns similar to those faced by the New Deal and other economic reform movements in the United States. Its proposals were not so radical as those of the C.C.F. (Socialist) and Fascist parties that had been gaining some popularity throughout Western Canada. Social credit was likewise a moderate alternative to the UFA government, which, nearly everyone agreed, had to be changed.

The transition from study groups to political party was organizationally not difficult. The Aberhart following was broad-based and secure; visibility throughout the province was high; the organization was centralized and efficient; and the system of communications among the various groups was well-developed. The first major challenge of the Social Credit party was to select candidates for the provincial election on August 25, 1935. With no preexisting selection mechanism and without knowing dedicated followers who could become strong candidates, William Aberhart, Ernest Manning, and a few colleagues formed committees in each of the legislative ridings (districts) to select from three to five delegates. These delegates would be interviewed by a central committee, which would visit each of the ridings. On the basis of the recommendations and interviews, this central committee would select the final candidates to contest the provincial election.

In May 1935 the Cardston district convention of the Social Credit party met. Several hundred enthusiastic supporters met to nominate their favorite candidates to run in the fall election, and Kirkham L. Lee, Nathan Eldon Tanner, and Grover Thomas were named as delegates.

Eldon Tanner, like Mr. Aberhart, was reluctant to enter provincial politics. However, his humanitarian interests, which had led to his involvement in teaching, Scouting, coaching, and serving in church and community positions, caused him to overcome his reluctance and enter the political arena. In his acceptance speech, he declared that his support for Social Credit was primarily in hopes of improving the conditions of children in the province. As a school principal, he saw many students come to school poorly clad, undernourished, and having received inadequate health and dental care.

Social Credit had much the same humanitarian appeal to Eldon Tanner as it had to William Aberhart. He was very much concerned with finding solutions to the problems facing the people in Alberta and in the western world generally. He recognized the inconsistency of poverty in the midst of plenty. At the time of the depression, governments were paying farmers to destroy their produce and livestock. He felt that if the government had provided the same money to consumers, they could have bought the goods, and the country would have begun to prosper. He also became impressed with Mr. Aberhart's view that the province could create its own credit instead of borrowing from the outside and sinking further into debt.

It was William Aberhart's right to choose the candidate from Cardston from the three delegates named. Although popularity was an important criterion, other factors such as honesty, leadership ability, and loyalty influenced the final selection. He chose

Eldon Tanner to become the Social Credit candidate from the Cardston riding. Of the sixty-three Social Credit candidates announced for the coming 1935 provincial election, four were Latter-day Saints: N. Eldon Tanner; Solon Low of Stirling, a high school principal and Eldon's good friend; H. E. Wright of Lethbridge; and James Hansen of Taber.

With only one month remaining before the provincial election, the campaign consisted primarily of candidates' stumping through their respective ridings and holding rallies at churches, granges, fraternal organizations, shopping centers, and schools. The campaign benefited greatly from organization of the previously existing Bible and economic study groups. The Social Credit theme song was also borrowed from Aberhart's Prophetic Bible Institiute, "O God, Our Help in Ages Past." Ernest Manning later observed that the challenge had an atmosphere wholly different from that of a political campaign. It had the flavor of a crusade.

Eldon wanted his family to understand his campaign. When his daughter Beth asked him why he joined the Social Credit party, he told her that "it was necessary for the government to issue purchasing power in different ways . . . even, if necessary, giving a dividend so that the consumer could buy the goods." His family knew of his concern for the poor, and especially the children of the poor. They supported him and helped him in all his endeavors.

The Social Credit platform contained ten planks, focusing primarily on organizational and economic proposals. Included among the planks were proposals to eliminate governmental debt; increase health, education, and other social welfare services; increase government efficiency; encourage agricultural and industrial production; and develop a program of conservation for Alberta's natural resources.

Many of Alberta's citizens ignored the significance of most of the party's tested proposals and focused instead on the promise of a monthly dividend. The success of the Social Credit party seemed to depend on this. Conditions of the time, the upsurge of

William Aberhart's grass-roots influence, and the popularity of
the message made the Social Credit campaign one of the most
successful in Canada's history. In the 1935 election, 62 percent
more votes were cast than in the 1930 provincial election. Social
Creditors garnered fifty-six of the sixty-three seats in the General Assembly, a landslide victory. The new opposition consisted
of only five Liberals and two Conservatives. The UFA party,
weakened by criticism and scandal, failed to retain a single seat
in the legislature it had controlled for fifteen years.

With the popularity of the Social Credit party, combined with
his own strong history of leadership and civic involvement,
Eldon Tanner had no trouble carrying the Cardston riding on
August 25, 1935. He received 2,037 of the 3,063 votes cast in the
riding, winning twenty-two of the twenty-five precincts. His
closest competitor, the UFA candidate, received 564 votes, while
the Liberal candidate received 480 votes. The other Latter-day
Saint Social Creditors from Southern Alberta easily carried their
ridings also.

Newspapers and magazines throughout Canada reported
the stunning results of the election, though some expressed
skepticism about the party's unconventional platform. The September 2, 1935, issue of *Time* reported that when news of the Social Credit sweep in Alberta reached Montreal's conservative
financial center, "their astonishment was as vast as their dismay."
Eldon Tanner, the respected small-town schoolteacher and
principal, found himself in the thick of provincial politics and
controversy.

Now that they controlled the provincial power, the Social
Creditors had to decide what to do with it. Not a single member
of the majority party had previously held an elected position in
the province. They did not, however, come to power without cre-
dentials. Of the fifty-six MLAs (Members of the Legislative Assembly), twenty-four held normal school or university degrees.
The new party also boasted of such professional backgrounds as
teaching, medicine, engineering, law, clergy, business, and agriculture.

*Official portrait
of Premier William
Aberhart,
Edmonton*

On August 31 Mr. Aberhart announced his cabinet. He would be Premier and Minister of Education. Other members of the executive council would include John Hugill, Attorney General; Charles Cockroft, Provincial Treasurer; William Chant, Minister of Agriculture and Minister of Trade and Commerce; C. C. Ross, Minister of Lands and Mines; W. W. Cross, Minister of Health; W. A. Fallow, Minister of Public Works, Railways, and Telephones; and Ernest C. Manning, Provincial Secretary and Acting Premier. Many of the new Social Credit officials were young, and Secretary Manning, at age twenty-six, was the youngest man ever to be appointed to a Canadian cabinet.

The creation of the world's first Social Credit government caused no small stir among the citizens of Alberta. Shortly after moving into office, governmental officials were deluged with inquiries as to the exact date the dividends would be issued. Some Albertans quit their jobs or planned early retirement in anticipation of an additional income. Eastern Canada and the world also reacted with surprise and wonder. The landslide victory appeared to widen the rift between Canada's financial east and agricultural west.

Regarding the press's suspicion of Social Credit before and after the election, Premier Aberhart recited the following parable, reflecting his self-confidence and sense of humor: "An old man with a corncob pipe lounged at the station platform and watched a newfangled locomotive as it stood hissing on the rails with steam up. 'By gum, it won't move,' he said. But the throttle was opened and the strange machine started down the track in a cloud of steam. Its ca-choo, ca-choo became more and more frequent and its speed increased. 'By gum,' said the old fellow, 'it won't stop'"[8]

Eldon Tanner shared this same confidence.

Premier Aberhart hired experts in the Social Credit philosophy to start the new machine moving ahead. To prepare for the opening of the legislature scheduled for February 6, 1936, the Social Credit government not only had to generate bills to be considered by the legislative assembly, but to select a Speaker of the Assembly as well. Although the choice of Speaker belongs to the majority party, the office is ideally nonpartisan. A number of names were mentioned in various caucuses. Eldon Tanner specifically pressed the name of Solon Low for the position. Mr. Low, who was born in Cardston, had taught school since 1923 and had recently been made principal of a new high school in Stirling. A Latter-day Saint, he had studied at the University of Southern California. He had read and lectured on Social Credit in Raymond and had organized a study group in Stirling.[9]

However, William Aberhart did not nominate Solon Low as speaker of the Assembly; he chose Nathan Eldon Tanner. Ernest Manning remembered no other name than that of Eldon Tanner discussed in cabinet for the position of Speaker. He said, "There was no question at all that Mr. Aberhart had been very

favorably impressed with Mr. Tanner's ability, personality, and
fairness, all things you look for in a speaker."

Once approved by the cabinet, the proposal was placed before a caucus of the Social Credit MLAs. Again, Mr. Manning recalls no opposition to Eldon Tanner, and on November 23, 1935,
the young Mormon bishop was nominated and confirmed by the
assembly. According to the official report:

> The Premier, The Honourable William Aberhart, address-
> ing the Clerk, nominated Nathan Eldon Tanner, member for the
> Electoral Division of Cardston, to take the chair of this Assembly
> as Speaker, seconded by the Honourable John W. Hugill. The
> Clerk having asked if any Honourable Member had another
> name to propose as Speaker, and no name being proposed, the
> Clerk of the Assembly then declared, that Nathan Eldon Tanner
> is duly appointed Speaker of the Legislative Assembly according
> to law.

Legislative tradition in Alberta allows the outgoing Speaker
to retain his gown and chair, so Eldon had to borrow a chair and
gown in order to be installed as the Speaker of the Alberta Legislature. Journals of the legislative assembly report:

> The speaker retired and re-entered the Assembly, robed, ac-
> companied by his Mover and Seconder, and standing on the
> upper step of the dais, thanked the Assembly for the honour con-
> ferred upon him in the following speech:
> "Honourable Members: Permit me to express to you my ap-
> preciation of the high honour you have been pleased to confer
> upon me by electing me as your Speaker. I shall rely upon the
> loyal co-operation of all the Honourable Members to uphold me
> in maintaining the rules, orders and regulations and the best tra-
> ditions of the Legislative Assembly."
> The Speaker then took his seat and the Mace was placed on
> the table by the Sergeant-at-Arms.
> His Honour returned to the Assembly and took his seat on
> the Throne. Mr. Speaker then said:
> "May it please your Honour, the Legislative Assembly have
> elected me as their Speaker, though I am but little able to fulfill
> the important duties thus assigned to me. If in the performance
> of those duties I should at any time fall in error I pray that the
> fault may be imputed to me and not the Assembly, whose servant
> I am, and who, through me, the better to enable them to dis-

charge their duty to their King and Country, hereby claim all their undoubted rights and privileges, especially that they may have freedom of speech in their debates and access to your person at all reasonable times; and that their proceedings may receive from you the most favourable construction."[10]

In this speech, the Honorable Mr. Tanner was not simply expressing false modesty. He had never attended a session of the legislature—and now he found himself moderating its deliberations. Because he was inexperienced and unskilled in parliamentary procedure, before and after his swearing-in he spent long nights poring over rules of order of the legislature. During the sessions themselves, he received coaching from Robert Andison, the clerk of the legislature.

Following the swearing-in, Eldon obtained a robe (he can be seen in his full official dress in an official portrait hanging in the corridors of the Alberta Legislature Building). He maintained this official dress when he presided over the legislature.

The Speaker of the Assembly is responsible for calling the House to order, offering the prayer, and determining when any MLA may speak. As he enters the legislative chambers, the sergeant-at-arms precedes him with the mace on his shoulder and calls to the House, "Make way for Mr. Speaker." (This must have amused the modest N. Eldon Tanner and left him a little bewildered.) Members of the assembly stand while the speaker enters and remain standing while the prayer is offered. The Speaker sits at the head of the assembly upon a raised platform; the majority party sits to the right of the Speaker on the main floor, with the opposition parties on the Speaker's left. During the Manning and Aberhart years, Social Credit had more representatives than could comfortably fit on the right side of the Assembly. Consequently, some of the party's back-benchers (a term given to MLAs who hold no other legislative position) were placed with the opposition on the left half of the assembly.

The legislators from the majority and opposition parties face each other across the main aisle running from the Speaker's dais through the center of the assembly. The assembly table in the

Official portrait of N. Eldon Tanner as Speaker of the Alberta Assembly, Edmonton

center of the assembly separates the two sides. On the table is placed a bouquet of flowers, symbolic of the harmony that should pervade the House. The mace, the symbol of authority in the legislature, is placed on the table opposite the Speaker. According to British parliamentary tradition, the legislature can not convene without the mace.

The Speaker of the House is actually the chairman of the legislature; he directs the discussions and determines whether or not they are in order or contrary to the rules of order. Ernest Manning, who succeeded William Aberhart as Premier, observed that Eldon Tanner was "an excellent Speaker. He was completely fair and scrupulously careful not to be biased to one side or the other. He inspired confidence. I would say he was one of our best Speakers."[11]

The first session that Eldon Tanner presided over as Speaker of the Alberta Legislative Assembly enacted the Social Credit Measures Act of 1936. It also enacted the Provincial Loans Refunding Act, which reduced interest the province paid on its bonded indebtedness. The second session of that same legislative assembly in August 1936 enacted the Alberta Credit House Act, which established an agency to issue loans at interest not to exceed two percent. Those eligible were Social Creditors who were registered and who desired to build a home or start a business, and the act involved making a covenant not to claim payment of Alberta credit in Canadian dollars nor to use credits to pay taxes. Retailers were also to give preference to Alberta-made goods and to accept payment in Alberta credit derived from a monthly dividend under the statute.

The Alberta Credit House, a board of five members, was established with headquarters in Edmonton. The Credit House seemed to have bank functions, but without banking and currency terminology, in order to avoid conflict with section 91 of the British North America Act of 1867, the Canadian "constitution." The Credit House Act also empowered the government of Alberta to modify or supplement any provision of the Act. The powers of the Alberta Credit House appeared to many to be administrative rule-making run riot. The Ottawa *Journal* suggested on August 23, 1936, that this statute constituted a violation of federal authority.

The Social Credit Board, notwithstanding the constitutional question, went to work and became known to some as "The Little Cabinet." In its enthusiasm, it opened negotiations with Major Clifford Hagen Douglas in England, who sent two associates to serve as board "technicians." This group framed legislation for a four-day session of the August 1937 session, resulting in the Credit of Alberta Regulation Act, which undertook to regulate the credit policy of chartered banks operating in Alberta. The act also denied access to the courts by unlicensed bank employees and amended the Judicature Act of prohibiting an attack on the validity of any provincial statutes in the courts.

These statutes were all disallowed August 17, 1937, by the Ottawa government through the ancient but modernized procedure of the Privy Council, that is, the Premier and government in power. The practice of "royal disallowance" was well known to the original thirteen states of the United States when they were colonies of Great Britain. Although greatly diminished in scope and in use, section 56 of the British North America Act made enactments of provincial legislatures subject to disallowance within one year after enactment. Such disallowance was to be exercised on the advice of the Ottawa cabinet to the governor general, meaning that the federal party in power decided. The Dominion had used disallowance some ninety-six times between 1867 and 1920, but following World War I, there was a shift to judicial review, and disallowance went into disuse.[12]

The British North America Act provided national authority over canals, railroads, defense, and currency, including banking, credit, and bankruptcy. The purpose of these sections was to prevent the provinces from interfering with the development of a national economy (the United States Constitution in 1787 represented an effort along similar lines) and to provide an economic base for national authority.

Eldon Tanner—first as Speaker and later as cabinet minis-

*Door to
Eldon Tanner's
office
in Edmonton*

ter—lived through and was part of the impact of the initial Alberta Social Credit legislation on this constitutional system. The initial bringing together in 1867 of Quebec, the Maritime provinces, Ontario, and the western territories provided basis for an uneasy balance of power. Elements of that unsteady relationship have remained, and successive national governments have had to cope with this issue. The Canadian Pacific Railway project, a great east-west communication system, was one effort to bind the nation together. Another was C. D. Howe's push for the Trans-Canada Pipeline, preceded by the experiences of two world wars. Increased Canadian independence from the English Parliament after the Statute of Westminster in 1926 did not relieve Ottawa of this domestic uneasiness. The rise and development of the Social Credit party in Alberta under William Aberhart and E. C. Manning, his successor as premier, added to the tensions in the confederation, including the debate over control of Alberta's gas and oil in later decades. The Social Credit party's influence was a symptom of a major shift in the balance of power in Canada. The authority of the Crown through the provincial governor general to practice the remnants of royal disallowance, and review by the Canadian courts of legislative authority between Ottawa and the provinces, were questioned.

The provinces were supposed to have more power. The monetary legislation of the Social Credit government was perceived by Ottawa to violate the British North America Act and was disallowed along with thirteen other Social Credit bills. Never before had disallowance been so consistently applied to a given body of legislation. This action not only threatened the already tenuous relations between eastern and western Canada, but also polarized the factions within the Social Credit party itself. Federal disallowance was thus one of the most serious challenges to William Aberhart's administration.

The reaction of government members in Alberta, according to E. C. Manning, "was one of keen disappointment and frustration. Eldon Tanner shared those feelings. The federal power of disallowance, once rarely used, but resorted to arbitrarily, led many members to feel incensed and even bitter. Eldon faced these difficulties with his usual quiet dignity."[13]

The Supreme Court of Canada contended that provincial legislatures were sovereign within their own sphere, and that enactments that did not usurp the powers of the federal Parliament in Ottawa were valid. Alberta had pressed the borders of its authority to the breaking point, and there were no further serious attempts to achieve social credit by legislation.

Social Credit legislation was just one of Premier Aberhart's plans to improve government and repair the provincial economy. Making use of his organizational skill, he also embarked on a program of reducing government operations and expense. Soon after his inauguration, he traveled to Ottawa to request a federal loan of $18 million to provide Alberta some initial operating capital. Because of the suspicion with which the untried Social Credit philosophy and the unproven band of Social Credit legislators were held in the more conservative east, the Premier succeeded in securing a loan of only $2.85 million, and that only on the promise that in the upcoming federal election Social Credit would not contest the West Calgary seat held by Liberal R. B. Bennett, then Canada's prime minister. Mr. Aberhart also hired Robert Magor, a prominent fiscal conservative and member of the Montreal Chamber of Commerce, to serve as his financial adviser as a gesture to the financial powers of eastern Canada in an effort to stabilize Alberta's government. This step was seen by many of the radical members of his own party as capitulation and abandonment of Social Credit's predominant anti-banking philosophy, a rift that continued to affect the Aberhart administration.

Though national attention had been focused on the Social Credit legislation and the constitutional issues raised, controversy caused the Alberta legislature to pass reforms of a more conventional nature, hoping to relieve the financial plight of the worker and homeowner of Alberta. These laws included industrial and labor legislation to protect workers and measures for debt relief. As Minister of Education, Mr. Aberhart made good on a campaign promise by consolidating many provincial school districts, which improved administrative procedures and reduced costs. But conditions in Alberta remained less than favorable. Hail and grasshoppers added to the problems of a renewed drought and continuing depression. Social Credit's first year netted a budget deficit of more than $5 million.

Footnotes

[1] J. R. Mallory, *Social Credit and the Federal Power in Canada* (Toronto: University of Toronto Press, 1954), pp. 59-61. John Walker, in "The Political Life of Nathan Eldon Tanner" (Brigham Young University, February 12, 1980), says the net income per Alberta farm in 1927 was $1,975; this fell to $54 in 1933.

[2] In foreword to John A. Irving, *The Social Credit Movement in Alberta* (Toronto: University of Toronto Press, 1959), p. vii. See also chapter 2, "The Prophet."

[3] W. E. Mann, *Sect, Cult and Church in Alberta* (Toronto: University of Toronto Press, 1955), pp. 119-22.

[4] C. B. Macpherson, *Democracy in Alberta: The Theory and Practice of a Quasi Party System* (Toronto: University of Toronto Press, 1953), p. 95.

[5] Ernest C. Manning, interview with Steven L. Olsen, 1981. James Moyle Oral History Program, Church Archives.

[6] Macpherson, *Democracy in Alberta*, pp. 144-56.

[7] John S. Barr, *The Dynasty: The Rise and Fall of Social Credit in Alberta* (Toronto: McClelland and Stewart, 1974), p. 20, in John Walker, "The Political Life of N. Eldon Tanner," p. 3.

[8] L. P. V. Johnson and Ola J. MacNutt, *Aberhart of Alberta* (Edmonton: Institute of Applied Art, 1970), p. 148.

[9] See Irving, *The Social Credit Movement*, chapter 6, "The Web of Politics," esp. pp. 210-12. He writes: "Under Low's dynamic leadership the Mormon population of Alberta went almost *en masse* into the Social Credit Movement." He also listed Solon Low among the "secondary leaders," p. 186. In the 1950s Mr. Low served in Canada's House of Commons as a Social Credit Member of Parliament.

[10] Alberta, Journals of the Legislative Assembly, November 23, 1935.

[11] Manning, oral history interview, p. 15.

[12] Mallory, *Social Credit*, esp. chapter 2, "The Historic Role of Disallowance in Canadian Federalism," and chapter 5, "The Attempt to Establish Social Credit."

[13] Ernest C. Manning to G. Homer Durham, May 29, 1981.

5

Minister of Lands and Mines

At the end of the second session of Eldon Tanner's first legislature on September 1, 1936, the Tanner family returned to Cardston from Edmonton. Just before Christmas, shortly after retiring for the night, Eldon received a phone call from Mr. Aberhart, who asked, "How would you like to be a member of the executive council?" Eldon replied, "Mr. Aberhart, I have no ambition whatsoever. I am happy here where I am." After the Premier asked him three times, he agreed to accept a post. He expected to be appointed Minister of Municipal Affairs, where his experience on the town council and school board would have been helpful. He received his second surprise when a wire from Premier Aberhart arrived a few days later asking him to report to Edmonton "as expeditiously as possible" to take over the position of Minister of Lands and Mines.[1]

The current Minister was C. C. Ross, a former petroleum control officer who had been chosen because of his expertise in mining. The major disagreement between Premier Aberhart and Minister Ross was over the administration of conservation programs for Alberta's natural resources, specifically the closing of gas wells in Turner Valley. Before the Social Credit party came to power, Alberta had had no systematic measures for conserving natural gas. Consequently, many millions of cubic feet of natural gas were flared because no ready market existed for its export. Mr. Ross's method was to close down the gas wells, even though they also produced large amounts of oil, until markets could be developed. Premier Aberhart favored a more gradual schedule of conservation. Mr. Ross, who was neither a Social Creditor nor a politician, did not want to be held to political decisions. When he confronted the Premier with this fact, Mr. Aberhart asked for his resignation and received it.

Eldon Tanner, who had great respect for Mr. Ross personally and professionally, called him and arranged for a meeting in Calgary. During the meeting, the new Minister protested that he knew nothing of mines and natural resources, that Mr. Ross was far better qualified, and that he (Eldon) should not accept the position. However, Mr. Ross assured him, "You are my choice. You're the man that I recommended when they asked me."[2] After being assured that C. C. Ross was definitely leaving the government, Eldon decided to accept the new assignment. He reported to Edmonton on January 7, 1937. His duties as bishop had kept him up all the night before. This sudden turn of events must have given rise in his mind to some sense of wonder. Two years before, he had never thought of running for political office outside his own community, but already he had served as Speaker of the Alberta Legislative Assembly and now he was a member of the cabinet, the first Latter-day Saint in the British Commonwealth to rise to such positions of prominence. His unique position did not last long, however, because Solon Low, also a Latter-day Saint, was sworn in as the new Provincial Treasurer, replacing Charles Cockroft, who resigned over a disagreement with Premier Aberhart. Solon Low and Eldon Tanner worked closely together throughout their governmental service. In addition to sharing religious and political philosophies, they were the best of friends.

After taking the oath of office, Cabinet Minister Tanner told the press that he intended to manage his department for the good of all the citizens of the province. His years of government service would prove how seriously he took this pledge. A speech from the floor of the legislature, as reported in the Calgary *Herald* January 6, 1937, praised his selection for this position:

Cabinet members and Members of the Legislative Assembly, with N. Eldon Tanner in the front row, fourth from right

Those who know Mr. Tanner intimately are confident that a splendid choice has been made by the Government and that he will maintain adequately the traditional dignity and responsibilities of his important office. We are proud that a teacher has once again been raised to the eminence, Mr. Speaker, and we voice the hearty congratulations extended to him by Alberta teachers everywhere.

Mr. Tanner is a man with strong personality, reserved and unassuming; he never speaks until it is absolutely necessary and then with considerable effect. He is a good organizer, has a fine head for business and enjoys the happy faculty of winning popularity without seeking it, while yet respect maintains the ascendency over popularity.

Having been sworn in as Minister of Lands and Mines, Eldon Tanner declared that departmental policy would be "to develop the natural resources for the benefit of the people as a whole. Development should keep in mind the best interests of both the province and investors." In a newspaper interview he added the reflection, "I feel as if I have been in public life all my life."[3]

His responsibilities included supervision of the province's wealth of natural resources, including oil, gas and minerals, timber areas, fish, game, and public lands. He was in charge of formulating legislation and regulations for administering these areas, guiding them to passage in the legislature, and seeing that they were carried out. His valued and competent secretary, Mary C. Livingstone, later commented that "this was the beginning of great activity in the development of the resources of Alberta."[4]

John Hargrave, a vital force in Britain's Social Credit movement, had arrived in Edmonton in December 1936. He bore the image of a true disciple to the hopeful. After becoming familiar with Alberta's Social Credit government, however, he issued the following critical observations: "I still feel that the first Social Credit government in the world is not yet publicly committed to the principles of Social Credit. . . . It lacks technical knowledge and as a consequence has, over the past sixteen months, groped its way like a man stumbling along on a pitch-dark night."[5]

Nevertheless, the government was attempting to deal with social problems. Compromise with opposing views was essential for any progress to be made at all. Nathan Eldon Tanner said he wished the legislature were more concerned with the welfare of the people and less concerned with politics. He stuck to his tasks. He made concentrated studies of oil, gas, and natural resources policies, especially those of the United States; conferred with experienced experts; and traveled and inspected at every opportunity. He promoted Alberta's potential in Ottawa, seat of the Canadian government.

In February 1937, six days before the third session of the legislature convened, the Alberta Supreme Court struck down two important pieces of Social Credit legislation, the Reduction and Settlement of Land Debts Act and an act reducing the rate of interest on the province's bonds. As a result, Alberta had to default on a number of bond payments valued at several million dollars.

Three weeks later, Solon Low presented the 1937 Social Credit budget to the House for approval. Despite the presumed commitments to issue the dividends, the government made no Major Douglas-type Social Credit proposals. Taxation was increased on banks, corporations, railways, insurance, gas, and power companies. Despite the increased taxation, the budget contained a projected deficit of $1.2 million, part of which was to be recouped by a reduction in the interest rate on provincial debentures. While the opposition denounced the budget as anticipating further defaults, the radical Social Creditors (the Douglasite movement) opposed it for its lack of "true" Social Credit legislation. Eldon Tanner arose and, in his first speech before the House as a cabinet member, gave a rousing defense of the budget for more than an hour.

The battle lines were too firmly drawn for his speech to have much immediate effect. Minus the Social Credit insurgents, the government lacked a majority to approve the budget. Despite its landslide election nineteen months before, the Social Credit government appeared to some to be fighting for its life. After weeks of debate on the budget, a compromise was reached between Premier Aberhart's supporters and the insurgents. In return for support on the budget, the government created the Social Credit board to propose specific legislation reflective of Social Credit philosophy.

Although Douglasite controversy followed the Premier wherever he went, this move quelled the insurgency for the time being and united the party in deed, if not in complete thought. It also gave the government the decided advantage in its continuing internal debate with the Douglasite Social Creditors. The Social Credit board was given sole responsibility for proposing Social Credit legislation. If the board failed, the Douglasite faction of the Social Credit party would receive the blame. The board, however, was placed under the authority of the Cabinet, which could modify any legislation proposed by the board. In reaction to the strong criticism received for failing to initiate the Social

Credit dividend, Premier Aberhart quipped, "I feel in my present condition like the girl in the labor room of the maternity hospital, who asked the nurse to relay the following message to her young man: 'If marriage is like this, the engagement is off.'"[6]

In the fall session of the legislature, three major pieces of Social Credit legislation were passed. In the opinion of John Barr, the Credit of Alberta Regulation Act, the Bank Employees Civil Rights Act, and the Judicature and Amendment Act "struck at the power of the banks in a way more profound than any legislation ever drafted in a free nation."[7] They empowered the province to license banks, to prohibit unlicensed banks from operating, and to deny bank employees access to the courts. This legislation was disallowed within weeks of passage. By the end of 1937, the Supreme Court had disallowed all such legislation enacted during this session, a major blow to the Social Credit board.

While Premier Aberhart and the government as a whole were receiving serious criticism from the press, Eldon Tanner maintained consistently favorable relations with the media. Although as loyal to the government as anyone else, he avoided political controversy as much as possible. At one point in his career he observed in a note in his diary, "Politics is no game for me. I do enjoy my work as Minister of Lands and Mines but do wish politics, elections, etc., could be carried on in the interests of the people and not so much along selfish and ambitious lines."[8] While avoiding the controversy that much of the media feeds on, he trusted the press and expected the press to trust him. He later said, in retrospect:

> I was always prepared to talk to the representatives of the different papers and radio stations. As we were preparing our program I told them what I had in mind, what I intended to do, with the understanding that they keep confidential what I told them until I told them to release it. That way I had them always working with me.
>
> There was one exception. One particular reporter used to attend the legislative sessions, and I told him, at the same time I told others but not along with them, of some actions we were going to

*Official
portrait of
Ernest C. Manning
as Premier,
Edmonton*

take in the government, with the understanding, of course, that it be kept confidential. But he'd have the information and be able to ask questions and discuss it before the action was taken. This man broke faith and thought he had a scoop on the other papers. I called him in and told him it was the last time he could talk to me, and I reported it to the government. It wasn't long until he was taken out of the picture entirely.[9]

Minister Tanner always conducted his office with the highest moral principles. Many times he was given the opportunity to gain personal advantage from his position. On one occasion a wealthy businessman sought him out for special treatment. The Minister assured him he would be treated like anyone else. Not satisfied, the man pressed his point and more or less accused Eldon of selling out to the major oil companies. Indignant at such tactics, Eldon ordered the man out of his office. "I don't know what you want to get mad about," responded the man. Eldon replied that accusing someone of selling out was good cause for making him angry. The man later wrote a long letter of apology.[10]

The legislation Eldon proposed as Minister of Lands and Mines reflected his interest more in good government and social welfare than in doctrinaire Social Credit philosophy. One major piece of legislation he was working on as early as March 1938 concerned aid to the Metis, a mixed French-Indian minority population near Lesser Slave Lake in northern Alberta. The legislation would provide lands for settlement and resources for homes, other buildings, and occupational training to this economically depressed population of 13,000 persons. These measures were necessary, he felt, to enable the people to improve their livelihoods and to compensate them for the increasing commercial development of their traditional hunting and fishing grounds.

At the same time, Eldon was shepherding legislation through the House to establish an oil and gas conservation board for the province. Conservation of Alberta's natural resources had been a major plank in the Social Credit platform. The waste of natural gas in the Turner Valley to the tune of millions of cubic feet per year was appalling to the government as well as to many citizens. The board was set up to take the technical features of conservation out of the political arena and place them on the shoulders of experts. Eldon was able to encourage William F. Knode of Corpus Christi, Texas, a leading authority in the natural gas industry, to chair the board. Other board members included C. W. Dingham, former director of the Department of Lands and Mines, and F. G. Cottle, former accountant in the office of the Board of Public Utility Commissioners.

In debate before the House, Eldon Tanner admitted that the bill contained drastic measures, particularly those which empowered the board to "take such steps or employ such persons as necessary to enforce its orders." He replied, however, that such measures were needed to halt this unjustified waste of natural gas, adding that the drastic measures would not be used unless necessary. The measure was approved by the House with only minor opposition.

Other major legislation introduced by Eldon Tanner during the eighth Alberta legislature included a provision for a permanent three-man board to administer drought areas in the province, primarily in central and southeastern Alberta, consolidating the Department of Lands and Mines into one administrative structure. The board would be assisted by five field men to make recommendations regarding relief, agriculture, dam construction, and municipal affairs. The increased efficiency this measure provided did not increase administrative costs in the department.

Minister Tanner also guided through the House legislation changing the terms by which provincial land would be apportioned. Instead of homesteads, perpetual leases would be granted to persons willing to break virgin territory. Payment would be made on a crop-share basis, not cash. The advantages of such a program, according to the Minister, were increased provincial revenue without the possibility of a farmer losing his land for nonpayment of taxes. "If there is no crop, there will be no crop-share payment to make," he said in his defense of the bill before the legislature. Furthermore, no crop-share requirement existed for the first two years of occupation. Under this program, an applicant could acquire a twenty-year lease with the possibility of renewing the lease for additional twenty-year periods, and could purchase the government lands after ten years of continuous residence on the land. The farmer was also required to make improvements, such as habitable dwellings worth at least two hundred dollars. Royalties collected from the program would be turned over to municipalities and school districts.[11]

In addition to his work in the Department of Lands and

Mines, Eldon was a member of the following standing legislative committees: Agriculture; Colonization, Immigration and Education; Municipal Law; Public Accounts; Privileges and Elections; Railways, Telephones, and Irrigation. He was also on the committee to nominate Members of the Legislative Assembly to these and other provincial committees. He resigned his position on the Committee on Municipal Law in 1940 and on the Committee on Privileges and Elections in 1945, but assumed a seat on the Committee on Private Bills, Standing Orders, and Printing in 1942. He retained his other committee appointments throughout his tenure in the legislature.

In 1939 Minister Tanner led a committee of four to England in an effort to cultivate interest there. He knew there was a great future for the underdeveloped natural resources of Alberta, and he tried to spread the word to Britain in the hope of attracting more private capital to his province. In those early years before the war, Alberta's finances and economy still suffered from the depression, and he found English investors wary of his approaches. Some of them had already had unhappy experiences with other Canadian promoters. He and his group worked for a month in England, staying at the Canada House in London. They finally succeeded in interesting a few investors who ultimately became involved in developing the provincial industry. But most slid away, leaving the major role to investors from the United States. Perhaps part of the cool reaction that the Tanner group found in England was a result of the fact that the nation's attention was focused on preparations for the war that everyone expected.

Despite the generally favorable press coverage received by Minister Tanner, Premier Aberhart and the Social Credit party were continually being criticized by the press. In an effort to silence this opposition, much of which was mudslinging politics, the Premier introduced a misguided Accurate News and Information Bill or "Press Gag Act," as it was popularly termed, October 5, 1937. This bill served only to further consolidate mounting opposition to the Premier, infuriate an already hostile press

79

(the Calgary *Herald* was awarded a Pulitzer Prize for its defense of freedom of the press in opposing this measure), and bring the inevitable election one step closer. As might be expected, the Supreme Court disallowed this measure along with other 1937 Social Credit legislation.[12]

By 1940 Social Credit representation in the House had been reduced by defections and floor-crossings from fifty-six to forty-seven members. A coalition of Social Credit defectors and opposition MLAs calling themselves Independents waged a strong campaign against Premier Aberhart. Recognizing the inevitable, he called for an election on March 21, 1940. Although he was severely criticized during the campaign, he was equally able to return the volleys. In one of his more famous speeches, he responded to his critics with all his finely polished oratorical skills: "The voters know who it is who has been fighting for their God-given rights during the past five years. So let them roll out their barrels of money, these big shots and their deluded henchmen. I say let them begin at once their double-dealing, gossip-mongering whispering campaigns . . . the mothers know who has brought comfort to saddened hearts."[13]

Though his grass-roots support had dwindled throughout the province, Premier Aberhart still had a large following. Expressions of confidence included such comments as these: "Even if heaven (i.e., the dividends) cannot be brought to Alberta in a short time, a little of the hell may be removed." "The people of Alberta are proud to have a Premier who is capable of preaching the Gospel to hungry souls on Sunday, and is working for the good of humanity all the rest of the week." A popular quatrain went like this:

> "They say Aberhart is a crank
> And he accepts the name.
> A crank is what you start things with
> And he'll get there just the same."[14]

Although the incumbent Social Credit legislators who remained loyal to the government ran again in their respective ridings, candidates to contest the other ridings had to be selected.

As in 1935, William Aberhart retained considerable control over the final selection of Social Credit candidates. The procedure of candidate selection was much as it had been in 1935, only more formalized. Caucuses throughout the province elected as many as three delegates and provided the provincial committee with general biographical information on each candidate, assessments as to the candidates' public speaking ability, community opinion of the delegates, their possible motivations for participating in Social Credit, and their length of time as supporters of Social Credit.

Each candidate then responded to a lengthy questionnaire. In it, the person was asked for opinions on such Social Credit policies as state health insurance, old-age pensions, relief allowance, education assistance, natural resource conservation, development of a system of highways, and debt adjustment. He was also asked to comment on his attitude toward the party with questions such as: "If your Constituency Executive came to an open break with Government on any matter, what would be your stand?" "Have you said to anyone that if not chosen, you would run as a candidate anyway?" And "If not chosen, will you definitely work for the candidate chosen?" This information allowed Premier Aberhart to select the most loyal candidates. After the insurgency of 1937, it was increasingly important to him to have party unity. His advice to his candidates was, "Prudence will get us what nothing else can. Remember, prudence means a combination of two important qualities, piety and practical sagacity."[15]

Like Premier Aberhart, Eldon Tanner was a strong campaigner, but unlike the Premier, he tried at all costs to avoid personal attacks. He consistently defended the accomplishments of the Social Credit government. He encouraged voters to examine the record and judge the government on that rather than on second- or third-hand reports of government actions or policies. He was honest with his constituency. He admitted, "The Social Credit government has accomplished less than it set out to do, but it has accomplished far more than any previous government and more than the government of any sister province during the past five years. Yes, it has come back with the cleanest record yet."[16]

Minister Tanner's assessment was fair. The government succeeded in none of its patently Social Credit legislation, because of federal disallowance. It had, however, reduced the provincial debt by approximately $2 million per year, improved governmental efficiency, and established measures to benefit from Alberta's natural resources when world economy improved.

The party platform emphasized these accomplishments and promised to continue in the direction of good, honest government and conservation. World War II was raging; accordingly, the party pledged "full support to the war effort, an extension of the government's health, education and public welfare programs, reorganization of the municipalities, and continued debt protection."

Toward the end of William Aberhart's first term, Albertans did find themselves with an increased standard of living. The outbreak of World War II also enhanced production within the province, increased employment, and reduced the demand for the dividend. Social Credit's accomplishments, the change in the world situation, and the fact that the Independents proposed no positive alternative to Social Credit justified the voters in returning Mr. Aberhart to power. In a new government he enjoyed a smaller majority than he had his first term; Social Credit captured 43 percent of the popular vote and thirty-six of fifty-seven seats in the House.

N. Eldon Tanner handily retained his Cardston seat. He was the unanimous choice of his party's twenty-five-member delegation to the Social Credit convention held in Calgary on February 12, 1940. At the polls he defeated the Independent candidate, S. H. Nelson. Although his margin of victory was only 350 votes (2,152 to 1,801), incumbent Tanner won eighteen of thirty-one precincts in his riding.

In his second term as Minister of Lands and Mines, Eldon continued the consistent and broad-based conservation policies of his first term. The Metis communities began to be established, beginning in 1940, on 1.5 million acres of land near Lesser Slave Lake. The project was so successful that by 1946 ten new communities had been established housing 1,352 persons. In addition, five schools were constructed to provide career training and equipment for 240 children at a time. Many formerly unemployed persons began careers in farming, ranching, mink farming, and fishing.

With respect to Alberta's natural resources, Minister Tanner initiated a campaign to establish provincial control over all mineral rights in the province. He was successful in retaining 93 percent of such mineral rights, the other 7 percent having been granted earlier to the Canadian Pacific Railway, Hudson's Bay Company, and other public and private groups who would not transfer them back to provincial hands. His aim was to enable the province to monitor the sensitive balance between conservation and development and between private investment and public welfare. He said, "We feel that we should retain control over all natural resources to see that conservation is always followed in development. The programs should be administered to get the most returns possible, and the people as a whole should share in the control."

In order to achieve this purpose, Eldon made a careful study of conservation methods of oil- and natural-gas-producing countries. He was also able to attract some of the most knowledgeable people in the field to administer specific programs of the department. In the end, his department devised a scheme to encourage development of Alberta's energy resources and at the same time secure sufficient revenue for the province to carry out its social programs. In order to search for oil, a company was permitted to rent from the government two tracts of 100,000 acres each. Companies were allowed to lease additional tracts in the names of subsidiaries and friends. The company paid a nominal fee of $250 plus a $2500 deposit for each 20,000 acres leased.

The system encouraged speed in finding oil by means of steadily raising the rent from seven to twenty-five cents per acre

Ernest C. Manning, former Premier of Alberta, as he was interviewed in June 1981

over the second and third years of exploration. If the company failed to find oil in three years, it had to vacate the area. If oil was discovered, an ingenious system took effect. The driller could lease a tract of land either two-by-four miles or three-by-three miles immediately around his well. Such leases were for one dollar per acre per year. The lessee could also lease at this same rate one-half of the original 100,000-acre reservation where the tract was located. This half would be determined by dividing the tract checkerboard fashion and leasing the company alternate blocks up to half the tract. Should companies fall behind in their lease payments, the government could place a lien on the company's equipment to the amount of payments in arrears. No more than four wells could be drilled on any one block to reduce the overall expense of drilling. Every barrel was taxed by the province at 13 percent of the value of the oil. The tax was graduated, however, so that small producers could recoup their investment before having to pay the higher rate.

The other half of the checkerboard blocks reverted to the control of the Alberta government. These were auctioned in smaller pieces to the highest bidder. In this manner, the exploring company was "paid" for his investment through lower rental fees. However, no company could sit on an oil strike for very long without other companies drilling for the oil it had found. Drilling had to begin within a year of discovery of oil; otherwise, the company would lose its lease. At the same time, the province retained ultimate control over the mineral rights and received large royalties for the right to explore for oil, drill for oil, and extract oil from the land. Nevertheless, the government consistently and forcefully resisted pressure to confiscate oil property or nationalize oil companies. Minister Tanner felt that appropriate regulations and incentives in a free-market system would accomplish greater good than under any other type of economy.

This system of leasing oil lands worked to the benefit of both the oil companies and the province. Companies could acquire large tracts of land for exploration at relatively low cost and plan an orderly program of drilling over this large area. Small companies that could not afford to gamble on unproven lands could bid for leases on the government's alternate blocks near established oil fields. In addition, the limitation on numbers of oil wells per section made it impossible for an unscrupulous operator to move into a producing field and quickly siphon his neighbor's oil. Nor was the farmer forgotten. Drilling could take place only after the drilling company agreed to pay the farmer "surface nuisance" payments, which ranged from $1100 to $1600 per year for five or six acres. The farmer was allowed to farm the land on which the well was dug, so long as he did not interfere with the drilling operation.

These incentives to development made Alberta's oil fields the fastest growing in the world. At the same time they preserved a return to the people of Alberta of approximately 50 percent of the total oil profits, which controlled the economic boom and helped avoid many of its familiar excesses. The amount of money invested in recovering Alberta oil rose from $36 million in the early 1940s to $200 million in 1951. Eldon Tanner's role in this process was summarized by one journalist in a single sentence: "In Alberta, the government, for all practical purposes involving oil, is Tanner."[17]

Not everyone, particularly the small oil companies, was in favor of Minister Tanner's scheme when it was first implemented. Oil companies had been enjoying a virtually free hand in developing Alberta's vast reserves with no concern for the people of Alberta. When the government began to levy tariffs and exact royalties, many became incensed. Wishing to receive input from such firms regarding his proposed changes, Eldon sent a draft of the regulations to a board of directors composed of presidents and managers of oil companies operating in Alberta and asked for their suggestions and criticisms. Two weeks later he met with them. It was not a pleasant meeting; they categorically refused the proposed legislation. Minister Tanner replied that he was not seeking their approval, only their amendments and suggestions. "They were very indignant," he recalled, "not any more indignant than I, but they were greater in number."

Eldon returned to Edmonton to pursue his program. A week later the group met with him in his office to make a second protest. He later described the meeting: "One of them said, 'I represent so many thousand shareholders in my company and I must look after their interests. What you're suggesting is more than they can stand. It doesn't give them a fair return.' I said, 'I'm sorry, but I represent a million people here in the province of Alberta and I'm looking after their interests. I feel this is just as great a responsibility as you have.' They said, 'Well, we can't do it.' So all of them got up and walked out."

They returned later that day in a more conciliatory frame of mind. Experiences such as these earned Eldon Tanner the nickname "hard apple," as one journalist put it, "in tribute to the way in which he has operated his department to squeeze out the most profit for Alberta but still keep the development capital flowing in."

Even after the regulations were approved by the legislature a short time later, Minister Tanner had conversations and lengthy correspondence with oil firms protesting the perceived high financial cost of developing Alberta's oil. Nevertheless, most of them stayed and worked within the guidelines, and over the years many other companies shared the wealth of Alberta's vast oil reserves.

An attempt to eliminate waste of natural gas in Alberta was passed in the Alberta legislature in early April 1941. The measure, introduced by Eldon Tanner, granted an exclusive franchise to a corporation, or to a group of companies to be named by the government, to establish a pipeline to gather waste gas and return it to the structure of the field. The purpose of the legislation was two-fold: to eliminate the practice of flaring natural gas and to maintain pressure in the oil fields so that a greater proportion of the subsurface oil could be removed. Under this plan, producers would have to sell their waste gas, give it away, or pay to have it removed.

During the ninth legislature beginning in 1941, Eldon introduced legislation to create a natural-gas control board. The two-man board would have power to renegotiate contracts relating to the transportation, processing, purifying, selling, purchasing, and storing of natural gas. The board did not, however, have the power to control the production of natural gas or to deal with municipal franchises respecting natural gas. Nor was the board empowered to regulate the pricing of natural gas; this was the responsibility of the public utilities commission. Rather, the board was a watchdog over the conservation of natural gas.

In addition to oil and natural gas, Minister Tanner's department was vitally concerned with the coal reserves of Alberta. In

1939 he addressed the legislature in a strong protest against policies of the Canadian railway that inhibited development and
transportation of Alberta coal. He pointed out that it was less expensive to ship goods from Toronto to Vancouver than from
Toronto to Edmonton, and that Canada imported $45 million
worth of coal from the United States every year. When he assumed the portfolio of the Department of Lands and Mines, Alberta coal was being extracted at an annual rate of 5.7 million
tons, valued at $14.7 million. His work with the dominion gov-
ernment over the next several years encouraged coal production
in Alberta, and by 1942 Alberta mines yielded 7.7 million tons of
coal valued at $22.5 million, the highest production year in Al-
berta history. Although coal production remained high during
the early 1940s, the coal industry presented a constant challenge
to the Department of Lands and Mines.

In his second term as Minister of Lands and Mines, Eldon
Tanner proposed legislation to divide the province into three
game zones within which farmers and their immediate families
could shoot game birds without a license. In another step to
minimize destruction to farmers' crops and livestock, war
surplus ammunition was distributed to farmers for use on pred-
atory animals.

A related conservation measure was the annual practice of
the Department of Lands and Mines of distributing trees to
farmers to erect protective windbreaks and to prevent erosion of
the soil. Memories of the Dust Bowl were too vivid for such a conservation measure to go untried. Minister Tanner also
authorized distribution of poisons to kill magpies and crows,
which were destroying a significant amount of farm produce in
Alberta. In all this legislation, he tried to strike a balance between
wildlife conservation and agricultural production. His general
policy, as reported in the High River, Alberta, *Times,* was: "Alberta wildlife is an asset which must be carefully protected. Every
denizen of forest and field; every bird that takes wing over
prairies, foothills and mountains; every fish that races the rapids
is the property of the crown and therefore of the people of Al-

berta. As servants of the people of the province, it is a duty of government to protect and encourage perpetuation of wildlife in all forms."[18]

Eldon Tanner continued to be an avid supporter of the government. Reminiscent of his rousing defense of the proposed 1937 budget, he gave an impressive seventy-minute defense of the proposed 1942 budget. His speech was received with thunderous bipartisan applause. The Edmonton *Journal* reported of this event that "most members [of the legislature] were prepared to agree that the applause was in recognition of the Minister's fine review of the work of his department."[19] Of course, Eldon Tanner would be the last to claim that the work of his department was due to himself alone. He fully recognized his initial dependence on a few civil servants who had been carried over from the past regimes.

Footnotes

[1] N. Eldon Tanner, Ursenbach interview, p. 38.
[2] Ibid., p. 39.
[3] Calgary *Herald,* January 6, 1937.
[4] Mary C. Livingstone, "N. E. Tanner," typescript, March 1981.
[5] Barr, *Dynasty,* p. 100.
[6] Johnson and MacNutt, *Aberhart of Alberta,* p. 164.
[7] Barr, *Dynasty,* p 100.
[8] N. Eldon Tanner, diary, June 9, 1945.
[9] N. Eldon Tanner, Ursenbach interview, p. 7.
[10] N. Eldon Tanner, interview by Davis Bitton, 1972. James Moyle Oral History Program, Church Archives. Hereafter cited as Bitton interview.
[11] Edmonton *Bulletin,* March 31, 1939.
[12] Barr, *Dynasty,* p. 109.
[13] Ibid., p. 116.
[14] Cited in Lewis H. Thomas, ed., *William Aberhart and Social Credit in Alberta* (Vancouver: Capp Clark Publishing, 1977), pp. 141-42.
[15] Harold J. Schultz, "A Second Term: 1940," *Alberta Historical Review* 10 (Winter 1962): 17-26.
[16] Cardston *News,* March 19, 1940.
[17] *Colliers,* August 9, 1952, pp. 68-69.
[18] High River (Alberta) *Times,* December 9, 1943.
[19] Edmonton *Journal,* February 25, 1942.

6

Developing
Alberta's Resources

In 1943, N. Eldon Tanner was appointed chairman of the Alberta provincial Post-war Reconstruction Committee. William Aberhart had been the first Premier of Canada to encourage military conscription. The Social Credit government was the first provincial government to guarantee the seniority of civil servants who left their jobs to enlist in the armed forces. Alberta was also the first to protect, through legislation, soldiers' property throughout the war and up to a year after the war's end. The provincial government supported the Canadian government in its production and rationing measures to aid in the war effort, and many Albertans served their country in the war effort. To recognize this service and to help Alberta's veterans reenter civilian life, the government, at Eldon's encouragement, established the Post-war Reconstruction Committee, and he was named chairman.

Before the committee could begin its assigned tasks, William Aberhart, the embattled architect of the world's then only Social Credit government, found his physical condition to be weak. On the advice of his wife and his doctor, he went to Vancouver for a rest. There, on May 23, 1943, he died of what was diagnosed as cirrhosis of the liver. He was buried outside the province he had served since 1910. "We were too unhappy in Alberta," said his wife. Nearly all of the cabinet, including Eldon, went to his funeral. One of the cabinet ministers remained in Edmonton, since tradition dictated that at least one member of the provincial government must remain on duty at all times.

Premier Aberhart's natural successor was Ernest Manning, who had been with the Premier from the beginning of the Prophetic Bible Institute and was its first graduate, and who had been a devoted supporter of Mr. Aberhart during the evolution of the Social Credit party. He had become at age twenty-six the youngest cabinet member of any government in Canada's history, and had established a reputation for impeccable honesty and as a sound, able administrator. His election as Premier by his party was expected and well-received. At thirty-four, he assumed the reins of the government of Alberta and held them firmly for the next quarter of a century.

Many years later, Eldon Tanner would point to Premier Manning, in a general conference address, as an example of the ideal public servant, "a man of great integrity" and "100 percent trustworthy and sincere, with no hypocrisy of any kind." The admiration was apparently mutual, since Premier Manning retained Eldon Tanner in the cabinet for ten years and finally accepted his resignation reluctantly.

While William Aberhart had been an enthusiastic crusader and polarized some opinions, Ernest Manning was a political realist. He never compromised his moral principles, but could appreciate divergent points of view. In his own assessment, "I didn't inspire either that intense devotion or that intense dislike, which I'd say now is an asset in public administration."[1] His political realism also allowed him to back away from hard-line, doctrinaire Social Credit policies. His government was characterized by fiscal responsibility and efficiency.

The general improvement of Alberta's economy, the requirements of the war effort, and the 1943 change in Social Credit leadership allowed the party to downplay the patently Social Credit proposals of Major Douglas. The rift between Premier Manning's policies and the original Social Credit philosophy became even wider during the war. As a result of all these changes, the Premier was able to establish Alberta's government and economy on a more secure foundation.

Eldon Tanner was a prime mover in these successes. In March 1944, he presented to the legislature the first interim report of the Post-war Reconstruction Committee. The ambitious report recommended public works projects costing $40 million, the construction of public buildings costing $6.25 million, a ten-year educational building program costing $20 million, and a road improvement program costing an estimated $130 million. One of the committee's more innovative proposals involved a land settlement scheme to bolster Alberta's agricultural base and to provide ready-made occupations for returning veterans. Under this plan, large sections of Alberta's prairies would be cleared at government expense; veterans from Alberta could then claim certain amounts of this land as homesteads. The government would recover its investment by share-lease arrangements with the landed veterans.

In May 1945 Eldon went to Ottawa at the request of Premier Manning to meet with the director of the Canadian Veterans Land Act to work out an agreement for the settlement of veterans in Alberta. In this program, if the veteran developed the land, he would be free from his obligation to the government in seven years, and after ten years he would obtain free and clear title to the lands he farmed. Because of such incentives, many thousands of veterans returned to Alberta to settle permanently. The land program benefitted the veterans most directly; other committee recommendations, such as job training, national health insurance, establishment of agricultural extension agencies, and a road improvement plan, were to have long-term beneficial effect on Alberta.

The final report of the committee to the legislature in 1945 contained a political philosophy that characterized Minister Tanner and the Manning government: ". . . if reconstruction is to have any meaning, it must be initiated on the basic understanding that the person and the family are the first beneficiaries of the rebuilding process." It also contained a glimpse into the concept of governmental operations under Premier Manning: "Reconstruction demands a process of social engineering, and social engineers will bear in mind that social power lies in the unity of the people. They will recognize that social power bears certain characteristics similar to solar power. It must be properly generated, properly transmitted, properly applied. And like all engineers, they will recognize that the longer the line of transmission, the greater the loss of power. . . . Government, therefore, will remain close to the source of power."[2]

The committee held its final meeting on March 19, 1945, and after its report was submitted to the legislature, the committee was dissolved and specific projects of the government relating to veterans were handled by the Veteran's Welfare and Advisory Commission.

In 1943, in addition to his other duties, Eldon assumed chairmanship of the Alberta Research Council, a board of educational, professional, and governmental experts whose purpose was to generate pure and applied research to benefit the province. Given Alberta's challenges in the 1940s as well as Chairman Tanner's principal orientation, the focus of the research sponsored by the council was economic, including the following: to determine the best and least expensive surfacing material for Alberta's expanding highway system, to determine the most efficient manner to extract tar from Alberta's vast Athabasca Tar Sands reserves, to investigate the most appropriate uses, domestic and industrial, for Alberta's varied energy reserves, to conduct a market survey of products produced in Alberta, and to test Alberta soils and different varieties of crops to determine the agricultural capabilities of the province. Eldon expressed the value of this research as follows:

> To make Canada a prosperous and progressive country, industries must be established and scientific research on a large scale must be carried on. Only as this is done, will we enjoy the growth, development and security which is possible.
> Scientific research is demanding more and more interest on the part of those engaged in industry, as well as government, all

over the world. Everywhere today we see and realize the importance and effect of scientific research in the progress of humanity.[3]

Before his government had become too comfortable in its
position, Premier Manning called a surprise election for August
8, 1944, one year before William Aberhart's five-year term ex-
pired. The early election was designed to ward off the growing
influence of the Socialist (CCF) party in Canada. In 1943 a Gal-
lup poll showed that the CCF party was the most popular party in
Canada, with 29 percent of the voters' preference. That year it
gained control of the government in Saskatchewan and captured
thirty-four seats in the House of Commons in Ottawa to become
Canada's official opposition party. Though it was not yet a strong
threat in Alberta, Ernest Manning figured that a provincial election would disperse the opposition before it had time to coalesce.

The 1944 Social Credit campaign was run on a platform of
sensible free enterprise, emphasizing the danger of "bureau-
cracy and regimentation" from the left. The radical reform spirit
of 1935 and 1940 were gone from the campaign rhetoric. At the
same time Mr. Manning emphasized the government's social
and economic achievements: highways; land for returning veterans; free tuberculosis, cancer, and polio care; increased old-
age pensions; maternity hospitalization; tax cancellation; and reduced insurance premiums.

The polarization of the issues routed the Independent coalition of Douglasites. Some of the former opposition sided with
the CCF, but many rejoined the Manning ranks. Opposition
presses were even forced to acknowledge the accomplishments
of the Manning government in contrast with the untried and
largely unknown socialist program. Although the CCF ran well
in many ridings, the Social Credit party was resoundingly returned to power with 52 percent of the popular vote and fifty-
one of fifty-seven seats in the House.

Eldon Tanner had no difficulty retaining his Cardston seat.
He received 2,104 of 2,696 votes cast. One difficulty the Minister

The Alberta Legislature Building, Edmonton

of Lands and Mines did encounter during the campaign gained the attention of the Toronto *Globe and Mail* and remains today one of the oft-repeated stories. Accurate or not, it has entered the folklore of the times.

> At a political meeting in Tanner's Province an inebriated man in the front row interrupted the previous speaker constantly with the refrain, "I am a Liberal."
> When his own turn came to speak Hon. N. E. Tanner decided

to deal with the heckler at once to leave the way clear for his later remarks. So he addressed the disturber at once and, levelling his forefinger, said: "You say you are a Liberal. Why are you Liberal?"

"Well, my grandfather was a Liberal, my father was a Liberal, my whole family are Liberals, and so I am a Liberal."

"If your grandfather were a jackass, and your father were a jackass and your whole family were jackasses, what would that make you?" asked the Minister. "A Social Creditor," was the instant reply.[4]

During Eldon's third term, Elder John A. Widtsoe, of the Council of the Twelve of The Church of Jesus Christ of Latter-day Saints, and his wife, Leah, visited Eldon and Sara on assignment from the First Presidency. The Social Credit philosophy was not understood in Utah, and Church leaders wondered if the Alberta government might be "up to some mischief." On August 31, 1945, the Tanners, the Widtsoes, President and Mrs. J. Y. Card of the Alberta Mission, and Solon Low spent an evening discussing politics at the Tanner home. Of Elder and Sister Widtsoe's reaction Eldon wrote: "They seemed very interested and approved of several principles. . . . Before they left Sister Widtsoe urged us to go right ahead and Elder Widtsoe said we seemed to understand the problem confronting the economic world and were prepared to offer a solution or partial solution at least."

Next day Eldon recorded in his journal: "The Widtsoes are lovely people. We need only to compare our General Authorities with other people . . . to realize how superior they are." Evidently he felt his views had passed a critical test.

In his third term as Minister of Lands and Mines, Eldon Tanner maintained the programs he had initiated previously: the Alberta Research Council, the post-war reconstruction work, the development of Alberta's energy reserves, and the conservation of natural and animal resources, in addition to his campaign for good government and fiscal responsibility. He followed a demanding speaking schedule to take his policies to the people of Alberta. Rarely did a week go by without several speaking assignments at luncheons and dinners. He addressed the Alberta Board of Trade and Agriculture, the Canadian Institute of Mining and Metallurgy, the Interstate Oil Compact Commission, the Kiwanis Club, the Lions Club, the Canadian Manufacturers Association, the Alberta Fur Growers Association, the Alberta Fish and Game Association, the Alberta Long Grass Growers Association, and the Chemical Institute of Canada, in addition to party rallies. He also recorded several radio broadcasts relative to departmental actions in order to be as responsible as possible to the people of Alberta.

During this term, Eldon Tanner served as Acting Premier when Mr. Manning attended the Dominion-Provincial Conference in Ottawa in August 1945. For each cabinet post, two or three "acting ministers" are authorized to conduct business in the appointed ministers' absence. Any one minister may be acting minister for several other departments. Eldon served as Acting Provisional Secretary and as Acting Minister of Economic Affairs on occasion, while serving as Minister of Lands and Mines.

Eldon's far-sighted legislation as Minister of Lands and Mines began to pay off in tremendous financial benefits for the province. In 1942 less than $300,000 was paid to Alberta from oil and natural gas rents, royalties, and leases. This amount had risen in 1944 to $1.1 million, resulting from 3.5 million acres explored by sixty-six active companies. During the same year 8,788,845 barrels of oil had been extracted from Alberta's soil, worth at 1944's low prices $14,468,061.[5]

Then on February 13, 1947, at 4:03 P.M., Eldon Tanner witnessed the beginning of the great Alberta boom. The Imperial Leduc No. 1 well, sixteen miles south of Edmonton, brought in the first major Alberta oil strike. Clouds of flame and smoke could be seen from the city as the well was flared. Minister Tanner was invited to turn the valve that started the flow of oil into the storage tanks.

As a result of this and subsequent strikes, the provincial government received $72 million in lease auctions alone from 1947

N. Eldon Tanner turns valve at oil field in Alberta

to 1951. Rental fees and royalties produced an additional $48 million. The Leduc well, after Imperial Oil Limited had spent $25 million in fruitless exploration, clearly established Alberta as a major world oil and gas center. As the returns from exploration increased, the lease auctions became increasingly competitive. On June 17, 1949, Minister Tanner noted with pride in his journal, "The day before yesterday a section (640 acres) of oil rights brought a bonus of $3,223,230." *Time Magazine* for September 24, 1951, reported that since Imperial Leduc No. 1 came in, forty-five new oil fields had been established, with an average drilling rate of two new wells per day. The report added that "more than 300 million U.S. dollars, one of the freest and fastest streams of American private capital ever sluiced into a foreign country, have been invested in Alberta oil." On May 22, 1952, the competitive bidding brought $3.1 million for one quarter section and $2.1 for another. Eldon noted in his journal, "All in all the sale brought approximately $10,000,000."

In 1952 the Atlantic No. 3 well in the Leduc field went out of control. Oil and gas were blown for hundreds of yards, "and the area resembled the geysers of Yellowstone," observed Eldon's secretary, Mary Livingstone. Atlantic No. 3 was said to be responsible for the increased international interest in Alberta's oil.[6]

Some have claimed that the ability of Alberta's economy to turn around so rapidly after the war was based on the moderation of the weather and the fortunes of a number of oil companies. It is certain that Alberta weather did moderate in the late 1930s and the 1940s, and that the oil boom came at a particularly opportune time for Alberta and the Social Credit party. It is also true that Alberta had prepared for these events by legislation designed to benefit the people of Alberta without diminishing outside investment interests. Had it not been prepared for the strikes, the province might have experienced much more of the boom-bust economy than it did. With Minister Tanner and his able staff taking the lead in Alberta's conservation policies, the government enabled the wealth acquired from its energy reserves to spread broadly across the province and to improve social services greatly, particularly in the fields of education and health care. The emerging wealth of the province encouraged other large-scale private investment. A plastics industry emerged to make use of the cheap energy and raw materials. Plans were begun for a steel mill in Alberta, using local gas to smelt iron from British Columbia. A similar arrangement using timber from western Canada resulted in Alberta's first pulp and paper mill. The skylines of Edmonton and Calgary began to

99

change as high-rise office buildings were constructed, reflecting the rapid influx of financial, transportation, and other business firms. An era of prosperity in Alberta had begun.

On January 24, 1947, Eldon Tanner wrote in his diary that he had had lunch with a Dr. Hume "and we discussed the possibilities of the Tar Lands. He says 120 acres is capable of producing over 350 million barrels. Premier Manning and I also discussed with James Lowrey and Marsh Porter the question of gas and oil conservation and also the Gas Utilities Act."

Shortly after the Leduc strike in the spring of 1947, Eldon and Sara left for a month-long tour of oil- and gas-producing areas of the United States. They traveled to Oklahoma, Texas, New Mexico, California, and other states, where they became familiar with the latest developments in legislations, operations, and technology, including that for synthetic fuels. Not only did Eldon learn more about the energy industry in America, but he also received many inquiries about Alberta's oil industry. In Tulsa, Oklahoma, he met with the Oil Compact Commission. There he consulted with Robert Hardwick, whom he described in his diary as "one of the recognized authorities in oil and gas development and conservation . . . and the best-informed lawyer in the industry I have ever met." He also met with representatives of Continental and Humble Oil companies and others.

March 1949 found him in Dallas, Texas, where he presented a paper on the oil and gas laws of Alberta at a meeting of the Southwestern Legal Foundation. A month later he went to New York with Sara and their daughter and son-in-law, Ruth and Cliff Walker. There he consulted with Imperial Oil and other interests. Such excursions to the East, including Ottawa, Montreal, and Toronto, increased as the oil and gas industries of Alberta developed. Correspondingly, his concerns with cabinet and legislative affairs mounted. A special session of the legislature convened July 4, 1949, to deal with issues involving oil and gas conservation. He wrote in his diary, "We have reached the point where there is more oil being produced than the Prairie Provinces can use." Such information at the national level did not escape the attention of C. D. Howe, Minister of Trade and Commerce, as well as the attention of American oil and gas interests.

Because of the oil strikes and the developing interest in natural gas, the market for Alberta coal declined substantially in the post-war era. As a result, Eldon introduced legislation to open all of Alberta's lands to coal mining subject to proper application to and approval of the Department of Lands and Mines. Before this was done, however, the department generated policies requiring reclamation of lands affected by strip mining. This was the first major strip-mining legislation in North America and went far to balance the need for a beautiful environment with that for the development of energy reserves. He also initiated mine safety legislation requiring monthly inspections of operating mines.

Another policy established by the department was that wildlife resources taken from the province for commercial use were to be taxed. In 1945 more than eight million pounds of fish were taken from Alberta waters by commercial fishermen. With the income received from this taxation, the province was better able to administer wildlife conservation. One effect was to make Alberta whitefish known throughout North America for their quality. The province was also able to pay higher bounties on predators, such as wolves, whose numbers had grown dangerously large in some areas of the province. The Ministry bolstered renewal of forests to an extent that $10 million in lumber was taken from Alberta forests in 1945 with detrimental impact on watershed and wildlife.

In 1947 Eldon completed a twenty-five-year dominion-provincial agreement to preserve forests along the eastern slope of the Canadian Rockies. The Eastern Rockies Forest Conservation Board was designed to administer the watersheds, trees, and wildlife of more than nine thousand square miles of Alberta's forests. By 1952, revenues from commercial extraction permits, tourist permits, and other kinds of taxation paid for almost all the maintenance costs of this vast preserve, including the building of trails and lookouts and other forestry work.

Riding high on the first wave of the oil boom, the Manning government was overwhelmingly confirmed in office in the election of August 19, 1948. Eldon too maintained his popularity in Cardston, being favored for his fourth term as an MLA by a more than two-to-one margin. He won all but seven of thirty precincts.

Premier Manning found in Eldon Tanner a man he could trust and admire. He sought Eldon's advice on many issues and policies of his administration, even those beyond Minister Tanner's departmental responsibilities. He confided in Eldon because of the latter's personality, expertise, and spiritual dimension.[7] He also knew that matters would be kept in strictest confidence. The respect was mutual. *Collier's* magazine on August 9, 1952, said of them both, "Oilmen classify both men as 'political freaks' possessed of 'fantastic honesty.' No one thinks there is the slightest chance of corrupting either."

Under Eldon Tanner, the Department of Lands and Mines had become enormous, and soon after the election, he conferred with Premier Manning on dividing the ministry into two separate units: a Department of Lands and Forests and a Department of Mines and Minerals. Mr. Manning agreed. Over the next few months, details of the division were worked out, and on March 30, 1949, the split was realized—with Eldon asked to serve as Minister of both departments!

Details of the swearing-in ceremony for the two departments have been provided by Ernest Manning, who recalls:

> The Imperial Oil Company had built an oil tanker in Chester, Pennsylvania, and named it the *S.S. Imperial Leduc,* after the oil field. They asked my wife to christen the ship, so we were invited down to Chester, and we asked Mr. Tanner and his wife to go along. . . .
> We were to leave Edmonton in the afternoon of March 31 [1949]. The day we were to leave, somebody in the government discovered that the bill terminating the old joint Department of Lands and Mines died at midnight that night under the old legislation and that two new departments came into being. . . . With new departments, there had to be a new minister sworn in, because the names of the departments were changed.

> We were to leave that afternoon, and we couldn't swear Mr.
> Tanner in before midnight, because that's when the old depart-
> ment would end. So we called Imperial Oil and they said, "Well, it
> doesn't make any difference to our boys. They can fly you down in
> the night as well as in the daytime." Our lieutenant governor in
> those days had a suite in the McDonald Hotel. So Eldon and Mrs.
> Tanner and my wife and I and some other members of the
> Cabinet gathered in the governor's suite at five minutes to mid-
> night, and at the stroke of midnight we swore Eldon Tanner in as
> minister of the two departments. There was a car waiting down-
> stairs; we tore down to the car and rushed to the airport, and
> twenty minutes later we were on our way to New York.[8]

Eldon's reputation was as secure in the oil industry and
among his constituents as it was in government. As Ernest Manning observed, "He did have the reputation, very widely and
firmly, certainly throughout the petroleum industry and among
the people at large, of always being absolutely impartial and
fair."[9]

Indicative of Eldon Tanner's professional reputation, the
government of Barbados invited him to be its guest in the spring
of 1950. Barbados was beginning to face the storm of energy reserves development that Alberta had begun to successfully
weather under Eldon's direction, and he was asked to help Barbados design a conservation policy that could balance conservation and development as Alberta's policies had done.

On Wednesday, April 5, 1950, Eldon and Sara flew from Edmonton to Ottawa, where they met with, among others, the
British high commissioner, Sir Alexander Clutterbuck. After
two days in Ottawa, they continued on to Bridgetown, Barbados,
where they were first taken to Government House as guests of
the governor general, Sir Alfred Savage, and Mrs. Savage, then
to a hotel.

Eldon was provided with an office, and he began negotiations, on behalf of Barbados, with the British Oil and Petroleum
Company (BPOC) and Trinidad Leaseholds. Gulf Oil Company
was also involved in the negotiations. By Saturday, April 22,
Eldon could report in his journal: "We are making good progress, but I am expecting some problems with the Trinidad

Leaseholds and the BPOC. Gulf seems to be coming along okay." Over the weekend, however, negotiations broke down with both BPOC and Trinidad Leaseholds, and during the following days he reported meeting with the Gulf representatives and making "very little headway." He noted that Gulf was in a much stronger bargaining position now that the other two companies had withdrawn, but that Gulf's representatives were "holding out for some changes, which we will likely have to grant." By April 27 Eldon thought he had the regulations drafted and acceptable to both sides. But the New York office of Gulf advised its representatives that they should not yet sign, and requested that the entire documentation be sent to New York.

Eldon and Sara had expected the negotiations would be completed by April 29, and so they had made airline reservations for their return to Canada. They now returned to Government House, since their hotel room had been released. The negotiations with Gulf continued for several more days, and on May 4, Eldon noted, "Though things do not look too bright, I still have hopes."

The next day, Friday, he was able to work out an agreement on all points with the Gulf Oil representatives. He reported this to the governor general at 10 P.M., and Sir Alfred promptly invited all concerned to Government House to celebrate.

After the celebration Sara and Eldon packed, and they were ready to leave at 5:30 the following morning. He said, "Though I did not get all I wanted for the island, I am satisfied that they got a good deal, and everyone seemed to be happy and appreciative." The Tanners arrived home at Edmonton on Monday, May 8, 1950, to find everybody well and happy. The next day Eldon was fifty-two years old, and he recorded in his journal, "They certainly made good progress on the Church while we were away."

By 1952 Eldon Tanner had decided that his contribution to the government and economy of Alberta had been made. The two departments over which he had presided were well organized and running smoothly. The legislation he had intro-

duced was producing huge social, economic, and cultural results. The government had reduced its debt payments from 50 to
5 percent of the provincial budget. His journal shows that he had
contemplated retirement from the government as early as 1947,
but had resisted some tempting offers from private firms. Five
years later, after discussing his decision with his family, he talked
it over with Premier Manning. Mr. Manning responded that he
had contemplated stepping down himself to let Minister Tanner
assume the premiership. Not being politically motivated, Eldon
respectfully declined the offer. He agreed to remain in the
cabinet until autumn to avoid the politics of a replacement just
before an election.[10]

Premier Manning publicly announced Eldon's retirement on
June 28. From that time until the election on August 5, Eldon
worked for the reelection of other Social Credit candidates and
for a smooth transition of departmental ministers. He did not
stand for reelection and was replaced as the Cardston delegate.
His Mines and Minerals portfolio was assumed by Premier Manning himself at that time.

Ernest Manning and the Social Credit Party were returned
once again to power with the majority of forty-nine of sixty-one
seats. The party's pragmatic policies would continue to dominate
Alberta politics for another two decades with Social Credit
majorities winning every election until 1970. The effects of
Eldon's tenure would be felt much longer than that.

Before the election, many articles commented on Eldon's impending resignation. On December 6, 1958, the Calgary *Albertan*
summarized his contributions as follows:

> As architect of Alberta's eminently successful government oil
> and gas policy, Mr. Nathan E. Tanner won the respect and ap-
> preciation of the people of this province many years ago. As
> Minister of Mines he worked out a system combining maximum
> returns to the public treasury with adequate incentive for the in-
> dustry. Such a policy created both the vast development of the in-
> dustry and the return of hundreds of millions of dollars to the
> government coffers. One has only to look around him to see the
> network of paid-for-roads, the public buildings, the new schools

and many other projects financed directly or indirectly by this oil revenue, to appreciate the results of the policy evolved by Mr. Tanner during his years in the provincial cabinet, and followed ever since. In the eyes of other governments it is perhaps the world's most successful oil and gas policy.

The Edmonton *Journal* questioned his motives but, finding no hint of scandal or impropriety, stopped short of making any charges. Elsewhere, Minister Tanner's record received only praise. One magazine article published before the election suggested that his impending resignation was the biggest news of the campaign because of his role as "a pillar" of the government. "It was he who administered the oil boom which has enriched a province already bountifully blessed with grain, cattle, timber, minerals and scenery. The administration will miss him." The article went on to affirm the reputation that he had established among industry leaders.

With his final term of office at an end and the press speculating about his future, Nathan Eldon Tanner must have paused to review with some satisfaction his public career. His rise to power, beginning with his election in 1935, had been sudden, unsought, and unexpected. He had been elected to his seat four times and had served in the Alberta government for nearly seventeen years. He had presided over the crucial years of one of the largest oil booms in North American history. Throughout his political career, his membership in The Church of Jesus Christ of Latter-day Saints had been widely publicized, and in every way he had reflected honor on the Church and his heritage. He had served the government well without compromising his principles or losing his independence. Indeed, one of his most memorable experiences during this period, often retold in later years, was a time when he stood to vote against his own government on a proposal that he could not accept. Warned by colleagues that this vote could cost him his government post, he replied that he "would rather be *out* honorably than to be *in* voting against my principles." He took particular satisfaction in an editorial that appeared in the Calgary *Albertan* praising his record. It read in part: "For the general good sense of the government's oil policies, most of the credit must go to Hon. Nathan Tanner, whose impending resignation from the Cabinet will be received everywhere with genuine regret. . . . We have not always agreed with him, but we respect him; and now, on his departure, we sincerely wish him well."

Eldon had always maintained that a man would go farther in this world on respect than on popularity. His own career in government had given evidence that he was right. V. A. Wood, director of Lands and Forests, wrote of his chief, "He was more interested in doing what he considered right than in making decisions for political expediency."[11]

The Honorable Mr. Tanner, in reflecting upon his resignation, recalled: "When I resigned the Premier didn't want me to resign. At least he said he didn't. But the papers tried to find some reason for my resigning, and as papers do, dug into everything they could to see if they could find something against me. I'm not boasting, but I'm very happy to say they were not able to do this. I think the reason they were not able to do this is because every night and every morning I prayed to the Lord that my administration would never be such that it would be a reflection on my character or the Church."

Although he had various personal business dealings while in government service, Eldon always scrupulously avoided any potential conflict of interest. Consequently, when he was offered top positions with a number of different oil companies, he refused. Once he decided to return to private business full-time, he resigned his government position and left a clean and admirable record.

Upon his retirement from the government, he was honored by many civic and business organizations throughout Alberta. At a dinner of the Edmonton Chamber of Commerce, he was awarded a silver tray on which was inscribed "Presented to Nathan Eldon Tanner by the Edmonton Chamber of Commerce, Nov. 12, 1952, in recognition of his outstanding contributions toward the development of the natural resources of Alberta while in the public service as a minister of the crown."[12] A newspaper article of the time said, "The oilmen with whom Tanner has worked in the past five years deeply respect him; they call him a 'hard apple' in tribute to the way in which he has operated his department to squeeze out the most profit for Alberta but still keep the development capital flowing in." At a retirement dinner in his honor in the Edmonton Masonic Hall, he responded to these many honors with a philosophy of service that had become a hallmark of his life: "The service we give is the price we pay for the privilege of living in this world. The type of service we give will determine the kind of world we will live in."[13]

Footnotes

[1]Manning, oral history interview, p. 48.
[2]Alberta Legislative Assembly, Alberta Post-war Reconstruction Committee, Edmonton, 1945; Alberta Provincial Archives, Edmonton.
[3]Calgary *Herald,* January 17, 1946.
[4]Toronto *Globe and Mail,* December 6, 1944.
[5]Alberta Legislative Assembly, Annual Report of the Department of Lands and Mines, Alberta Provincial Archives, Edmonton. At 1981 world prices, the figure would be about $270 million.
[6]Livingstone, "N. E. Tanner."
[7]Manning, oral history interview, p. 45.
[8]Ibid., p. 38.
[9]Ibid., p. 44.
[10]Manning, oral history interview, pp. 42-48.
[11]Letter to G. Homer Durham, February 19, 1981.
[12]Edmonton *Journal,* November 13, 1952.
[13]N. Eldon Tanner, scrapbook.

7

Family and Church:
The Edmonton Years

While serving as Speaker of the Alberta Provincial Legislature in 1936, the Honorable Mr. Tanner continued to maintain his residence in Cardston. He had to be in Edmonton only about three months: January, when he prepared for his new role, and February and March, during the legislative session. Afterwards, he returned south to teach school. Those three months were not without their difficulties in Cardston as well as in Edmonton, where Eldon was getting established in his new government position.

The family had only recently purchased their first home in Cardston. Sara went to Edmonton with Eldon, and they left their daughters in Cardston with conscientious and trusted friends. However, after a short time in Edmonton, they sent for four-year-old Helen; they felt she should not be separated from her parents for the three-month legislative session. Her sisters put her on the train in Cardston, and Solon Low, another newly elected member of the legislature and a friend of the family, met the train at Lethbridge and accompanied her on to Edmonton on what, to that time, was the biggest adventure of her life.

Eldon was still serving as bishop of the Cardston First Ward,

Note: This chapter is based on research and a draft by Dale Beecher.

and after a busy week in Edmonton, he would drive the 325 miles to Cardston on weekends to take care of ward business. The highway at that time was surfaced largely with mud and snow, and he usually had to drive it at night, arriving at his destination just in time to face the duties of the day. But this schedule lasted only one year. On the night of January 3, 1937, he worked in the bishop's office all night to finish tithing settlement and other year-end business of the ward. At daybreak he drove to Edmonton for an appointment with Premier William Aberhart before beginning his new assignment as Cabinet Minister.

Being Minister of Lands and Mines would prove to be a full-time job. For Eldon, it required the same intense study needed to teach trigonometry when that, too, had represented unfamiliar ground. There was also the challenge of becoming acquainted and working with the permanent civil servants. As stated by Ernest C. Manning, "Neither Eldon Tanner nor any of the others had ever been in the House, let alone been a Speaker or a Cabinet Minister. He was in the same position that we were in as minister when we started. We didn't even know where the offices were, let alone how you ran the country."[1]

It became necessary to move the family north to Edmonton. The Tanner rented a house "in the highlands" on Sixty-second Street. They did not buy one at that time, their daughter Beth recalls, because they fully expected to be turned out of office in the next election.[2] Later they rented a twin-home on Ninety-ninth Avenue. There they remained until 1944, when they purchased a home on Eighty-seventh Avenue near the University of Alberta. They enjoyed this house, remodeling it to meet their needs as a family, and remained in it until Eldon left the government in 1952. Their home in Cardston, rented out at first, was sold in 1944 for $4,850.

Eldon lost no time in introducing his family to their new life in Edmonton. Beth recalls that on the evening they arrived at their new home, tired from traveling all day along winding and often difficult roads from Cardston, her father asked each of the girls to name the direction he was pointing. Disoriented in un-

Sara and N. Eldon Tanner with their daughters Isabel, left; Ruth, Zola, Beth, Helen

familiar surroundings, they did not respond well. Patiently he drove them around the city until they could each name the directions without hesitation.

The family's orientation did not stop here. Beth said, "Mother and Daddy took us through a dairy, to a meat packing plant, and to a bakery. It was a real education to see things we had never seen before."[3] The idea of buying everything with money instead of a half-barter system seemed strange to the family after the depression life in Cardston. Helen remembers: "At five I learned you could buy milk and bread from stores. I thought milk came from cows and bread from the oven."[4]

Other forced experiences stood them in good stead. Helen recalls: "Because of Daddy's position in the government, we were exposed to teas, formal dinners, parties, morning suits, tails, white gloves, hats, etc."[5] One of the social highlights of every year was the formal opening of the legislature, which the family customarily attended. Eldon's journal for the Edmonton years details a whirlwind of social activities undertaken by members of the family, often together, but just as often alone. In addition to the numerous official events he and Sara attended, there were frequent shows, dances, dinners, and informal evenings with friends. It was rare that Cabinet Minister Tanner recorded in his journal, "We spent the evening together as a family at home."

In spite of social responsibilities and her husband's hectic schedule, Sara was not kept busy enough in a rented house with most of the family gone all day, so she took up ice skating. First she leaned on a chair as she went around the rink; then she ventured forth with a broom. Finally, with no support but her own derring-do, she took off, solo, in fine style. She remembers that "the first summer we were all quite lonely and spent our leisure time exploring the Edmonton countryside as a family, and going on picnics and excursions together. This experience, I believe, was the beginning of our closeness as a family."[6]

An equally major change in their lives related to the Church. In Cardston Latter-day Saints were the single largest religious group and had been prominent from the town's founding. In Edmonton, the Church was virtually nonexistent. Helen remembers, "Mother and Dad told us that most of the people we would meet would never have met another Mormon, so that we would represent the Church for the people."

Beth remembers how the family arrived in Edmonton only to find that their furniture was still on the road. Sensing their dilemma, some neighbors invited them over for refreshments. Upon discovering that they were Mormons, the neighbors offered them Postum, respecting their belief in the Word of Wisdom. On another occasion, Helen was asked by a local minister, "Where did you get those pretty brown eyes?" Without hesitation she replied, "From Heavenly Father." The minister was so impressed that he developed his next sermon around her response.[7]

Members of the Church in and around Edmonton had met informally for several years. The group consisted of a couple of families, a sprinkling of students attending the University of Alberta, and some servicemen stationed in Edmonton. A few months before the Tanners moved in, the group had been made a dependent branch of the Calgary Ward, under the presidency of Alfred R. Strate. The coming of the new cabinet officer's family raised the membership from fifteen to twenty-two.

It was an informal organization. The only regular meeting was Sunday School, held in a little social club, the Scona Hall, on White Avenue and 103rd Street. An occasional Mutual Improvement Association meeting was held in someone's home on Sunday evening. Often the group would go out for a picnic at Borden Park, on the river near Fort Saskatchewan, or to Cooking Lake. In inclement weather, they would get together at one of the homes.

Once the Tanner family became involved with the branch, the loneliness was ended. Sara became hostess for branch council meetings and unofficial gatherings of Church members.

"Our house was open to LDS servicemen, LDS students, and missionaries," she recalls. "It was not a question of whether we would have company to Sunday dinner, it was simply a matter of how many. We ate every dinner in the dining room, always with a clean cloth and linen napkins. On Sunday evenings after dinner, we and our guests would sit around and discuss our religion and beliefs. There were many questions answered. Many a young man, serviceman, student, or missionary, understood and established their beliefs as a result of these discussions."[8]

In July 1938 the Edmonton congregation became an independent branch of the Lethbridge Stake. Elder Stephen L Richards of the Church's Council of the Twelve Apostles visited the little group and set apart Alfred R. Strate to continue as president. Counselors were N. Eldon Tanner and Arthur M. McMullin, with John H. Sheppard as clerk. The membership at the time of reorganization was sixty-one, a sizeable increase from a year earlier, though still small. Most of the new members were farmers from the Mormon settlements in southern Alberta who had come north for the cheap land. They tended to live at distances from one another and from the city, which precluded full activity.

On March 19, 1939, Eldon was set apart as president of the branch by President A. E. Palmer of the Lethbridge Stake. His counselors were Arthur M. McMullin and Vi A. Wood, with Harold Russel as clerk. This presidency would continue as a working unit for over thirteen years, until the Tanners left government service and moved to Calgary in 1952.

The new branch president immediately applied his experience as bishop, as well as the administrative expertise he was gaining in government, to transform the little branch into a dynamic organization. First he instituted a monthly meeting in which auxiliary programs and procedures were correlated and made truly functional. In June 1939 seventeen members drove to Cardston for the first Edmonton Branch temple excursion. That fall the branch adopted a budget system for activities and maintenance. President Tanner stressed effective, instructive meetings and good attendance.

The organization was still minimal and required multiple assignments to fill the few positions required by the Church programs. Thus, the branch presidency did double duty as Sunday School superintendency. President Tanner also taught Sunday School and joint Mutual Improvement Association classes, which included everyone but the twelve- and thirteen-year-old Beehive girls.

Activity in the branch enriched the lives of Sara and the Tanner daughters as well. Sara became both Relief Society president and teacher of the theology class. Ruth played the piano for meetings and was secretary of the joint Young Men's and Young Women's MIA. Beth served in the Primary presidency and was Gold and Green Ball queen in 1945. Zola sang solos in meetings and accompanied others on the piano. The girls were all popular in MIA activities, and with so many young men in the branch, they never lacked for dates.

The branch had outgrown Scona Hall, and in 1938 they began renting the Orange Hall on Eighty-third Avenue. President Tanner remembers that he and others often had to sweep out the beer bottles and cigarettes and sweep the floor on Sunday mornings before Sunday School could begin. Mutual was held on Sunday evenings except on the first Sunday of the month, when there was a special evening sacrament meeting. Priesthood meetings were also begun that year.

Within two years the branch outgrew the Orange Hall, and the more spacious Odd Fellows Hall on 59th Street was rented for Sundays and for other meetings during the week. In 1940 a record ninety members attended the Mothers' Day service.

Through the next few years President Tanner and other branch leaders progressively pulled the branch into shape, until by the mid-1940s it was running as smoothly as a large established ward. It is evident that he thoroughly enjoyed the whole process. He loved administration and had special talents for it. He cared little for self-aggrandizement and even less for political games, but in the tiny branch as much as in his expanding government post, he gained experience and found a field on which to try his organizational skill and financial genius.

115

His counselor, Vi A. Wood, recalls, "When I was in the branch presidency with Brother Tanner I learned a great deal about dealing with people and relations with people. President Tanner had a faculty for making everybody feel that they were worthwhile. He could always build up a person's ego and make him feel he was important. I remember talking to him about this, and he said he got that from his father's example." Brother Wood also noted that President Tanner "had a very good relationship and influence with young people. He often said 'Don't make issues over little things, for example, how a man parts his hair, but on the fundamental issues like smoking, drinking, morality. Be prepared to take a stand, and people will respect you for it.'"[9]

One more organizational change challenged Eldon in the presidency of the Edmonton Branch. Following the general conference of October 1939 in Salt Lake City, he and stake president Asael Palmer called on the Presiding Bishopric, Elder John A. Widtsoe of the Council of the Twelve, and President David O. McKay, then second counselor in the First Presidency. Unsolicited, they suggested to these Church authorities the establishment of a separate mission for western Canada, headquartered in Edmonton.

Later in the month President Tanner followed up this visit with a letter to President McKay detailing the advantages of a new mission. He described the demography of the area and the prospects for proselyting, enclosing large maps of all the towns with the most convenient transportation lines. A letter in February 1941 from Elder Joseph F. Merrill of the Council of the Twelve showed that the General Authorities were seriously considering the idea. Because of World War II in Europe, the European missions had been closed, and there were now many missionaries needing a place to go. In September 1941 the First Presidency established the Western Canadian Mission with central offices in Edmonton. The branch there hoped that full-time missionaries concentrated in Alberta would strengthen the Church in numbers and activity.

The entrance of the United States into the war in December 1941 diverted resources intended for the new mission. But despite the war and the dearth of young men at the university, the branch prospered. On November 18, 1942, a special meeting was held. Elder Clifford E. Young, Assistant to the Twelve, presided, and mission president Walter Miller conducted. By unanimous vote of the congregation, the branch was taken from the Lethbridge Stake and made part of the mission. The branch presidency under Eldon Tanner would continue in office.

Though the branch was still relatively small, it was close-knit. The branch choir sang regularly at meetings, and a recreation committee kept members involved with parties, dances, and dinners. Vi Wood recalls: "We almost, you might say, operated as a large family, and probably some of the most pleasurable experiences of my Church activity were during these years when we were a small branch and a very unified branch. The members all came out and enjoyed association with one another."[10] Part of the closeness was explained by common roots, with most of the families hailing from southern Alberta. A number, such as Vi Wood, were attracted to Edmonton by Cabinet Ministers Tanner and Low, who filled government jobs with men whose qualifications and integrity they knew and trusted. The branch records are full of familiar Mormon colony names, such as Pitcher, Pilling, Redd, Nalder, and Stevens.

The feeling of closeness was not restricted to permanent members of the branch. Eldon Tanner's journals frequently report students and servicemen dining with the family Sundays and other occasions. During Christmas and New Year's celebrations, Eldon and Sara spread a large table for these young single members, many of whom were away from home for the first time. One of President Tanner's motives was to encourage Mormon youths to remain in Canada for their education and professional training, thereby strengthening the ranks of the Church there.

Because of its size, the branch occasionally had problems staffing and sustaining some of the Church programs. The branch welfare program, for instance, began with a community garden on a plot of rented land. Though everyone pitched in, the branch presidency did more of the gardening than anyone else. Later, a welfare committee, with Eldon Tanner as chairman and Marie Low and Morgan Pitcher as members, tried to increase interest in the garden effort. On one occasion Eldon's daughter Beth recalls branch members agreed to harvest some garden produce on a holiday morning. When they arrived at the garden, they were disappointed to discover President Tanner absent, so they decided to pay him a visit at his home. When they arrived, they announced to Sister Tanner that they had come for breakfast. Not knowing any differently, she stopped her preparations for canning the garden produce and prepared a large breakfast. Then someone asked where President Tanner was. Sister Tanner replied that he had been unexpectedly detained in Ottawa on business and that he would join them as soon as he returned. The workers quietly finished their breakfast and returned to the garden to complete their tasks.[11]

Scouting was another program that never flourished in the branch despite Eldon's concern. Because a suitable Scoutmaster could seldom be found, the post was usually filled by anyone available or willing at the moment. The troop did function, but it was handicapped by having no suitable meeting place and not enough boys to allow a full range of activities. President Tanner tried various solutions, including incorporation with a large non-Mormon troop. But even the resources of a master organizer and provincial Scout commissioner were not enough to surmount the problems. He was never satisfied with this effort, but would use the experience in judgments he was later called to make.

President Tanner was valued as a teacher, at the pulpit, in the classroom, in any situation. The branch minutes frequently remark on powerful doctrinal talks he gave. In a branch correlation meeting in 1943, he anticipated the Prophet's dictum of nearly two decades later when he told the officers to form enlistment committees to reach inactive members and to "discharge their responsibilities so that we may all be missionaries."[12]

His journal entry of March 25, 1945, says: "I do enjoy teaching the Gospel Messages class." In September of that year he records that he was chosen to teach the senior interest group in Mutual. Thus the branch president worked in the ranks when he was called upon, even when, apparently, the request came from the ranks rather than a call from higher authority.

Through the years the branch tried to get a meeting place of its own. While a site was purchased in 1944, a building permit could not be obtained because of war-time scarcities. It was also difficult to persuade the Presiding Bishopric in Salt Lake City that a building was needed for fewer than two hundred members. The branch president did not give up, however. In September 1945, while Elder and Sister Widtsoe were in Edmonton for a mission conference, Eldon recorded in his diary, "I was pressing hard for an institute to be built here . . . and feel that we might succeed as well to get a good chapel and recreation hall." That fall the need for additional facilities was evidenced when he began teaching a missionary course in Sunday School. At the commencement of the university term, enrollment in his class shot up to sixty-three.

Finally a building permit was granted, permission was given, and a fund-raising campaign began. Ground was broken for the Edmonton chapel on June 6, 1949, and construction got under way with characteristic intensity. The masonry was completed by late November, but the shell could not be enclosed before January arrived with record low temperatures. Heaters had to be installed to keep mortar and plaster from freezing. On January 14, 1950, when the thermometer registered minus forty degrees Fahrenheit, roofers were at work putting on shingles. The branch moved into part of the building, with some work still unfinished, in September 1950.

As the Edmonton Branch chapel was being completed, President Tanner again pushed hard for an institute of religion at the university. This was opposed by some who feared that it would divide the congregation, leaving neither branch nor student group as a viable unit. He saw it through anyway, and the institute building would be nearly completed when he left for Calgary in 1952. By that time the branch membership would be 350. The branch would be divided in 1955, and in 1960 the former branch president would be back in Edmonton as an Assistant to the Council of the Twelve, with Elder Richard L. Evans of the Council of the Twelve, to organize five wards and a new stake. His long-ranging judgment, as was usually the case, would again be vindicated.

Life was very full during these years for the Tanner family, a whirlwind of responsibilities in the Church, in government, and in the community. But though they led busy lives, they remained close-knit, and they thrived on the opportunities available to them. More than anything else, Eldon's diary is a record of family comings and goings, birthdays, boyfriends, progress in school, music lessons. His most important business was his family. He continued to take time to help Sara with the washing and other household chores. Whenever a child telephoned him at work, the call was put through. Helen remembers one memorable occasion:

"At the age of eight, my girl friend and I, with long braids down our backs and little purses on our arms, put our dolls in their carriages and walked the several blocks to the government building, pushing the doll carriages. We went up the big marble steps into the huge foyer, up the elevator to the top floor, down the big wide hallway, in through the big heavy door. Daddy's secretary announced us and we were invited into the big executive office and introduced to the men he was meeting with. We introduced our dolls and we were thanked for coming."[13]

Their departure was conducted with the dignity accorded a corporate executive.

Eldon often enjoyed sports and outings as opportunities to be with his family for relaxation and subtle teaching times. Beth recalls that because of his demanding work schedule during the daytime and evening hours, he used the early morning hours to play tennis and to golf, fish, swim, and work around the home, yard, or garden with his daughters. These were times when they, as a family or individually, could be with their father to enjoy nature and discuss their interests and concerns. On at least one occasion he expressed to them his disappointment at not being as good a father as he knew he should be, but the girls felt that he was available whenever they needed him, and the time he did spend with them was quality time.

Though Eldon had to make time count, he also knew how to enjoy life, and he played as hard as he worked. "We can't waste a minute of our holiday," he would say. Daughter Beth said of vacations, "We'd have to get up at five or six in the morning so we could enjoy every minute."[14]

One memorable family trip to Seattle, Washington, by automobile was described by Isabelle:

"There were seven of us, Mother, five girls, and Dad. Before we left, Dad said, 'I know we are going to have a really good time. I also know that if anyone gets cross or irritable it will be because they are not well, so we will give them a good dose of soda to make them feel better.' You can bet that everyone was most congenial. It was an exciting trip. We experienced many firsts: eating raw oysters in the half shell, taking a trip on a ferry, each taking turns steering the vessel, staying in a lovely motel, and shopping for clothes in the shops. The ride down and back was a series of games, contests, and competitions."[15]

Occasional pack trips with his friends were highlights of Eldon's year, breaks from the incessant demands of the office. He and his companions would pack their camping gear and grub on their horses and head into the mountains for a few days. For one fun-filled trip shortly after his election to the provincial legislature, he and four friends planned a week of fishing and camping at various campsites along a predetermined route from Waterton Lake through Kootenay Pass and back. Grant Woolley, one of the group, recalls that upon arriving at a fishing hole where they found trout abundant, Eldon and another man stripped, except for their hats, and plunged into the icy glacier water and attempted to catch fish with their hands. Unsuccessful, they built a fire and began hooking the fish from the stream into the frying pan in two minutes.[16]

Another memorable trip is recorded in his diary. In August 1945 he and a son-in-law, Cliff Walker, took the train to Vancouver, where they met Ernest Tillock, Jack Reed, and Jack's young son Bruce. They embarked on Jack's cabin cruiser, living on it for four days. Eldon wrote in his diary: "Sunday August 12, 1945: Ernie and I got up and took the row boat and fished for a couple of hours. It has been a lovely day. After breakfast, we traveled up the coast of Bowen Island, and while Jack and I loafed and exposed our bodies to the sun, Cliff and Ernie rowed and fished. I caught a blue cod in the morning, and they caught two or three trout. We then took up anchor and went to Gibson Landing and had supper.

"August 13, 1945: Cliff and I find that we are quite badly sunburned."

Eldon's idea of an ideal holiday was one in which he could just "loaf," or in other words, "spend two or three days resting, listening to the radio, having good food, and beds, no phones, and with good company." He caught a lot of trout, salmon, cod, and flounder, but if asked about his biggest catch, he would say, "That would be just another fish story."

During his years as a business executive he fished occasionally with business associates. One September he spent a three-day weekend at a private resort on the Mirimachi River in New Brunswick, at the invitation of the International Paper Company. There he fished, canoed, relaxed, and enjoyed the scenery. Pleased with the fine facilities and the beautiful landscape, he wrote that he "should like to spend two or three weeks there, it being so lovely." He spent one entire day wading the river in hip boots while lure-fishing and was successful in catching "six nice salmon." At the conclusion of this experience, he noted, "Boy!

This is the life of a millionaire," though he was a long way from being one.

About the time Eldon was elected to public office, he took up golf, principally for relaxation. He made this discovery: "If I play in the morning, or anytime, that is what my interest is, and I forget the other things."[17] When weather permitted, he met once or twice weekly with Sara or other family members, business associates, or friends, for nine or eighteen holes. In later years Franklin D. Richards, a partner on the Salt Lake golf courses, would describe Eldon as "a good golfer."[18] This would be borne out by Eldon's occasional scoring in the low 40s on par 35 courses and by a story told a grandson, David Spackman, who frequently caddied for him. Eldon was golfing with family members at Waterton, and his ball had to be chipped up over a rise in the ground to reach the green. "Well, Grandpa chipped it just right," said David. "Over the rise it went, bounced onto the green and right into the hole. Everyone was amazed but Grandpa. He just smiled and said, 'That is just exactly what I wanted to do.'"[19]

Eldon would say, however, "If I find I can beat anybody, I am going to quit playing golf, because that's evidence I am spending too much time at it and not enough at what I am assigned."

Eldon's recreational activities were usually people-oriented. He attended concerts, movies, plays, school productions, and spectator sports events with family and friends as much for the company as for the entertainment. He did not join many of the clubs and social organizations that opened their doors to him in his early years with the government; his preference was for participation in picnics, boating, Ping-Pong, Church socials, and similar activities that he could enjoy with those close to him.

Eldon's diary entry of July 15, 1945, for example, says: "Grandpa, Grandma, Sara, Helen, and Maxine Merrill, a cousin, and I went up to Cameron Lakes this morning to fish. We caught six trout and came back about 3:30 p.m. Sara and I played a game of golf, finishing about 6:30. After a good supper of trout, peas, potatoes, turnips, and cantaloupe, Grandpa and Grandma went to a show. Sara and I visited downtown, and Helen and Maxine went to a dance."

At home he and Sara enjoyed going to and giving dinner parties. The more casual or informal gatherings, particularly those with family and close friends, usually involved games, such as table tennis, Rook, cribbage, and charades.

Beth remembers, "We used to have family night regularly. My father believed that this was something we should do. . . . We really had special times together as a family. My parents encouraged our reading and improving ourselves in any way we felt we wanted to."[20]

Eldon enjoyed taking his wife and daughters dancing, especially to Church Gold and Green balls. He was a skillful stepper from his academy days, when he won prizes for his graceful and fancy footwork.

Another favorite recreation was dining out. Wherever the Tanners lived or traveled, they had their favorite places to eat. Meals were something to detail in one's diary. There was the sumptuous feast enjoyed at the home of the Governor General of Canada. Eldon noted that the menu consisted of "grapefruit cocktails, celery and olives, consommé, filet mignon, scalloped potatoes with cheese, green frozen peas, cauliflower, rolls, baked Alaska, sherry, coffee, port wine, also cigars." He was quick to add, "We did not take coffee, cigars, wine, or sherry."

Eldon was involved with his family as disciplinarian. According to his daughters, he rarely administered corporeal punishment, but in their younger days, when a spanking was warranted, they got one. On such occasions their father would take the offender into a separate room to administer the punishment. He was deliberate but forceful, and the moment was not soon forgotten. But only once does Beth remember him being really angry—when Helen broke a bottle over a neighbor girl's head!

As a father, Eldon was sometimes indulgent. He loved to bring home surprise gifts for no particular reason. Once he gave a daughter a two-piece bathing suit, shocking for the time. He explained that it was better to give in to little things than create big problems. But he could still be strict. Helen recalls that they "were to be home from a party at a certain time. Always before midnight—often by 10:00 or 10:30. It didn't matter if refreshments had not been served or that no one else had left."[21]

Eldon gave his daughters, as well as those working under him, all the responsibility they could handle. He would tell them that they could do anything they wanted to do; the decision was theirs. But he constantly taught them and voiced his opinions on important matters. Ruth reported, "I never had reason to doubt his judgment or advice. When we asked for advice we were often reminded, 'What would your Heavenly Father want you to do?' or sometimes he would say, 'You know how I feel about it. You make the decision.'"[22]

Eldon himself recorded a teaching moment in connection with one of the girls:

> My daughter and her girl friend were at our house, and they were going to a party; then two young men came and called for them. I sat and talked to them . . . about different things, and just before they were ready to leave, I said, "Now, have a good time, kids." But just as they were going out of the door, I stepped over to my daughter and said, "Now, behave yourself."
> And she said, "Well, Dad, make up your mind."
> Then I said to those young people so they could all hear me, "Have a good time, kids, the best time you will ever have in your lives, but the kind of time that tomorrow, next week, a month from now or a year from now, ten years from now, you can look back on tonight and say, 'I had a good time,' and have nothing to regret or be sorry about."[23]

Eldon and Sara saw to it that their daughters had many opportunities and much encouragement to associate with eligible men, and Eldon spent many hours discussing with them courtship and marriage. One evening after four young men had left, Zola, Beth, and their father had a talk late into the night on choosing a mate. Pleased, Eldon wrote in his journal, "The girls' attitudes are very good."

The Tanner daughters were encouraged to obtain good educations. They all excelled in music and other activities as well as academic subjects, with the full support and encouragement of their parents.

Ruth attended the University of Alberta, earned a master's degree at Washington State, and later obtained a Ph.D. at the University of Wisconsin. She worked in Montreal and taught at Winthrop College in South Carolina prior to her marriage. While she was in college, her father provided her with money for support, but so that she would not take education for granted, they agreed she would later pay him back. However, when she showed determination to go on to graduate school, having earned a fellowship, he wrote off the debt. He was sure by that time that she respected schooling as something to be obtained by one's own efforts.

Beth graduated from the University of Alberta in Edmonton and taught for a time before her marriage. She remembers her early days at the university. She was grateful to be able to live at home, because she could try out new ideas and philosophies on her father. Although she mustered the strongest possible arguments in favor of these philosophies, she would hope that her father could dissuade her with equal logic and compelling arguments. Apparently he understood her purpose in arguing, for he would always patiently discuss any matter she brought to him and help her find perspective.

Zola went away to college, to Brigham Young University to study music. There she fell in love and got married before completing her degree. Isabelle studied languages and business at Alberta College in Edmonton, then worked as a secretary before her marriage. Helen, the youngest daughter, married at age nineteen. She had always been active in theater work and took leading roles in high school and church productions. This interest carried over into her adult years, and when her children were grown, she went back to the University of Alberta to study directing.

The first wedding in the family was that of Isabelle, who married Willard S. Jensen on December 16, 1942. Harmonious with Church policies of the time, President Tanner performed the ceremony himself in their home before the couple traveled the next day to the Cardston Temple to have the marriage sealed.

Before Ruth married a long-time friend of the family, Cliff Walker, her father spent his summer vacation taking the couple on a pack trip in the mountains. The courtship had been going on and off for years. Eldon wanted them to enjoy each other's company and to be sure they really knew each other before taking the big step. They were married September 24, 1946.

The year 1949 saw two marriages, Edna Beth to Grant Lawrence Spackman on July 28, and Zola to Howard S. Rhodes on September 5. Helen married Lowell L. Williams on August 17, 1950. Some years later they were divorced, and she married John Edward Beaton May 30, 1972. All the girls had married and left home before Eldon and Sara left Edmonton in 1952.

Having grown up on a ranch, Eldon liked horses and open spaces. On his frequent trips to his constituency in southern Alberta, he would tour his small farm, which he had rented to a local farmer on a crop-share basis. He gave advice on the buying and selling of livestock, the construction and upkeep of buildings, and many other farm-related issues. He seemed as comfortable on the farm and as expert in its operation as he had become in legislative chambers. While he was in Edmonton, he purchased another small farm four miles from the city and rented it to a local farmer for a fair price. With these farms, his family garden, and the branch gardens, he remained—and encouraged others to remain—close to the land.

Although members of the Tanner family enjoyed themselves, times were still not easy and they were not yet well off. In the spring of 1945 Ruth sent Beth $125 so she could spend the summer with her in Montreal. She indicated that Beth could earn that much while working there and thus get some experience and pay for the trip at the same time. While her parents were disposed to let her go, they finally decided against it when they found the total cost would be $200. Those extra dollars were simply too much to handle.

The entire family was involved in financial decisions. On August 29, 1945, Eldon wrote in his journal, "We discussed going to Salt Lake tonight. It was left for Sara and the girls to decide. Sara and Zola voted to go and Helen and Beth to wait until next year. I should like very much to go and take the family and may do so yet, but we have spent over $2,400 during the last twelve months on improvements on the house and for Zola's schooling."

September 25, 1945: "We had our first family meeting this evening to discuss finances. The idea is to determine how we can live on $300 net after having paid tithing and income tax. It seems to be a real problem. Zola is to be our treasurer with each receiving an allowance."

If not wealth, at least the family enjoyed good health. Eldon himself rarely missed a day's work because of sickness. There were a few occasions when he would go to the office just long enough to take care of urgent business and then leave early.

Eldon's daughters remember the full schedule their father kept while in government in Edmonton. His diary shows that it was even more than they remember. A few hours' sleep on a train was all the rest he needed to keep going from 6 A.M. to midnight, on many occasions for three or four days running. In one journal entry he recorded: "I have been meeting people all day and am now on the midnight train leaving for Edmonton. I breakfasted with Alex Snowden at 8:00 A.M. I met the grazing committee at 9:00, spoke to the Western Stock Growers at 11:15, met McLeman from Vancouver at 2:15, H. G. Jensen, William Pilling, and others at intervals until the banquet of the Alberta Transport Association at which I spoke. For once I am really tired."

"In spite of his position and schedule," recalls Helen, "he still got up with us in the night if we were sick. He prepared breakfast every morning and set up the washing machine rinse tubs every Monday morning at 6:00 A.M."[24]

On Sunday, January 21, 1951, he wrote in his diary: "I have certainly had a busy day today. We had priesthood meeting where I was in charge, Sunday School where I taught a class, a baptismal service where I was in charge, branch presidency meeting with me as president, building committee meeting, sacrament meeting, and after sacrament meeting I had to meet Mr. McKinnon, chairman of the P. & N.G. Conservation Board, to discuss with him their report on the question of gas export. Left him at 11:30 and am now on the train on my way to Calgary."

As a cabinet minister, his days were filled with negotiations with railroads and oil companies "in an endeavor to work out satisfactory arrangements whereby unitized operations and pooling of royalty can be practiced." Such business often took him on the train to Calgary, where he spent long days, returning late at night to Edmonton.

Eldon was not immune from human frailties and occasional bloopers, as indicated in some diary entries:

November 25, 1945, in Montreal: "I got up this morning and took a taxi to church but gave him the wrong address and came back to the hotel without attending church."

December 26, 1945: "Sara and I went to the dinner in our tux and evening gown and had to come home and change as we were the only ones in monkey suits."

May 15, 1950: "I gave the convocation address at the nurses graduation. (Not so good.)"

Eldon was practical, modest, and approachable in spite of his leadership positions. His family and close friends always called him Eldon. A few professional acquaintances called him "Nat." The press occasionally listed him as Nathan. His journal shows that among events reported like the dropping of the first atomic bomb or high policy cabinet meetings, he gave equal import to family matters, such as, "Cliff came over again and helped me paint."

Life always afforded memorable experiences, even considering the busy routines of the Tanner family. In April and May 1939, when the Province had first sent Eldon Tanner, its Lands and Mines Minister, to Ottawa and then to England in the interest of Alberta's fledgling oil industry, Sara went with him. Accompanying them were friends Bill and Margaret Knode, Walter and Ethel Campbell. The weekdays were busy, but on weekends they toured France, Holland, Belgium, and Scotland. There was shopping and sightseeing in London almost every weekday.

While they were in Europe, Eldon and Sara had left their daughters in the charge of Jeannie Low, a trusted family friend and nurse. Although she was a competent caretaker, Ruth, who was away to school when her parents left, felt that she and her sisters could fend for themselves, so she relieved Jeannie of her duties. Shortly after Jeannie's departure, Helen had an attack of appendicitis. She was taken to the hospital and there contracted pneumonia. Their parents were contacted and apprised of the situation, but they could not return from England quickly enough to be of any help. Consequently, while Eldon and Sara worried in England and he finished his mission for the Alberta government, the cause for concern fortunately resolved itself in Edmonton. All were well upon the parents' return several weeks later.

Eldon and Sara lived extremely active lives, allocating available time to family affairs, Church activities, and personal transactions such as selling his pigs, a tractor, and a few pieces of land. On Wednesday, May 9, 1945, he recorded in his diary:

> I am 47 years old today according to the best information I have at my disposal. The world and all concerned have been very kind to me during these years. I have a lovely wife, loved and respected by all, and one who has always been prepared to carry a little more than her share of the load. I'm enjoying good health and all the comforts of life necessary to one's happiness. My family of girls is . . . a credit to anyone, and we are proud of them. I only hope that I can prove worthy of the blessings I have been blessed with.

Five months later, on October 8, 1945, while Sara was away visiting family, he noted in his diary:

> Sara is 47 years old today. This morning Helen and I went shooting but saw nothing, so we did some target shooting with the .22 rifle. The girls got a very fine dinner with roast chicken and the trimmings and did as well as anyone could. Zola also put up

seven quarts of tomato juice. Cliff came for a while this afternoon and we played table tennis. . . . Zola and Beth are going to a dance with Harland and Merve S.

Eldon apparently regarded 1945 as an exceptionally eventful year. A year-end wrap-up in his diary mentions victory in Europe and Japan; the dropping of atomic bombs on Japan; Prime Minister Winston Churchill's defeat by the "socialist" Clement Atlee; the death of Church President Heber J. Grant and the succession of George Albert Smith. In that same year he noted that he was a central figure in refinancing the province's $113 million debt and in making an "outstanding submission" to Canada's provincial conference. Sara's father died, and there were illnesses recorded, including an operation on his uncle Hugh B. Brown.

His journal faithfully recorded weather conditions, including temperatures. The tone is always optimistic. "It has been a lovely day," or "The weather has been lovely again," whether in January or May. Occasionally a poetic line appears, such as this entry for March 13, 1945: "Spring is tripping over the meadows, scattering sunshine everywhere."

On Thursday, March 6, 1947, President David O. McKay of the Church's First Presidency phoned from Salt Lake City "to inquire if it would be possible for me to act as mission president of the Western Canadian Mission and carry on with my work in the government. I don't see how I can, and do justice to either one of them, but I am willing to accept the call and resign from the government. However, I am to call President McKay in two or three days." Two days later, after he phoned President McKay and described his work, he wrote: "He thinks it would not be advisable for me to undertake both jobs, and I fully agree. He made it quite clear that my work in the government was most worthwhile and that I should continue there."

That spring the Tanners attended Eldon's parents' golden wedding anniversary celebration at the Lion House in Salt Lake City. Of the dinner and following reception, he wrote: "It was really a grand success. All of the sons and daughters and in-laws were present, and all the grandchildren except Zola and Helen were there. Also, Willard Jensen and John Jensen, the only great-grandchildren. Cliff, Ruth's husband, was not able to be there." The following day Eldon and Sara went to Ogden to have brunch with Elder S. Dilworth Young of the First Council of the Seventy and his wife, Gladys Pratt Young. The Youngs were leaving soon to preside over the New England Mission.

As for Church work during these busy years, it would be impossible to tabulate all the administrations to the sick, meetings addressed, Sunday School classes taught, and travels on church business. But time was found to attend general conference sessions of the Church in Salt Lake City. On Friday, April 6, 1951, after driving to Utah, he recorded in his diary: "Sara and I went down to the opening session of conference. We could get seats in the gallery only, because we were not more than a half hour early. It is grand to be able to be in attendance at conference." The next evening he could not get into the Tabernacle for general priesthood meeting, though he arrived thirty-five minutes early for the 7:00 P.M. session. The Assembly Hall on Temple Square was also filled, so he went over to Barratt Hall on the old Latter-day Saint Business College campus (where the LDS Church Office Building plaza now is). There were fifteen hundred priesthood holders in Barratt Hall, he recorded, "besides many who left."

On Monday, April 9, he attended the special solemn assembly in the Tabernacle at which President David O. McKay was sustained as President of the Church, following the death of George Albert Smith. Stephen L Richards and J. Reuben Clark, Jr., were sustained as first and second counselors respectively. Eldon wrote: "I have never experienced the presence of the Spirit of the Lord before as I did in that meeting. Many others said the same thing."

From Salt Lake City Eldon and Sara flew on to Dallas, met their friends, the William Knodes, and then continued on to Mexico City. Eldon and Bill Knode went to see Senator Bermudas, Director-General of Petroleos Mexicanos, and, according to Eldon, "we had a good visit with him." In Mexico City Eldon and Sara, typical tourists, ate at one of the city's fine eating places, witnessed a bullfight, and visited a sixteenth-century cathedral, the national palace with its murals depicting the history of Mexico, a flower market, leather factories, Chapultapec Castle, the great pyramids of the Sun and Moon, and an aqueduct built by the Spaniards in the seventeenth century. They later flew to Acapulco, where they went deep-sea fishing, relaxed, and enjoyed seeing the multimillionaires' and movie stars' homes.

Eldon's influence and visibility had gradually increased, and by 1950 he was a full-fledged VIP, recognized over much of Canada. This meant that the pace of his life-style was constantly increasing. The diary reflects a growing popularity and "grand" treatment. In November 1950 Sara was chosen to christen the *Imperial Leduc,* a tanker of the Imperial Oil Company. Held at the Collingwood shipyards near Toronto, the ceremony was "imperially" ostentatious despite an incessant flurry of snow. At a luncheon afterward, it was Sara who spoke rather than Eldon. He recorded in his diary, "Sara looked lovely and did the christening beautifully. The shipyards gave her a lovely sterling silver tray after the luncheon. Sara responded admirably."

Eldon's most enjoyable social contacts were invariably with family and Church members. Not to have company for Sunday dinner was an event to write into the diary. The company were generally members of the branch. It was more than duty reflected in the personal interest he took in every one. The comment "There are certainly a lot of fine people in this branch" appears frequently in his journal.

The whole family was nearby in these days. While Ruth and Cliff Walker had moved to Calgary, the rest were all in Edmonton. The close-knit family group did things together constantly: little holiday trips, parties, Christmas holidays, home evenings. They were all available to each other for working on a house, tending children, or other interfamily needs.

Eldon seemed to enjoy himself no matter what company he was with. One young Latter-day Saint girl, in an extemporaneous address at MIA, remarked that the most exciting trip she had ever taken was hiking up Old Chief Mountain with N. Eldon Tanner, Ora Williams, and her father.

In the summer of 1951 Eldon and Sara had an opportunity to return hospitality to Sir Alfred and Lady Savage, the governor and first lady of Barbados. The Savages visited in Edmonton, where they were shown nearby oil fields as well as entertained at many social functions, including an elaborate luncheon at the Mayfair Golf and Country Club and a reception and dinner arranged in their honor by Premier Manning and the cabinet. And, as might be expected, Eldon took them to see the new Latter-day Saint chapel in Edmonton.

In later times, after government service, business positions, and general Church responsibility, Eldon's associates from earlier years would recall that he was always the same pleasant Eldon to them. In the 1960s, upon learning that he and his wife were visiting in Canada, some long-time friends invited him to spend a few days in the mountains with them. He was pleased to be invited, and asked if his grandson, who was also named Eldon, could go along. Eldon sensed how uncomfortable his friends felt when they gathered, wondering how formal or unformal to be when addressing him. He introduced his grandson as Bud. "His name is Eldon, but on this trip we call him by his nickname, 'Bud,' because on this trip *my* name is Eldon," he said. This put his friends at ease, and they all enjoyed three pleasant days.[25]

During their trip to Barbados, for the first time the Tanners had come face-to-face with a predominantly black population. Eldon noted that he felt comfortable in the situation and was "not conscious of them to any great extent." But he was somewhat surprised to see that most of the children from infancy to early adolescence went about clothed only in shoulder-to-waist shirts. This was one of the early eye-opening experiences that would prepare him for dealing with the multitude of cultures and traditions he would be called upon to work with when he was appointed a General Authority of the Church ten years later.

Nearly every visit to a new place evoked an entry in his journal about the scenery and some expression of the quieting feeling it usually induced. He wrote about the beautiful white sand beaches and extensive sugar plantations of Barbados, the grain fields and olive groves near Tiberias in the Holy Land, the Nile River and the great pyramids of Egypt, picturesque Loch Lomond in Scotland, and the breathtaking scenery of the Bavarian Alps.

Through the years Eldon was on the lookout for ways to improve the family's financial situation. Business opportunities continually sought him out, for he was known as a first-rate administrator. To many, he was referred to as "Mr. Integrity." His daughter Ruth reports: "He has been in many positions where it has been easy or common to accept bribes or show favors or to be tempted to be a bit worldly. But he never gave in to such temptations." He was known as a fair man to deal with. On October 5, 1945, he recorded in his diary one such dealing: "Earl and I arranged for him to provide salt and winter pasture and feed for the cows [in Hill Spring] and he was to get 33 percent but I have decided to raise it to 40 percent as he is doing a good job and I think it is worth that."

Not everything worked out. In 1945 he had, with difficulty, been able to secure a permit to start a frozen food plant. However, his political opponents called foul, claiming he had used the influence of his position, so in order to avoid the appearance of wrong-doing, he gave the business up. That same year he seriously considered an offer from the owners of the Cardston *News* to sell him the newspaper. The deal looked profitable, but the price was out of reach.

For a while he and his son-in-law, Cliff Walker, were involved in buying chinchillas, but they soon sold the animals. In 1946 Eldon sold his livestock in southern Alberta and began looking for more land for ranching. However, he never entered into

135

speculation or development to any great extent. Only sound investments, coupled with the desire to help his family, determined his actions.

After careful consideration, Eldon bought into Cash Foods, a grocery store that was developing into a chain. In February 1947 he and Cliff organized a sales agency, Walker Agencies, Ltd. It soon was representing such firms as Prudential Mortgage and Loan and Hoover and Chester, a distributor of propane. But the Tanner fortunes were not turning appreciably. His income was still modest.

Over these years there were any number of offers to get in on some business venture or other. Eldon looked at most of them carefully, but was cautious and reluctant to spread himself too widely. He wrote on November 3, 1949: "I had a meeting with the executives of the Western Canadian Petroleum Association. They wanted me to head up their association with a salary commencing at $15,000 and expenses. I didn't feel that I could accept without it being embarrassing to either the Government, the Association, or myself."

During the Edmonton years Eldon Tanner's personal philosophy matured. It started out with the basic principle he had learned from his father and which he had passed on to his children: the principle of dependability. His daughter Ruth recalls, "No wonder that as I was growing up I thought the one and only virtue was dependability. I didn't know there were any other virtues. My father instilled in me that no matter how much talent you had, or how much you could do, or what you had done, if you weren't dependable, it was of little value."

The theme of Eldon's philosophy expanded steadily from the personal to the interpersonal, from the provincial to national scope and beyond. Following World War II he wrote in his journal:

> During the war, and as a result of the war, we have been enjoying prosperity. Now there is great fear that there will be a depression with all its evil effects. In fact, the proposals set out by the Dominion Government are definitely admitting that there will be

a depression and are planning to meet it. My contention is that we should all be bending every effort to prevent a depression and in fact if we can, and don't do it, it is a reflection on our intellect. If we would accept and apply the principle of Social Credit we would go a long way toward solving this problem. However, in order to really solve this and other major problems and to enjoy lasting peace we must accept and apply the principles of true Christianity.[26]

As his interests expanded, he read considerably to keep abreast of what was happening in the world, maintaining a steady interest in foreign affairs. For example, "I am reading *Thunder Out of China* and find it very interesting. We seem to know very little about what is going on in such countries and what is behind it all."[27]

From international to universal values, he expressed a real concern for the people of the world, if not a complete grasp of historical precedent: "I have never known of the people of the world being so much at cross purposes, not knowing which way to go nor whom to trust."[28] With this entry he demonstrated firm grasp of the higher principles that were ruling his life: "There are more people in high places talking of the need of accepting Christianity and of good will, but few seem to understand that it must be *applied* in their lives."[29]

Eldon's journal also brings the universals to focus on the outlook of the individual. On Barbados he met some "idle rich" retirees who were there for nothing but to soak up the sun. He then commented: "It is a good thing to have responsibility and something definite to work for." Reflecting back on the year 1950, he wrote: "Certainly it does seem that people should be able to accept their responsibilities and learn to live in peace. All that would be necessary would be for us to accept and live the Gospel of Jesus Christ."[30]

In this, he was not being naive. Rather, he was reaffirming his determination to spread the gospel as far as he could. During the Edmonton years Eldon's journal and the Edmonton Branch minutes show that as visitors came to Edmonton, and as he had contacts with Salt Lake City in his efforts to get a mission, a chapel, or an institute building, he was becoming well-acquainted with most of the General Authorities of the Church. And they were also taking notice of him.

And finally, as one reads Eldon Tanner's journals for these years, it is apparent that there is no undue concern about reaching the top of his profession; in fact, his journal never mentions personal aspirations for place or position. The entry for May 9, 1951, however, again illustrates what he considered important in his life: "I am fifty-three years old today and am enjoying the best of health. I am happy; I have a lovely wife and family; our home is paid for; I have a little laid by; we are active in the Church; all the members of the family are well and living good, clean lives. What more could a fellow wish?"

Whatever a fellow could wish is open to conjecture. But new doors were opening to Eldon Tanner, and one day in 1952 he and his beloved wife, Sara, determined to leave government service and walk through one such door that beckoned.

Footnotes

[1] Manning, oral history interview, p. 16.
[2] Beth Tanner Spackman, interview by Charles Ursenbach, 1979. James Moyle Oral History Program, Church Archives.
[3] Ibid.
[4] Helen Tanner Beaton, "My Father: Nathan Eldon Tanner" (talk given at a fireside in Phoenix, Arizona, 1969).
[5] Ibid.
[6] Sara M. Tanner, Life Story.
[7] Spackman, oral history interview.
[8] Sara M. Tanner, Life Story.
[9] Vi A. Wood to G. Homer Durham, February 19, 1981.
[10] Ibid.
[11] Spackman, oral history interview.
[12] Edmonton Branch minutes, August 29, 1943.
[13] Beaton, "My Father."
[14] Spackman, oral history interview.
[15] Isabelle T. Jensen, memorandum to G. Homer Durham, August 4, 1981.
[16] Grant Woolley, letter, 60th Wedding Anniversary Scrapbook.
[17] N. Eldon Tanner, diary, September 11, 1949.

[18]*Church News,* November 17, 1973, p. 3.
[19]David Spackman, letter, 60th Wedding Anniversary Scrapbook.
[20]Spackman, oral history inteview.
[21]Beaton, "My Father."
[22]Walker, "My Father."
[23]N. Eldon Tanner, *Seek Ye First,* p. 9.
[24]Beaton, "My Father."
[25]Donald C. Remington, letter, 60th Anniversary Scrapbook.
[26]N. Eldon Tanner, diary, January 17, 1946.
[27]Diary, January 22, 1947.
[28]Diary, January 31, 1947.
[29]Diary, Febraury 1, 1947.
[30]Diary, December 31, 1950.

8

The Industrial Years,
1952-1960

By 1952, after seventeen years of service in the Alberta Provincial Government, Nathan Eldon Tanner felt that his governmental contributions to Canada's emerging energy industries had been made, and he wished to return to the private sector. He had discussed with his family his retirement from the government he had helped form and maintain in power, telling them that he considered his mission for the government of Alberta complete. He saw his contributions lying in three general areas: conservation of Alberta's extensive natural resources, establishment of fiscal responsibility, and establishment of an efficient administrative system.

Eldon also discussed his retirement with Premier Manning. After hearing him out, Mr. Manning offered to step down himself to let Eldon assume the reigns of the Social Credit government. Minister Tanner respectfully declined the offer. He felt that Premier Manning was an able, forthright leader and would carry on with distinction without him. He also lacked political ambition and felt that he would be involved in too many political conflicts if he stayed.

This chapter is based on extensive research and drafts by Steven L. Olsen.

Eldon's retirement from government was announced after the legislature adjourned April 10, 1952. At Premier Manning's request, he remained in the cabinet until after the fall election in order to minimize the political implications of choosing his successor. A number of opposition newspapers tried to create a political issue of the resignation but were not successful. The Social Credit Party was returned to power by a large majority.

When Eldon and Sara had gone to Barbados in 1950, he had met Charles Merrill, a partner in the investment firm of Merrill, Lynch. Cliff Walker, Ruth's husband, had developed a number of oil ventures, and Charles Merrill wanted to finance an oil company in Alberta. He was aware of the quiet efficiency and influence of N. Eldon Tanner, the Alberta oil minister. In 1951 Cliff became Mr. Merrill's representative in Alberta to organize his investments in the oil industry, and as a result of this contact, Eldon was offered a position in the company. Though he had declined many similar offers in the past, he seriously considered this one, partly because of his desire to return to the private sector and partly because Mr. Merrill had had no prior interest in either Alberta or the oil industry. It would be a new approach, a new enterprise with no past involvements.

Merrill Petroleums was formed in September 1952 from the merger of three oil firms in Calgary: Merrill Canadian Oil No. 1, Cascade Drilling Company, and Merrill Development Company. From this merger the new company acquired eight rotary drilling rigs, varying interests in eleven producing oil wells in Alberta, and extensive oil and gas holdings throughout Alberta and the state of Montana. Merrill Petroleums was capitalized from an issue of three million shares at five dollars per share.

Officers in the company included N. Eldon Tanner, president; Orville W. Matheny, former vice-president of both Merrill Development and Cascade Drilling, vice-president; Clifford R. Walker, former president of Cascade Drilling, secretary-treasurer of Merrill Development, and vice-president and managing director of Merrill Canadian, secretary-treasurer; Edward S. Magowan, former president of Merrill Canadian, and Edna V.

N. Eldon Tanner speaking over the radio at Canadian ceremony

Adams, directors; and Mary C. Livingstone, assistant secretary-treasurer.

With Eldon Tanner as president, Merrill Petroleums rapidly gained prominence in Alberta's oil and gas industry. Within two years, its stock rose from five dollars per share to twenty-six, and the company expanded its operations to twenty producing oil and gas wells.

Moving to Calgary where he could lead a more private life, managing a successful company without the pressures of politics, and being able to devote considerable time to church work—these all combined for a rewarding career for Eldon Tanner. His life at this time was stable and happy.

Two years later, in 1954, he was thrust back into public life to face the strongest challenge of his already eventful career. Four years earlier, Clint Murchison, a multimillionaire from Texas, had applied to the Canadian government for permission to construct a gas pipeline from the vast reservoirs on the Alberta plains to supply the growing demand for natural gas in eastern Canada. Murchison, known as a "natural-born horse trader," was the prototype of an oil tycoon. He had acquired substantial holdings in a variety of businesses, including oil and gas companies, pipelines, banks, motels, drive-in theaters, insurance companies, transportation lines, manufacturing firms, a supermarket chain, an airline, a publishing house, and a candy company. His business philosophy was "If you trade in peanuts, you can trade in watermelons, too. We buy anything that adds up."[1] The promise of energy development in Alberta aroused his interest. While much of the exploration in Alberta had focused on oil, he saw great financial opportunity in tapping Alberta's largely unwanted gas reserves, estimated by one study to be many trillion cubic feet. These reserves, for the most part, were being flared in order to recover quickly the desirable oil deposits.

Clint Murchison was not the only one interested in Alberta's natural gas. Four other firms were also bidding to transport Alberta's natural gas to markets outside western Canada: Westcoast Transmission, Northwest Natural Gas, Prairie Transmission Pipe Line Company, and Western Pipe Lines, Ltd. Of the five firms, only Murchison's firm, Trans-Canada, proposed to provide service exclusively for Canadian customers. Western Pipe Lines was looking to the northern plains states for its market, while the other three set their sights on the Pacific Coast states of the United States.

Former Minister Tanner's brainchild, the Alberta Oil and Gas Conservation Board, reviewed these proposals with an eye to serving Canadian interests first. Alberta's conservative gas policy was a far-sighted move to develop the natural and human resources of the province. It also reflected the attitude of many Albertans who saw their province's resources as the future life-blood of Canada, to be protected against the voracious appetite of its neighbor to the south, the United States. Many Albertans also felt that access to low-cost energy was an undeclared right of citizenship in the province.

The "Canada first" policy eliminated from the competition those proposals which would have exported Alberta gas primarily to American West Coast markets. Because Western Pipe Lines had been incorporated in 1950, before the "Canada first" policy had become politically prominent, its program of exporting gas to the United States survived this nationalistic feeling.

The dilemma facing the Canadian and Alberta governments was this: Western Pipe Lines, a Canadian company, was proposing an economical and realistic, but politically unacceptable, program to export more Alberta natural gas to America. On the other hand, Trans-Canada was proposing a politically favorable transmission route and policy, but one whose terrain and economics were highly questionable. Trans-Canada, furthermore, was a subsidiary of an American company owned by Clint Murchison, and at that time in Canadian politics, the only thing worse than exporting Canadian energy reserves to American markets was an American company controlling those reserves.

The conflict was between Canada's political and economic interests. If the pipeline were built with American capital, Canada would benefit economically from industrial development but would relinquish a degree of control over its resources. If the pipeline were built entirely within Canada exclusively for Canadians' use, the chance of securing the required capitalization would be substantially reduced.

The political and economic battle between Western and Trans-Canada produced a stalemate. While neither company was gaining the advantage, neither was Canada nor the United States receiving any benefit from these protracted negotiations. One historian of Canada's gas industry has suggested that the conflict between Canada's political and economic interests had more detrimental consequences for Canada and Alberta than for Western and Trans-Canada.

> Alberta's failure to act more positively and promptly on export eastward had left its mark on the future. It meant that pipeline construction was to be postponed beyond the days of low cost labor and material and cheap interest rates. It may have meant that the last chance to finance an all-Canada line without government help and public controversy had already vanished.[2]

In January 1954 the stalemate was resolved, four years after the first pipeline proposals had been submitted, when Alberta Premier Ernest Manning informed Clarence Decatur Howe, Canada's Minister of Trade and Commerce, that Alberta would grant permission to only one company to export Alberta natural gas eastward. Minister Howe contacted the representatives of Western and Trans-Canada and informed them that they should merge, making a "shotgun marriage." For several years, little love had been lost between these two companies as they battled for favor of the Canadian government; now they were being forced together with Mr. Howe's ultimatum that the pipeline would have an all-Canada route. Despite the protests of the Western group, the determined and impatient Minister Howe insisted, "The all-Canada line is national policy. I will *make* it feasible."[3]

Within a short time, details of the merger had been worked out, and the new company, Trans-Canada Pipe Lines Company Limited, became a legal entity. The first act of this corporation was to select a board of directors. The respective directors of Western and Trans-Canada were on the board, as well as persons representing competing governmental, sectional, and industrial interests. The first thirteen members read like a who's who of the gas and oil industry in Canada: Clint Murchison, Ray Milner, Deane Nesbitt, Senator Peter Campbell, Edouard Asselin, Alan Williamson, Gordon Osler, Frank Schultz, Ross Tolmie, Jules Timmins, Murdoch MacPherson, John Fell, and Edward Bickle. The first responsibility of this board was to select a fourteenth member who would serve as chairman and chief executive officer (president) of the company. Upon recommendation of Premier Manning and C. D. Howe, the choice of the board was Nathan Eldon Tanner. President Tanner later recalled details of his recruitment:

> In less than two years after starting Merrill Petroleums, I was approached by the Trans-Canada Pipelines Company . . . to see if I would be president of the company. . . . I told them I was happy where I was and wouldn't go to Toronto, where they wanted to have their head office. . . . They said, "Can we come back and see you?" I said, "Well, if you want to. . . ."
> The next day I received a call from Premier Manning. He said, "Tanner, these people want you to do this job and I think this is your opportunity to be of great service to your country." I said, "Mr. Manning, you are hitting below the belt. I have given sixteen years to my country, and you seem to know where to hit me." Well, I got a call that very day from Mr. C. D. Howe, who was the Senior Minister of the Canadian Government, telling me that he wanted me to take the job. He was very complimentary and said that I was the only man who could hold these two companies together. Flattery, you know, will get you anything. I did feel that when the two asked me to do it, I should accept.[4]

William Kilbourn, the leading historian of the Trans-Canada pipeline, offered the following critical assessment of Eldon Tanner's role in the project's development: "Tanner probably did not play as important a role in Trans-Canada's survival and ultimate success as half a dozen of the original sponsors on the board. Nor did his ability or style ever qualify him to be a member of the power *elite* of Canadian business and public life. But his quiet diplomacy was to be important both to the morale of the employees and for relations with a great range of persons outside the company."[5] Many will disagree with the first part of this opinion, for without the quiet diplomacy and demanding devotion he expended, the project might not have survived.

Although Eldon Tanner felt unqualified in most aspects of his new position, his executive assistant, J. C. Saks, summarized his performance as follows:

> He became involved with people of varying dimensions in the human sense, people who were schooled in various disciplines—the financial discipline, the legal discipline, engineering, consulting, accounting, from very diverse backgrounds and occupying positions of great importance in the business community throughout North America. During the very serious times . . . I think it was an inner quality of Eldon Tanner's, due entirely to his religious background, [that] very sophisticated, very hardnosed, and sometimes parochial individuals . . . gathered strength and inspiration from . . . which enabled them to keep going when many times they would have thrown in the sponge.[6]

The new chairman's political savvy, business acumen, and interpersonal skills amply prepared him to direct the Trans-Canada venture, the magnitude of which was comparable to the construction of the Canadian Pacific Railway in the late nineteenth century. In addition to his determination to serve his country, Chairman Tanner was attracted to the post with a five-year contract that included an annual salary of $35,000, equivalent to the salary he was receiving with Merrill Petroleums, plus a guaranteed retirement income of $15,000 should the project abort. He was also offered the same stock options that the initial sponsors had received—a substantial block of stock worth eight dollars per share. Because of his long career as a public servant, he did not have the personal wealth to exercise this option; consequently, the directors offered him, for one dollar per share, a block of their own stock, which they had purchased at eight dollars. Although very attractive, this offer was considerably below that which most senior executives in established American oil firms were receiving at the time. As a matter of fact, Chairman Tanner attracted to the firm several highly placed and respected executives from lucrative positions in the United States with salaries considerably higher than his.

147

In perhaps his major coup, Eldon induced Charles Coates to become his executive vice-president with a salary of $45,000 and equally impressive benefits. The incentive, however, must have been more than monetary. The imposing and dynamic Coates had been expected to succeed Gardiner Symonds as president of Tennessee Gas Transmission Company, the first, largest, and most prosperous big-inch natural gas pipeline in America. The adventure and opportunity to be associated with the world's largest natural gas pipeline project might have attracted the former football player. The quiet and deliberate personality of his superior might also have influenced his decision. Whatever the reason, his appointment as executive vice-president of Trans-Canada on August 11, 1954, surprised the natural gas industry. At the same time, A. P. Craig, a former Westinghouse executive and advisor to C. D. Howe, joined Trans-Canada as a vice-president in charge of negotiating sales contracts along the pipeline route.

Another invaluable assistant to the new Trans-Canada chairman was Mary Livingstone. In all, she was his secretary for twenty-four years. Through the years, she and Eldon Tanner expressed considerable mutual respect for each other's work. Of him she recalled: "He always had the admiration and support of his staff. His quiet manner and availability at all times were always appreciated by his staff. I can honestly say that in all those years I never heard a cross word from him. That is not to say he was not demanding—he was, but in a way that I was a partner in what had to be done."[7]

One of the few skills Chairman Tanner admitted to was the ability to choose good assistants. "I am not boasting, but I think I did [delegate] quite well," he said. "if you have the right kind of men and give them responsibilities and follow through, things are going to go well."[8]

Trans-Canada established its first headquarters in Calgary, in compliance with Eldon's conditions. The company's first offices, ironically, were located in the basement of the building occupied by Merrill Petroleums. As J. C. Saks quipped, "Eldon

Tanner and I did not start on the ground floor in the pipeline business. We started in the basement." The main offices were moved shortly thereafter to the Toronto Dominion Bank building, where there was enough room for expanded operations and personnel. These new accommodations also provided a higher profile for a company that was fighting for its political and economic life.

Soon after Eldon assumed the reins of Trans-Canada, C. D. Howe announced the government's all-Canada policy on natural gas: "The policy of the government of Canada is to refuse permits for moving natural gas by pipe across an international boundary until such time as we are convinced that there can be no economic use, present or future, for that natural gas within Canada." This policy shaped the natural gas industry in Canada well into the 1960s.

On May 14, 1954, the Alberta government authorized Trans-Canada to remove a total of 4.2 trillion cubic feet of natural gas from the province over a twenty-five-year period. On July 26, the Canadian Board of Transport Commissioners approved construction of the proposed pipeline from the Alberta-Saskatchewan border to Toronto and Montreal, subject to completion of financing arrangements by December 31, 1954. Some time earlier, the Alberta government had constructed a provincial gas-gathering system, the Alberta Trunk Lines, in order to avoid the undesirable situation of externally controlling the direction and price of Alberta gas and to keep jurisdiction over gas-gathering systems with Alberta. After four years of government negotiations, the formal apparatus had finally received government sanction. Approval, however, only laid the groundwork for the real challenge that lay ahead—to get the pipe in the ground and the gas to the markets.

Although the pipeline project had received bipartisan approval in both Edmonton and Ottawa, many serious complications later arose that delayed and almost completely frustrated the project on numerous occasions. The basic problems were these. The government had already required an all-Canada

149

route with a Canada-first distribution priority. Industrial centers in Ontario and along the Saint Lawrence River promised to be the best Canadian market for Alberta natural gas. In the mid-1950s, however, these markets existed only in potential and were two thousand miles from the energy source. There was also the serious but unanswered question of the economics of transporting gas eighteen hundred miles before reaching its first substantial market. Furthermore, to reach eastern markets exclusively within Canada, the pipeline would have to traverse the Laurentian Shield, a pre-Cambrian mass of solid rock. Such a route would add hundreds of miles to the pipeline route and an estimated $50 million to the estimated $300 million construction cost.

Gas companies in Alberta—for the most part American based—were reluctant to contract with Trans-Canada for gas it might not ultimately be able to sell, while eastern utility companies were likewise reluctant to contract for Canadian gas that might ultimately cost much more than American gas imported near Niagara Falls. Because of the planned construction period of several years, investors outside the petroleum industry were reluctant to wait that long for a return on their investments—a return that might not be realized at all. American utility and gas transport companies were also reluctant to contract with Trans-Canada because of the prevailing Canada-first attitude in the Canadian government. Contracts with American firms had the additional difficulty of having to be approved by the U.S. Federal Power Commission, which was reluctant to grant import permits to a company whose financial soundness remained uncertain at best.

As president of Trans-Canada, Eldon Tanner was principally responsible for resolving these dilemmas. Under his direction, the previous contract with Northern Natural Gas was successfully renegotiated. He was also successful, to some extent, in reducing the price demands of both the utilities and the gas companies until long-term markets could be established and the pipeline put into smooth operation. He told the Canadian Club in Toronto that the contending companies were "going to have to take a little less" in the initial years of operation in order to get the project off the ground.[9]

Despite his efforts to reconcile competing interests and despite his persistent air of confidence, Eldon could not bring the divergent interests together before the initial financing deadline, December 31, 1954. The deadline was extended to April 30, 1955, then to October 30, 1955, then to May 1, 1956, and finally to March 31, 1957. During this period of intense negotiations, Trans-Canada was able to secure two-thirds of the required supply contracts with oil companies drilling in Alberta. However, the delay in achieving complete capitalization caused the company's contract with Northern Natural Gas to lapse, which left only one purchase contract—with the American firm of Tennessee Gas Transmission—still in effect. Eldon Tanner, who had hoped to finance the pipeline exclusively from the private sector, was now forced a final time to seek government loans for Trans-Canada's initial capitalization.

The question of government assistance to finance the pipeline had been raised initially in October 1954, when the Trans-Canada board could see that the initial financing deadline was not going to be met. Although Cabinet Minister Howe reiterated his basic support of the project, he declined public assistance at that time. The financing difficulties facing Trans-Canada included sales contracts whose signing was delayed for any number of reasons. Potential major buyers of natural gas were in serious financial difficulties themselves, and contracts were often all but signed until last-minute, unacceptable demands were made by one party or the other. In early 1955, Union Gas Company of southwestern Ontario was the only promising market for Alberta natural gas.

In order to meet the April 30, 1955, financing deadline, Trans-Canada proposed that the federal government agree to meet any payments due for the first few years of the company's operations on the first mortgage bonds that the company was unable to make. Feasibility studies indicated that the extent of government aid under this program would not exceed $25 million, which would be paid with interest prior to any payments to other security holders. When Walter Harris, the Canadian Minister of Finance and rival of C. D. Howe in the cabinet, received the formal request from Chairman Tanner, he interpreted it as a request to guarantee the bond issue. Not wishing to engage in public financing of private industry, the cabinet denied the request on January 12, 1955, over Howe's objections.

The next step for Trans-Canada officials was to negotiate a major loan through the Bank of Canada. After a series of intense negotiations, Governor James Coyne, director of Canada's national bank, agreed to loan the company $65 million if it could guarantee 30 percent of its projected capital requirements, or $105 million. The latter amount was to be obtained through public securities. The agreement was to be finalized March 13, 1955, at a meeting in the board room of the Bank of Canada. At this meeting, Mr. Coyne presented a new condition for the loan, namely, that until the loan was repaid, shares held by the bank as security for the loan would be voting shares. That is, the bank would retain controlling interest in the pipeline.

The board of Trans-Canada reluctantly agreed to this condition, but Canadian Gulf, Trans-Canada's major supplier, categorically refused to make any contract with the company that could be potentially controlled by any level or kind of government agency. Chairman Tanner's announcement of the failure of these negotiations read:

> To date the company has been unable to negotiate a type of financing assistance that does not result in an agency of the government of Canada being in a position to control the company and such an arrangement makes it impossible for the company to purchase its gas requirements. Under the circumstances the directors of Trans-Canada have most reluctantly reached the conclusion that there are no further steps within their power which can now be taken to arrange the financing to meet this year's construction program. Trans-Canada will continue its efforts to arrange the financing of its project from private capital sources.[10]

Because a major snag in financing the pipeline involved construction through the Laurentian Shield of the northern Ontario section, alternate routes were explored by Trans-Canada officials. One alternative proposed was to route the gas from Winnipeg through the United States and back into Canada at Detroit. Another possibility was to build the line in three stages. The Toronto-Montreal stage would import Tennessee Gas near Niagara Falls to develop gas markets in eastern Canada. The Alberta-Winnipeg stage would develop markets in the western prairies and create the possibility of exporting gas to the United States. The final stage across northern Ontario would be constructed after the other two stages were successfully established. A third alternative was to reroute the pipeline through Ontario, avoiding the Laurentian Shield. The first alternative was not compatible with Canada's all-Canada policy. The second was favorable to Trans-Canada, Tennessee Gas, and the Alberta government. The United States Federal Power Commission (FPC) remained unconvinced of Trans-Canada's financial soundness; consequently, the commission consistently denied requests by the pipeline company to export gas to the United States. In a rather forceful refusal to TCP's proposal, one FPC official commented,

> It is completely lacking in firm purchase contracts. It lacks firm market commitments in eastern Canada. . . . In the absence of pipeline experience over the proposed line, or reliable cost estimates, the Commission is without knowledge whether gas can be sold in competition with other fuels in Trans-Canada's potential market. It is difficult to see how any project could more completely fail to meet the standards enunciated by us.[11]

Despite the reluctance of the FPC to assist Trans-Canada, the Canadian Board of Transport Commissioners granted the company permission on September 21, 1955, to construct the Toronto to Montreal line. Trans-Canada would import gas from Tennessee Gas at Niagara Falls to develop the eastern markets while the rest of the pipeline was being constructed. Once it was completed, Tennessee Gas agreed to reverse the flow of gas across the border and to purchase off-peak gas from Trans-Canada. To finance this section of the line, Deane Nesbitt, Trans-Canada's chief negotiator, persuaded the Royal Bank of Canada and the Canadian Bank of Commerce each to loan 50 percent of the estimated construction cost. This loan constituted the first proof of financial soundness that Trans-Canada had been able to obtain for any major portion of the pipeline.

Regarding the third alternative, a variant of the proposal to build the line in three stages, Trans-Canada's engineering firm, Bechtel-Nammix-Hester, found that a longer route across southern Ontario would actually cost less than the northern Ontario route and avoid much of the Laurentian Shield. J. C. Saks remembers one consequence of this decision.

> Money being so vital, a careful choice had to be made as to how to get across Ontario. The initial plans showed a northern Ontario route. In some strange way, we suddenly found out that there was a great deal of buying of land on pieces of outcrops, swamps, and so forth along a line traversing northern Ontario. . . . It appeared that there was land speculation going on having to do with the route of the proposed pipeline. . . . When Trans-Canada finally announced what route it was going to take, there was tremendous criticism. Fellows were talking about "Well, I'm not going to get my beer parlor. I'm not going to get my motel. I'm not going to get the fortune that I planned to make. You guys can't do that."[12]

Even though real progress was being made toward financing the pipeline and obtaining the necessary supply and purchase contracts, increasing pressure was being brought to bear to complete the project, whether by free market economics or nationalization, both of which would have necessitated major changes in company and government policies. Premier Manning, for example, declared that if the pipeline were not constructed in 1956, Alberta would begin to look elsewhere to sell its rapidly increasing gas reserves.

A workable solution to Trans-Canada's dilemma was finally

proposed by Howe's office. A crown corporation would construct the problematic Ontario section of the pipeline at an estimated cost of $118 million and lease it to Trans-Canada with an option to buy. A Canadian crown corporation is a public enterprise, organized and managed by the Canadian government, but on the order of a private business rather than the civil service. Crown corporations had been created to manage the nation's largest harbors, to create a national broadcasting network, and to establish the Canadian National Airlines.

The proposed corporation, to be called the Northern Ontario Pipe Line Crown Corporation, would enable the all-Canada line to be constructed in accordance with government policy but without jeopardizing Trans-Canada's financial position. On February 22, 1956, the Ontario legislature approved the crown proposal without a dissenting vote in order to avert a rapidly approaching energy shortage in eastern Canada. Anticipating the advantages of this crown corporation, Eldon Tanner wired Trans-Canada's directors, "Good progress is being made on all fronts. We are happy to advise that the whole program looks more encouraging."

A shortage of big-inch pipe in the United States, however, dampened the enthusiasm created by the crown corporation. Trans-Canada's supplier, United States Steel, required a commitment of $40 million to build additional mills to manufacture the pipe needed for the 1956 construction season. At the time, Trans-Canada's original sponsors did not have that kind of money readily available. They worked out arrangements with three American-based companies—Tennessee Gas, Continental Oil, and Gulf Oil—to each purchase 17 percent of Trans-Canada's stock, for a total of 51 percent, or controlling interest. Western Pipelines and Canadian Delhi then would each retain 24.5 percent. C. D. Howe agreed to these arrangements on condition that these companies divest their interest in Trans-Canada once the stock issue went public. The agreement was formalized February 8, 1956.

Although this move considerably improved Trans-Canada's

outlook, it jeopardized final approval of the crown corporation charter by an increasingly anti-American House of Commons. In addition, Minister Howe, determined to have construction of the pipeline begin in 1956, worked out an interim financial arrangement in which the government would loan Trans-Canada up to $80 million, or 90 percent of the estimated construction costs for the Alberta-Winnipeg section. Trans-Canada would have until March 31, 1957, to repay the loan at 5 percent interest, and until December 31, 1956, to complete construction of the first third of the pipeline. Default on the loan would cause Trans-Canada's assets to transfer to government hands. Combining the costs of the crown corporation with this short-term loan, the Canadian government was proposing to finance half of the estimated pipeline construction costs.

Because the issue of extensive government support of a private industry was extremely sensitive in Canada at this time, negotiations between Messrs. Tanner and Howe were originally held privately. As time wore on, and with the "help" of leaks to the press by both Trans-Canada and the Canadian government, the agreement entered the fierce arenas of politics and public opinion. The ensuing debate produced one of the hottest political battles in Canadian history. Before it was over, the careers and health of a number of members of the House of Commons would be ruined; the Liberal Party, which had held power in Canada more than two decades, would be on the verge of ouster; and the viability of Canadian parliamentary democracy would be tested to its limits.

The "Great Pipeline Debate" initially centered on the role of government to ensure the success of private industries. The major political parties, which uniformly supported the pipeline in principle, became violently opposed to the specifics of its financing and construction. Conservatives objected to the government's assisting a private company owned principally by American interests and whose greatest potential markets were in America. Socialists, on the other hand, felt the government should nationalize Trans-Canada Pipe Lines Company if the company supplied half of the required financing. The Liberals, supported by the few Social Creditors, favored C. D. Howe's proposal. The proposal was also supported by the provincial governments of Alberta, Manitoba, and Ontario. Since the coalition of Liberals and Social Creditors enjoyed a large majority in Parliament, the pipeline bill was virtually assured of passing.

The Conservatives and Socialists, however, were so opposed to the proposal that they vowed to filibuster it to death. A legislative confrontation over a technical procedure initiated the filibuster on May 8. One week later, as the pipeline bill was being introduced in committee, C. D. Howe rose to move "that at this sitting of the committee of the whole on the resolution respecting the constitution of a corporation to be known as Northern Ontario Pipe Line Corporation, the further consideration of the said resolution shall be first business of the committee and that the consideration of the same shall not be further postponed."[13]

Limiting debate on business before the House, or cloture (British *closure*), had been invoked by the Canadian Parliament only seven times previous to the pipeline debate. From May 8 to June 5, cloture was invoked numerous times and at every stage of the bill's passage—resolution, second reading, committee, and third reading. Never had cloture been invoked before debate on a measure had begun nor on each clause of the bill in committee. Because of this radical move to ensure passage of the bill, little of the subsequent debate concerned the bill's substance. Instead, procedural questions relating to the appropriateness of the cloture rule occupied the legislators' attention.

At various points during the debate, shouts of "shame," "the club," and "the guillotine" could be heard on the floor of the House. Charges and countercharges were volleyed in various forums between proponents and opponents of the bill. Despite the cloture rule, the opposition delayed as best they could action on the bill by raising many points of parliamentary procedure. Shouting down the otherwise impartial Speaker of the House was an extreme but necessary method to gain his attention during the floor sessions.

As the debate continued, the opposition became aware that the office of Speaker was being removed from its traditionally nonpartisan role to force the bill through Parliament. Efforts to correct this breach of parliamentary tradition were repeatedly ignored. Finally a Conservative, Donald Flemming, was expelled from the House for defying orders to respect the Speaker and the order of the House. By contrast, Liberal Prime Minister St. Laurent remained aloof through much of the debate, offering only token concessions to the demands of the opposition. These were summarily rejected.

One night during the fiasco, N. Eldon Tanner, who had been observing the proceedings from the gallery day and night for two weeks, left his spectator's position to confront Prime Minister St. Laurent. He later recalled, "I have never talked straighter to a man in my life." He told the Prime Minister that he was shirking his responsibility by not speaking out on the pipeline issue. On May 22 before the House, Prime Minister St. Laurent defended the government's all-Canada policy and expressed confidence that the government's assistance of Trans-Canada would be approved by the electorate in the elections the following year. He avoided any direct mention of the cloture rule.[14]

The final showdown occurred on June 1, subsequently known in Canadian parliamentary history as "Black Friday." On the afternoon of May 31, the Speaker of the House had surprisingly allowed a motion to debate the ethics of his actions as Speaker over the previous weeks. This was the chance for which the opposition had been waiting; the debate, it felt, could now be extended for another year beyond the deadline for commencing construction on the pipeline. Such a delay might have been the final blow against the already embattled pipeline.

The following day, however, as the first Conservative rose to speak, the Speaker of the House ruled him out of order, apologized to the House for saying he would allow this debate, and rolled back the proceedings of the House to Calendar Thursday, the period immediately before the original motion was made. While enraged Conservatives and Socialists tried to shout the Speaker down, Liberals, sensing imminent victory, pounded on their desks and sang several choruses of "Onward, Christian Soldiers," "Hail, Hail, the Gang's All Here," and "I've Been Working on the Pipeline." Although the opposition proposed to censure the Speaker for his actions, the measure was turned back by the Liberal majority.

The rest of the debate was anticlimactic. The bill passed Parliament on June 5, 1956, and received Senate approval two days later, six hours before Trans-Canada's construction deadline for the year.[15]

The aftermath of the debate demonstrated how stormy it had been in the opinion of the electorate. A poll had shown that the government proposal was favored by only 17 percent of Canadian citizens. Nearly half (45 percent) of those polled preferred that the pipeline be built with private Canadian financing, and 29 percent favored governmental control. Not only was the Liberal position unfavorable in Canada, but the actions of the legislature that ensured its passage was blamed on the Liberals. In the 1957 parliamentary elections, the Liberals lost sixty-six seats and the majority they had enjoyed for twenty-two years. A post-election survey revealed that nearly 40 percent of the electorate who had defected from the Liberal cause did so because of the pipeline debate. To minimize the chances of a similar incident in the future, the Conservative House of Commons removed the office of Speaker from partisan politics and began legislative reform to streamline necessary action on measures before the House.

Despite the long-term political consequences of the pipeline debate, it did insure financing of the pipeline construction for the 1956 season. Within hours of the final approval of the bill, large-diameter pipe began moving from Pennsylvania to Canada. Before the end of June more than half of the construction contracts had been awarded. By July, however, a steel strike closed all the American mills. This interruption prevented Trans-Canada Pipe Lines from meeting the government-imposed construction deadline of December 31, 1956, though the cause of the interruption did not require that Trans-Canada forfeit its assets to the government.

Within a year of the approval of government loans, Trans-Canada had secured sufficient contracts so that it had to draw only slightly more than half of the $80 million loan. Some of the companies with which major contracts had been signed included Consumers Gas Company of Toronto, Winnipeg and Central Gas Company, Northern Ontario Natural Gas Company, and Quebec Natural Gas Corporation.[16] In addition, contracts were concluded with Tennessee Gas Transmission and Midwestern Gas Transmission of the United States. The contracts with eastern Canada utility companies fostered a promotional campaign to increase industrial and domestic consumption in the key provinces of Ontario and Quebec.

The Canadian government was now led by John Diefenbaker and the Conservatives, who opposed government financing of a company owned by American interests. Accordingly, Trans-Canada arranged a transfer of its ownership from primarily American companies to primarily Canadian concerns. A $111 million stock issue, of which $81 million was offered to Canadian investors, insured that by completion of the pipeline, Canadian interests would own 73 percent of Trans-Canada Pipe Lines.

The issue was to be made in debenture units consisting of one thirty-year subordinate debenture worth $100 and five shares of common stock, each worth $10, for a total of $150 for each unit. Trans-Canada arranged for the widest possible selling, favoring investment quality purchases more than profiteering. The opening date of issue was February 26, 1957, and by the end of the day, allotments had been made to over 35,000 individuals and corporations, the largest number of shareholders to whom a new issue had been allotted in Canadian history. Within a week, the value of a debenture unit had increased from $150 to $165. With the success of its stock issue, Trans-Canada could repay Canada its $50 million loan plus interest well before the established deadline.

In 1955, the seventy-three-mile line from Niagara Falls to

Toronto was completed, bringing gas from the United States to stimulate emerging markets in eastern Canada. By early 1958 the line from the Alberta-Saskatchewan border to Port Arthur, Ontario, was finished, and on October 10, 1958, the difficult and uneconomical section from Port Arthur to Toronto was completed. Alberta gas arrived in Toronto seventeen days later, at which time the gas flow through Niagara Falls reversed direction. This meant that Trans-Canada had begun exporting gas to the United States to help equalize the existing balance of payments between Canada and the U.S.

During peak construction periods more than five thousand men worked on the pipeline. Nine million cubic yards of earth and rock were excavated and over 650,000 tons of pipe were laid into the 2300-mile trench. The line crossed eight lakes, ninety-nine rivers, and numerous streams, roads, and rail lines.

The 2300-mile Trans-Canada pipeline cost $375 million to build. Within a decade this initial investment had doubled to nearly $730 million in pipeline facilities. Profits in 1970 exceeded $20 million and were growing rapidly. Eastern Canada thus gained a stable supply of reasonably priced fuel, and the pipeline had become 90 percent Canadian-owned. Moreover, construction of the pipeline spawned a pipeline manufacturing industry in Canada that continued to flourish long after Trans-Canada's demand for pipe had decreased. Finally, the impact of Trans-Canada on the life of Alberta, Ontario, and Quebec is immeasurable in terms of the material quality of life it contributed to these provinces.[17]

Nathan Eldon Tanner was a prime mover in this development. He was heavily involved in many of the negotiations with governments, including the U.S. Federal Power Commission, and with utilities and oil companies. Although he was well remunerated for his efforts, he sacrificed enormous human costs. Because he refused to move from Calgary and relinquish his position as the first president of the Calgary Stake, he spent many long nights traveling between Alberta and eastern Canada. Mary Livingstone, who made most of the pre-jet plane reservations, said, "It seemed he was in the air as much as he was on the ground for a period of three years."[18] According to J. C. Saks, his administrative assistant, Eldon Tanner could "drop off to sleep immediately upon fastening his seat belt in an airplane when we flew on the 'cardiac specials' leaving Calgary in the evening, arriving in Toronto for a directors' meeting early in the morning, around six o'clock, to go through a full day's work."[19]

On one occasion during some serious negotiations, President Tanner returned to Calgary for a meeting of the Calgary Stake presidency. His first counselor, Charles Ursenbach, recounted the incident: "He came back after a very difficult week and he was just a bronze, yellow color—he was sick. I said to him as we were sitting there together, the two of us, 'Eldon, it isn't worth it. You're ruining your health. Why don't you quit and tell them you don't want any more to do with it?' He pounded the desk, and said, 'Charles, don't talk to me like that. You know very well I never quit until I'm beat, and I'm not beat on this.'"[20]

Because he was in the middle of one of the most serious political and economic challenges to face Canada in the twentieth century, he received some unfavorable publicity from the opposing parties and groups. The most serious embarrassment came from a commission appointed by Prime Minister John G. Diefenbaker, the Conservative successor to the Liberal Louis St. Laurent. Selected to recommend a policy on exporting Canada's energy, the commission at one point criticized President Tanner and Executive Vice-President Charles Coates for exercising options on Trans-Canada stock when the government had underwritten its initial operations. It asserted, first of all, that the offer of 10,000 shares at a price considerably below par value in order to encourage him to accept the reins of Trans-Canada was "an unusual transaction." Second, it felt that the two men should not have exercised their options once the government had approved the loans to Trans-Canada.[21]

These references in the otherwise complimentary Royal Commission report endeavored to make N. Eldon Tanner and Charles Coates political scapegoats. Otherwise, the report commended the operation. Although the government had underwritten the crown corporation, its policies had forced the company, which had pursued private financing from every conceivable angle, to receive that much government support in order to succeed. And that support was the logical extension of the government's initial all-Canada route and Canada-first distribution policies.

As to Messrs. Tanner and Coates, the commission acknowledged that both men had left lucrative, secure, and promising positions at considerable professional risk to build the pipeline. Compensation on the order that they received was neither inordinate in the oil and gas industry in North America nor was it excessive in relation to their service to Canada as Trans-Canada's driving forces. Finally, of all the company's activities over the previous decade, the exercise of stock options, which followed the customary practice of free enterprise economics, was the only one criticized by the Royal Commission. Be that as it may, Eldon Tanner's conscience was clear. He relinquished the presidency to Charles Coates after the 1957 election, which brought the Conservatives to power. He retained his position as chairman of the board until 1958 and remained on the board until after he became a General Authority of the Church.

Of his service to Canada as president of Trans-Canada, the Calgary *Albertan* editorialized:

> When a gas pipeline across Canada was being proposed and negotiated, the project was bogged down for a time by confusion and rivalry and by difficult federal government conditions. It was agreed at that time that the one man in all Canada who could bring the various interests together and build a line conforming to government policy was Mr. Tanner. . . . The line has been built and is now in operation. It is a national institution, a major force in the economy of the country. And again the chief architect has been Mr. Tanner. . . . We move a vote of thanks for the work he has done for Canada.[22]

In honoring him as the Man of the Year, the *Journal of Trade and Commerce in Western Canada* said of Eldon Tanner, "Coupling a philosophy of service to community with personal determination so strong it shows in the jut of his jaw, Nathan Eldon Tanner, president of Trans-Canada Pipeline Company, has completed a record of success in government and business unequalled in Western Canada."[23]

Footnotes

[1]See Earl Gray *The Great Canadian Oil Patch* (Toronto: MacLean-Hunter Ltd., 1970), pp. 178-80.

[2]Ibid., pp. 187-88.

[3]The Honorable Mr. Howe, like Eldon Tanner, was born in the United States. Trained at Massachusetts Institute of Technology as a civil engineer, he taught at Dalhousie University for a time; he later formed his own construction company and became a millionaire by age thirty-nine. In 1935 he was elected to Canada's House of Commons, and was soon appointed Minister of Railways and Canals and Minister of Marine. In his twenty-three years in the Canadian government, he became, as one observer said of him, "minister of just about everything." At the time of the pipeline debate, he was Minister of Trade and Commerce and one of the most influential persons in Canada. *Who's Who in America* 29:124.

[4]N. Eldon Tanner, Bitton interview, pp. 15-16.

[5]Kilbourne, *Pipeline,* p. 49.

[6]James C. Saks, oral interview, Calgary, 1979, pp. 4-5.

[7]Livingstone, "N. E. Tanner."

[8]N. Eldon Tanner, Bitton interview, p. 13.

[9]Gray, *Canadian Oil Patch,* p. 195.

[10]Kilbourne, *Pipeline,* p. 76.

[11]Ibid., p. 70.

[12]Saks, oral interview, p. 6.

[13]For an extensive account of "The Great Debate," see chapter 9 in Kilbourne, *Pipeline,* pp. 111-33.

[14]Ibid., pp. 126-27. According to Professor Kilbourne, N. Eldon Tanner has heard Trans-Canada Pipe Line Company denounced as "Tanner's Tomboys" and "Murchison's Minions."

[15]Gray, *Canadian Oil Patch,* pp. 201-15; *Time,* June 18, 1956, p. 40.

[16]*Business Week,* October 27, 1956, p. 194; January 25, 1958, p. 166.

[17]Gray, *Canadian Oil Patch,* p. 218; Edwin O. Gould, *Oil: History of Canada's Gas and Oil Industry* (Seattle: Hancock House, 1976), p. 167.

[18]Livingstone, "N. E. Tanner."

[19]Saks, oral interview, p. 4.

[20]Charles Ursenbach, interviewed by William G. Hartley, 1973. James Moyle Oral History Program, Archives, Historical Department of The Church of Jesus Christ of Latter-day Saints.

[21]Gray, *Canadian Oil Patch,* pp. 216-17.

[22]Calgary *Albertan,* December 6, 1958.

[23]*Trade and Commerce in Western Canada,* January 1956.

9

Stake President and
Scout Executive

Not only did Eldon Tanner serve his country as president and chairman of Trans-Canada Pipe Lines, but at various times during the period of 1952 to 1960, he was also chairman of the board of Merrill Petroleums; a director of Toronto-Dominion Bank, Page-Hersey Tubes Ltd., Waterous Equipment Ltd., Jenkins Groceteria Ltd., Sturdie Propane Ltd., Alberta Gas Trunk Line Company, Consolidated Freightways, Inland Cement Company Ltd., and Alberta Ytong Manufacturing Company Ltd.; member of the board of governors of the University of Alberta and member of the advisory board of National Trust Company; and president of the Canadian Gas Association.

The position he honored more than any of these, however, was president of the Calgary Stake of The Church of Jesus Christ of Latter-day Saints. He held the position from the creation of the stake November 14, 1953, until his call as a General Authority of the Church in 1960. He initially resisted the Trans-Canada offer partly in deference of his church calling. He rarely, if ever, missed an executive meeting or stake conference because of his work responsibilities. This part of his life requires an excursion back to the time he left government in 1952.

Note: This chapter is based on research done by Steven Olson and Don Enders.

From Edmonton, the Tanners had relocated to Calgary in 1952. There Eldon became a ward teacher in the only ward in the city. Shortly thereafter he was called to serve on the high council of the Lethbridge Stake, of which Calgary was a part. His principal assignment on the high council was with the Aaronic Priesthood, continuing his long-standing tradition of working with Scouting and young men. His service on the high council lasted only six months, however.

Elders Harold B. Lee and Mark E. Petersen, of the Council of the Twelve Apostles, went to Alberta in November 1953 to dissolve the Lethbridge East Stake and create the Calgary Stake. The journal of Elder Lee relates the calling of Eldon Tanner as the stake's first president: "Saturday, Nov. 14, 1953--We went into a series of interviews throughout the day and particularly with Eldon Tanner. . . . Satisfied ourselves to his soundness and his loyalty to Church principles and leadership. . . . We finally selected him for our stake president, and he chose Charles Ursenbach and Frank H. Pitcher as counselors, and together they set up a skeleton organization which were sustained and set apart at the Conference."[1]

Charles Ursenbach, the new first counselor, reveals a human side to the events: "Up to [the time of the calling] we'd been 'Brother Petersen' and 'Brother Lee' and 'Brother Tanner' and so on. After the formal organizing, we sat down and talked and it was 'Harold' and 'Mark' and 'Eldon' and 'Charles' and 'Frank'—a nice, friendly visit. Brother Lee said, 'There's no hurry for you brethren; all you have to do is have your stake formed by ten o'clock tomorrow morning, with all the officers and high councilmen selected and interviewed.'"[2]

Under the guidance of Elders Petersen and Lee, the new stake presidency began the task of organizing the stake that evening, working until 1:30 A.M. Nevertheless, time did not permit President Tanner to issue all the calls that night. Mary Pratt, the stake Primary president, for example, later wrote a letter to President Tanner in which she remembered how she was called:

At the organization of the Calgary Stake: front, left to right, Mrs. David O. McKay, Fredda Kenney, Carolyn Pitcher, Sara M. Tanner, Lucille Ursenbach; standing, Frank Pitcher, left, N. Eldon Tanner, President David O. McKay, Donald Kenney, Charles Ursenbach

> Sunday morning at 7:45 A.M. our telephone rang. I was awake so I got out of bed to answer the phone. You, my friend, President Tanner, were on the other end. You came right to the point. You told me that it was 1:30 A.M. when you and the General Authorities finished organizing the stake—all positions were filled but the Primary. You went on to say that you asked several persons who they thought should be president of the Primary, and then you said everyone said Mary Pratt. To put it into your own words, you said, "You are the stake Primary president. When you come to the Palace Theatre, come and sit up on the stage." I was speechless, but it didn't matter, because I never got a chance to say yes or no, for you said, "I'll see you at the meeting"—and hung up.[3]

At the time the stake was organized, there were twenty-four hundred members within its boundaries, which extended from Red Deer a hundred miles to the north, to Rosemary Ward and Brooks Branch, a hundred and twenty miles to the east, and to Claresholm, eighty miles to the south—some 21,600 square miles. Complicating the great distances separating the various church units was the fact that some of these units were not as stable as others. President Tanner paid particular attention to these challenges in calling his leaders. He sought the best people for leadership positions and then delegated to them a major responsibility for unifying this new, diverse, and widespread stake. Many of the stake-level officers, including his two counselors, remained in their positions throughout President Tanner's tenure. This lent stability to the programs. However, as the minutes of the Calgary Stake reveal, many other offices, including stake boards, bishoprics, and branch quorum presidencies, saw rapid turnover, which presented a constant challenge to keep programs and activities running smoothly.

President Tanner was constantly trying to create additional church units wherever he felt the membership was sufficiently strong. In many cases, this campaign was successful. The number of units in Calgary, for example, grew from two to six wards during his administration. In other cases, he was disappointed by the attitudes and activities of the members. The Gleichen Branch was organized as a dependent branch on the

Blackfoot Indian Reserve, but because of white-Indian conflicts among the members, it was later dissolved.

One of President Tanner's first campaigns was to construct a stake center in Calgary to serve the needs of the local wards and to be a center of stake activity. Up to this point, stake conferences were held in local movie theaters. This arrangement was adequate for stake conference but not versatile enough for the broad-based program President Tanner wished to administer. On January 18, 1954, he received a favorable response from the Presiding Bishopric in Salt Lake City to his request to build a stake center. The stake presidency continued to make progress in the design of the building, the location and purchase of a suitable site, and fund-raising activities. On April 17, 1955, ground was broken for construction, and on September 16, 1956, President David O. McKay dedicated the Calgary Stake Center. The structure cost approximately $400,000 and was completely paid for before its dedication.

The cost of the building was kept low since President Tanner was able to receive loans of equipment from contractors, builders, and other workmen. Meetings and work sessions were held early in the morning and after work at night for stake members to contribute what efforts they could to help pay for the building. In addition, a variety of fund-raising activities was sponsored by the different organizations in the stake. The Relief Society contributed $400 from a square dance and $151 from the sale of box lunches at stake conference; the Young Men's MIA contributed $200 from an Armistice Day dance; and the Primary contributed $100 from a shoe sale and $500 from a contest sponsored by a toothpaste company. There were amateur boxing matches, professional entertainment concerts, fairs, dinners, and service projects, each of which contributed its small share. The members also made sacrifices of time and money. All of these efforts together paid for the stake center and unified the stake membership.

Unity and harmony were two of N. Eldon Tanner's main themes as stake president. He reminded stake officers of them in executive meetings, he preached them from the pulpit, and he lived them in his daily life. He helped many members turn their lives around to be more in line with the teachings of the Church.

To help the people in the Calgary Stake and to ensure the success of its programs, President Tanner had a philosophy of planned involvement of everyone. "One person, one job" was his motto. As ward and stake leader Bruce Bullock remembered, "We worked very hard to effect that program, and we did it by challenging people who weren't active and inviting them to do it, and it worked."[4] Wallace Hanson received the benefits of this philosophy:

> President Tanner called me up, and he had just finished as Minister of Lands and Forests at that time, so I thought it was probably something in connection with the work. I went with him to lunch at the Petroleum Club, and he brought up this thing. . . . He would like me to take a part on the welfare committee. I remember my answer to him was, "Well, I have the same answer for you as I had for Bishop Jensen when he asked me to take a job. I don't keep the Word of Wisdom." He said, "Well, I didn't ask you if you kept the Word of Wisdom," and I said, "No, you didn't." He said, "I'm not asking you now either, but we want you to do this job." He let it be known that if I took the job, I knew what he expected me to do. So we left it there, and he said, "Call me tomorrow and tell me what you decide on it."
>
> I've always been grateful for two things: One is that he asked me in the first place and showed the confidence in me. And the other is that I had sense enough to say yes the next day, because it certainly changed the whole tenor of my life.[5]

President Tanner's overriding concern for people did not stop with members. At all times he sought to uplift, inspire, and teach. Later, as one of the Twelve, he related the following experience of his days in Canada.

> I was driving along and had two young men with me in my car, and a young man thumbed a ride with us. I asked the boys who were with me if we should take him with us, and they said yes. I picked him up, and after we had driven along a little way he said, "Do you mind if I smoke in your car?" I said, "No, not at all if you can give me any good reason why you should smoke." And I said, "I will go farther than that. (I was stake president at this time.) If

you can give me a good reason why you should smoke, I will smoke with you."

Well, these two young men looked at me and wondered. We drove on for some distance, about twenty minutes, I think, and I turned around and said, "Aren't you going to smoke?" And he said, "No." I said, "Why not?" And he said, "I can't think of a good reason why I should."[6]

Given President Tanner's managerial skills and his love for people, it is not surprising that the Calgary Stake increased rapidly. In 1953, stake membership hovered around 2,400; by 1960, it had grown to 3,566, an increase of more than 40 percent. At the same time, the percentage of stake members attending meetings also increased. The Presiding Bishopric's Office at that time published monthly bulletins ranking stakes in the Church according to a number of criteria. President Tanner paid careful attention to the position of the Calgary Stake. For months Calgary was in the top ten. Finally it became the top stake in the Church, according to the PBO ranking, and it continued to receive the highest ranking in the Church from February to December 1960. President Tanner recalls this achievement:

If some stake in the Church could stand first, it could be the Calgary Stake. We set about with that in mind, not to just be the first in the Church, but we thought that it would be an incentive to do better work throughout the different auxiliary organizations. And if any organization was falling behind, we placed the responsibility on them so that they would make it possible for us to stand where we should. It took us over a year to do that—to get to the point where we stood first.

It's interesting to know how we did it. Sara and I were down in Hawaii visiting with Ruth and Cliff who were down there as well. And at the time Jack Armstrong and his wife were there also. Jack and I were out playing golf one day, and I got a phone call for either of us, and Jack went in to take the call. He came back and said, "President Ursenbach just phoned to say that the Calgary Stake stands first." The way they judged that was they had twenty-three questions that they asked, on twenty-three activities, like attendance at sacrament meeting and priesthood meeting, fast offering, etc. Then when President Ursenbach told him we stood first, Jack came back and said that was the information he just got. He said, "Now are you satisfied?" I said, "Yes, I'm satisfied we can do it. Let's keep on doing it." And we did for eleven months.[7]

$$* \quad * \quad * \quad * \quad *$$

In addition to his Church and business responsibilities, Eldon Tanner was active in the community, particularly in Scouting.* He had been an active Scouter from his early teens, and as an adult, he received nearly every award presented to adult leaders by the Boy Scout organizations of Canada and the United States.

His Scouting career began at age fourteen in Aetna, when his uncle Henry Tanner, convinced of the value of Scouting in the lives of boys, was appointed Scoutmaster and organized the first troop in the province of Alberta. This was about a year before Scouting was officially adopted as a program for boys in the Church. Eldon and his close friends Heber Jensen and Milton Hansen became the nucleus of the troop.

Uncle Henry, convinced of Eldon's influence with other boys and of his budding leadership ability, soon appointed him junior troop leader and eventually assistant Scoutmaster. Much of the troop's Scouting activities were enjoyed on Scoutmaster Henry Tanner's farm, south of the small farming community. There, in homespuns and decked out in red Scout neckerchiefs, they enjoyed learning to tie knots and cook out of doors, and had lessons on conduct.

Eldon developed a great love for his Scoutmaster. He felt him to be "about the nearest there was to being perfect." Uncle Henry started Eldon out in the usual way by having him repeat the Scout Promise and the Scout Law. Because of the older man's example, the words came to mean something to the impressionable young man. "He gave me ideals, helped me set goals, made me realize what it was to make a promise, especially on my

---

*Note: This section is based on studies and a draft by Don L. Enders.

173

honor," recalls Eldon. Teaching the practical aptitudes of Scouting was important to Henry Tanner, but he was equally desirous of using the time with his boys in troop meetings, hiking, or camping in the wilds of Alberta to help them understand their duty to God and the importance of cleanliness and morality.[8]

The lessons Eldon learned in his youthful Scouting years served as a model when he himself later assumed the position of Scoutmaster. An exacting disciplinarian, he insisted that rules and regulations teach self-discipline, and that it was the responsibility of the teacher-coach-Scoutmaster to enforce them. Because he mingled love and confidence in youth with his firmness, however, he was successful in curbing the previously unbridled "toughs," whose reputations improved until "they were considered the most well-rounded and mannerly" in the area.[9]

Willard Brooks, one of the youths of Hill Spring, became one of Eldon's Scouts, his student, a cadet, and an ardent athlete. He described Eldon Tanner as "my ideal of manhood . . . who influenced me to achieve scholastically and to be an upright citizen." Years later, he recalled, it finally dawned on him just how smart his Scoutmaster was, "introducing those extracurricular activities so that he could prove to us boys that he could handle any or all of us in case we ever had a mind to challenge him in or out of the classroom."[10] That Eldon Tanner was capable of making his programs for youth successful is evidenced by his wrestling squad: it became the winningest team in the province during his stay at Hill Spring. His philosophy was: "I had confidence in young people and I expected them to do things. I think young people do pretty well what you expect them to do, not what you want them to do."[11]

Eldon would not advance students in school, Scouting, athletics, or church unless they deserved it, stating that he took that stand because "people . . . should benefit through their own efforts and should be judged by what they do."[12] As a Scoutmaster, he did not hesitate to involve parents when adult assistance was needed. A major project was the cutting of logs back to the Belly River Flats for a place to house his Scouts. Fathers, mothers, and sons, working together at such projects, fostered the success of the Scouting program as well as lessened some of the burden of organizational demands, thus allowing the Scoutmaster more time for camping and working with the Scouts.[13]

When Eldon moved to Cardston to take the job of school principal, he was again appointed Scoutmaster. In 1935, when the family moved to Edmonton and he assumed his seat in the provincial legislature, his effect on Scouting in Canada began to be felt farther afield. He was appointed to the local council, then the district, and then the Alberta Provincial Scout Council. In April 1945, when he was asked to accept the post of Provincial Scout Commissioner, he wrote in his diary, "This is a real compliment, but I feel that I may have my time fully occupied now; however, I shall decide definitely before long."

His private deliberations continued until November 26, 1946, when he accepted the appointment. An editorial in the Edmonton *Bulletin* observed, "He is deeply interested in boys' welfare and possesses a wide humanity that will contribute much to the movement. The appointment could hardly be improved."[14] He performed his duties well, despite his other responsibilities, and was elected to a second term in January 1949.

As Provincial Scout Commissioner, Eldon also served on the national Scout council. His duties took him to various provinces throughout Canada and brought him in contact with prominent people of that country, the West Indies, and England. In his official Scouting capacity he made the personal acquaintance of Elizabeth II, first as princess, then as queen; of her parents, King George VI and Queen Elizabeth; and of Lord Rowallen, head of Scouting in the British Commonwealth. His influence was so strongly felt by youth and adults alike that he became generally known as "Minister of Lands, Mines, and Scouts"; the latter part of the title, he says, honored him as much as any other.

In Canada he spoke to many groups of Scouts and Scouters, talks that appeared in the press and were heard on radio by thousands of youths; he was also privileged to present numerous and distinguished awards to Scouts and Scouters. His influence

N. Eldon Tanner, as Provincial Scout Commissioner, greets Her Royal Highness Princess Elizabeth of England (later Queen Elizabeth II) and the Duke of Edinburgh

in urging large and continued private funding for the Scouting program for both boys and girls in Alberta resulted in a greatly improved program.

Eldon Tanner's philosophy of Scouting was based on the premise that an investment in the Boy Scout movement brings greater returns than money invested anywhere else. He was once quoted as saying that young men should "go out and have a good time in life, but the way to have satisfaction from one's work and life is to live according to the commandments of God,"[15]

Because he believed that Scouting develops these attributes and fosters love of country and God, he realized that a devoted Scouter's influence for good is enormous. "It is impossible to place a value on a good Scouter," he said. "I have seen a good, capable Scoutmaster, who understood and loved boys, come into a community and take over a Scout troop where only a small portion of the boys were active, and where there was much delinquency. After he had been there for just a few weeks, the boys were coming out of the back alleys and from every nook and cranny to be part of his troop."[16]

For his long service to Scouting in Canada, President Tanner received many awards, the most significant being the Thanks badge, the Silver Acorn for service at the provincial level, and the Silver Wolf for service to Canada as a whole. Following his appointment as a General Authority of the Church in 1960, he would continue to work on local and national levels to foster Scouting throughout the Church. In 1963 the Boy Scouts of America awarded him the "50-Year Veteran Award." He received the Silver Beaver for his devotion to Scouting on a regional level, and in 1969 he was awarded the Silver Buffalo, one of ten nationally known public figures to receive the award that year.

Despite his heavy involvement in business, Church, and Scouting, President Tanner still found time to participate in local civic affairs. During the family's sojourn in Calgary, he was

The Tanner home in Calgary, where the family lived for just a few months before Eldon Tanner was called to serve as a General Authority in the Church

active in the Calgary Chamber of Commerce, Rotary Club, the Canadian Forestry Association, the Calgary Exhibition and Stampede, and the Alberta Motor Association.

Stake President, Scout Executive

With his stake growing rapidly and still at the top of the Church in attendance, with his experience in education, government, and business, with his concern for civic improvement, and with his deep sense of morality and commitment to people, it is not surprising that Nathan Eldon Tanner was chosen as a General Authority in 1960. After stepping down as president of Trans-Canada Pipe Lines, he had planned to retire to his 300-acre ranch on the outskirts of Calgary. Sara Tanner remembers the plans they had made: "The last four years in Calgary I spent planning and building and living for eight months in my dream house, and we had what we thought was an ideal set-up—plenty of house and land, good help, grandchildren close, horses for them to ride, and we were planning to build a swimming pool for them in the summer of 1961. Then came the call to Eldon to be a General Authority, and our life changed overnight."[17]

The Tanners finished the home in May 1960, and in October he was called to be a General Authority. But, as Sara said, "It's only a house." Consistent with the rest of their lives, they forgot comfort and security when a higher calling came, because, as Eldon Tanner said of himself, "I have put my hand to the plough."

Footnotes

[1]Journal of Harold B. Lee, November 14, 1953.
[2]Ursenbach, Hartley interview, p. 64
[3]Mary Pratt, letter to N. Eldon and Sara M. Tanner, sixtieth wedding anniversary, December 1979.
[4]D. Bruce Bullock, interview by Charles Ursenbach, 1979, p. 64. James Moyle Oral History Program, Church Archives.
[5]Wallace Hanson, interview by Charles Ursenbach, 1973, pp. 10-11. James Moyle Oral History Program, Church Archives.
[6]Conference Report, April 1965, p. 93.
[7]Ensign, November 1972, p. 17.
[8]Violet H. Tanner, interview by Charles Ursenbach, 1974, p. 27. James Moyle Oral History Program, Church Archives.
[9]Ensign, November 1972, p. 14.

[10]Ruth Walker, "My Father," p. 16.
[11]Ibid.
[12]N. Eldon Tanner, Ursenbach interview, pp. 23-25.
[13]Beaton, "My Father," p. 2.
[14]Edmonton *Bulletin,* January 4, 1946.
[15]*Deseret News,* August 24, 1965.
[16]*Church News,* February 15, 1964.
[17]Sara M. Tanner, Life Story.

10

The Call as a General Authority

"Mark my words," eagerly commented a young missionary to his companion in Bradford, Yorkshire, in the early 1950s, "my branch president in Edmonton, Alberta, will become a General Authority some day." Told more as a tribute than as prophecy, this statement was not unique. Many persons felt that way about Nathan Eldon Tanner. Despite hearing intimations of this type from friends and relatives, however, he hardly expected what the future had in store.

Conference time in Salt Lake City was always viewed by Eldon and Sara Tanner as a time of refreshing. As president of the Calgary Stake, he attended as many general conferences as possible. Spiritual renewal and instruction from Church leaders were anticipated each spring and autumn. Laced between each conference session were visits with relatives and friends.

As the Tanners prepared to attend the semiannual general conference in October 1960, they sensed that the Church appeared to have passed almost imperceptively into a new stage of growth. Since Eldon's calling as stake president seven years before, the Church membership had increased by nearly half a million. Ninety-seven stakes had been created, and eight new mis-

Note: This chapter is based on a draft by James L. Kimball, Jr.

sions had been organized, extending the work even further, especially in South America and the Far East. Even traditional fields of labor in the United States, Canada, Europe, and the British Isles were bearing increased fruit. To oversee the work in Europe, a supervisory European Mission office had been reinstated in January 1960 under the direction of Elder Alvin R. Dyer, an Assistant to the Council of the Twelve, with headquarters in Frankfurt, Germany.

At the close of the afternoon session of the first day of the conference, Eldon Tanner received a call from his uncle, Hugh B. Brown, a member of the Church's Council of the Twelve Apostles. He invited Eldon to come that evening to the Browns' residence on Douglas Street on Salt Lake City's East Bench. The visit, while cordial and sociable, ended on a sober note. Almost as an afterthought, Elder Brown told his visitor that President David O. McKay wished to see him in his office at nine o'clock the next morning. His uncle then closed the conversation with the comment that he hoped his nephew "slept well." Although characteristic of Elder Brown's affable wit, the remark seemed to convey a deeper meaning to Eldon Tanner. Despite his uncle's best wishes, his sleep that night was much less than restful.

At the appointed hour early Saturday morning, N. Eldon Tanner was ushered into President McKay's office. The tall, white-haired figure of David O. McKay had never appeared more kindly and dignified to Eldon than that morning as he entered the office in the northeast corner of the Church Administration Building. Within a few but never-to-be-forgotten minutes the interview was over and the world was changed for the sixty-two-year-old stake president from Calgary. He had accepted a call and a charge from the Lord's prophet to serve as an Assistant to the Council of the Twelve Apostles. His counsel and wisdom would now expand from Merrill Petroleum, Trans-Canada Pipe Lines, and Calgary to the world-expanding Church. His influence would extend beyond a city, a province, or the two adjoining nations.

To service increased needs in the Church, Franklin D.

Assistant to the Council of the Twelve

Richards and Theodore M. Burton also were called as Assistants to the Twelve during the same conference. As Eldon spoke Saturday, October 8, 1960, in the Salt Lake Tabernacle, he said:

President McKay and brethren and sisters, I stand before you this morning in all humility. I wish to express my sincere appreciation of the confidence shown by the General Authorities, President McKay, and those associated with him, in calling one so unprepared to hold such a high office in this The Church of Jesus Christ of Latter-day Saints. No one with any less ability could be called to this position. I would like to assure President McKay and members of the General Authorities and you, my brethren and sisters, that I shall do my best and am prepared to dedicate my life and my best to the work of the Lord.[1]

He then spoke feelingly of the spiritual debt he owed to his pioneer forebears, his parents, his beloved Sara, and their five daughters. He could not refrain from mentioning, with some pardonable pride, his deep love for his then twenty-two grandchildren. Sensing the importance of his new sphere of responsibilities, in conclusion he acknowledged that he loved the Lord with all his heart, and pledged to serve Him and His prophet "with all [his] might, mind, and strength." Eldon Tanner was set apart Sunday afternoon, October 9, 1960, by President McKay.

To leave his Canadian homeland, family members, and many friends was not easy. A new home lovingly planned and built among beautiful surroundings and vistas, and so recently occupied, would be left behind. These emotional ties, bonded by many years of sharing himself in government, business, and Church activities, would always remain a gentle if distant magnet to bring him back. Nevertheless, the work of the Lord loomed uppermost in his thoughts, efforts, and desires. He considered it an act of special graciousness and kindness that his first stake conference assignment was to the Taylor Stake in southern Alberta.

Counseling with his brethren and members of the Church in formal and informal meetings, some late in the night, now became a way of life. His door was open to all. Those who came away were often heard to remark about his friendly concern for them. Elder Tanner, like Bishop Tanner and Stake President Tanner before that, was a good listener, well-met, courteous, and always eager to build up others' esteem.

As the new year 1961 dawned, Eldon and Sara were beginning to get accustomed to living in Salt Lake City. They had acquired a pleasant home on Pheasant Way in the Salt Lake City suburb of Holladay. Then one day in January Elder Tanner announced to his wife that he had been given a special assignment: to accompany President McKay to England and Europe, to assist in the creation of three stakes and tour seven missions. They would be gone five weeks, returning in time for general conference the first weekend in April.

President McKay and his party left Salt Lake City the last week in February. The first item of business was a district conference in London and dedication of the Hyde Park Chapel on Exhibition Road, across from the Science Museum and the Imperial College of Science and Technology. The building, a modern four-story structure, had a large pipe organ designed for organ recitals for the interested public that daily thronged the area to visit the chapel and other attractions nearby, such as the Victoria and Albert Museum. The occasion marked a new era for the Church in the British Isles, serving as a precedent for an extensive building program that would spread throughout the "green and sceptered isle of England" and the continent of Europe. J. Howard Dunn, former chairman of the Church Building Committee, has stated that N. Eldon Tanner's influence was vital in getting the Church building program moving in these lands. Further, Elder Tanner's vision of future needs generally exceeded that of the building committee.[2]

The dedication on February 26, 1961, was an emotional and spiritual event, made more memorable by a special Singing Mothers chorus of British and American women. Dr. Frank W. Asper, Salt Lake Tabernacle organist, played the splendid new organ. Capping the meeting was the creation of the London Stake, with Donald W. Hemingway as president.

A week later, on March 5, Elder Tanner assisted in the organization of the new Leicester Stake, with Derek A. Cuthbert called as president. (Some seventeen years later, on April 1, 1978, Elder Cuthbert would be sustained as a member of the

First Quorum of the Seventy.) This was followed by a tour of the Central British Mission with the new mission president, James A. Cullimore (who was named an Assistant to the Twelve five years later, in April 1966). From there Elder Tanner flew to Rotterdam for the creation of the Holland Stake on March 12, with Johan Paul Jongkees as president; then back to England to organize the Leeds Stake on March 19, with Dennis Livesey sustained as president.

The whirlwind tour was tiring and arduous. Even the ever-busy April conference sessions seemed like a rest when compared with all that was accomplished over the preceding weeks.

During the course of that general conference, Elder and Sister Tanner received the call for him to serve as president of the newly created Western European Mission, a successor to the historic European Mission Office, with headquarters in London. Although humbled at the prospect, they were nevertheless excited and exhilarated. While each had served in many Church positions, neither had ever served a full-time mission, and the opportunity to perform this service constituted an important fulfillment. To go to the land of their ancestors was an added blessing.

They had to be ready within a few weeks. Some things could be taken with them; many others had to be stored. The new house would have to be rented during their absence. Personal expectations aside, each knew their European assignment presented a formidable challenge. Mormonism had been preached in Europe and the British Isles since 1837. Converts had been made by the thousands, and great numbers had immigrated to the western valleys of America to build up Zion. By their hard work they had stamped their imprint on the western land and on their children and their children's children. By the end of the nineteenth century, emigration had become just a trickle, and by 1921 the Church population in Europe had become fairly well stabilized and constant. Then, after World War II, Church membership in Europe had begun a slight but steady upward climb, though it remained small in contrast with total populations. By 1957, some 40,000 members were living in ten missions in Europe and the British Isles, with no stakes or wards. That year 2,319 individuals were baptized into the Church in the entire area. From that date until 1961, when the Tanners received their European call, the Church in Europe experienced a substantial increase. By 1961 there were some 55,700 members in thirteen missions, and in that year 9,712 persons were baptized.

In the seven-mission area that constituted the West European Mission, many converts were young in years as well as new to the restored gospel. Their experience and knowledge of Church doctrine and procedure was limited, though their enthusiasm was unbounded. All needed training, leadership development, and seasoning. Missionaries also needed the understanding, mature counsel that would help their efforts to teach and improve the testimonies of both prospective and newly baptized members.

After a short good-bye visit to Alberta, Elder and Sister Tanner arrived at London's Heathrow Airport on the last day of April, less than one month from the time of their mission call. They found living quarters in suburban London, near a village with the colorful name of Leatherhead. Their house, also in proper English fashion, possessed a name, "White Hayes"; it had recently been purchased for them by the Church. Though the home was twentieth century, the surroundings were timeless. The majestic green Surrey countryside conjured up images of knights and ladies, of kings and queens, of poets and prophets. Nearby, the famed racecourse at Epsom lent a festive air to the centuries-old land, which, in the words of a familiar rhyme, was "a place of many well-remembered nooks, that of walking in old story books."

Almost before unpacking was completed, Elder Tanner was holding formal and informal meetings and seeking counsel from local officers. The next few months saw a continual round of mission tours and conferences. Daily consultations were held on every aspect of Church business, from stake personnel changes to the construction of buildings, working with mission presi-

Sara and Eldon Tanner outside their home at Leatherhead, Surrey, England

dents, and meeting the needs of members of the U.S. military services stationed in Western Europe. It seemed to both Elder and Sister Tanner that more time was spent in automobile, train, or airplane travel, or waiting, than at home in Leatherhead. Yet there are many who remember the Tanner hospitality and warmth. Sister Tanner remembers the time some young women from Canada were invited, along with President and Sister Selvoy Boyer of the London Temple, to Christmas dinner. Somehow the oven would not do its duty, and the whole group, with much humor, was forced to go instead to the home of the Boyers, also in Surrey, to spend what was left of Christmas day.

To his friends, his business associates, and his Church associates, Eldon Tanner was open, approachable, and concerned. His work in Canadian business and government had been set within a transplanted system of British politics and culture, and this gave him understanding, credibility, and the advantage of knowing how to approach British friends on less than "foreign ground." His Canadian citizenship and passport were additional assets. His governmental experience increased people's trust in the man "from the Provinces" who had made good in other than religious pursuits.

These qualities were especially visible in two areas. First was his solid contribution to the burgeoning Church building program in Britain. Under Wendell B. Mendenhall of the Church Building Committee, an expanded chapel construction project was begun. One thrust was erection of Church structures in Great Britain with chapels, cultural halls, classrooms, and Relief Society rooms as had been the practice in more settled areas of the Church. No longer were the Latter-day Saints to be a "rented hall" church only. Soon the image every convert had in his heart about the Church was to be made substance for people to see, admire, and appreciate, even if the buildings were modest in contrast with the grand cathedrals of Salisbury, Canterbury, Ely, or Westminster Abbey.

The second thrust of the building program was to tailor the costs of construction to the economic abilities of the Saints. The use of local labor missionaries for a number of years assisted in this process. By the time Elder Tanner arrived in England in the spring of 1961, sixty-three sites for Church units had been purchased in Great Britain alone. Before the year was over, thirteen edifices were under construction. To this on-going process Elder Tanner brought a superb sense of support, counsel, and direction. He was able to secure cooperation from local authorities. Quietly and earnestly he taught the Saints the blessings that could be theirs if they helped support labor missionaries. In areas where the size of buildings seemed too large for the small congregations they were designed to serve, he convinced the dubious that they "could do it," that with work and closeness to the Lord, their numbers would increase. His sincerity, openness, and eye to the future overcame many timid objections. His reputation for honest dealings and realism went before him, winning over the non-Mormon as well as the Saint. His way was calm. He listened to every side, let his petitioners tell all they wished to say, and then evinced concern that the best thing be done. His way was not to bully, but to encourage action and to support decisions made.

Many trips were made to branches to convince members of the worth of their Church commitments, ranging from the building of chapels to the building of souls. The latter, he felt, came first. His support of the building program was a substantial reason for improved acceptance of the Church in Britain despite some hardship and sacrifice experienced by the members.

A second accomplishment of President Tanner's administration was his supervision of Deseret Enterprises. This agency began before his arrival, but was supported by the Tanner methods of support and quiet direction. Deseret Enterprises included a bookstore, a publishing house, and a temple clothing factory for the English-speaking membership of the Church outside the United States. Again Elder Tanner's experience in British style and his ability as a diplomat helped him persuade otherwise reluctant government and financial officials to grant privileges to the Church. Not only in quality of members and buildings but also in quality of performance and expectations, Eldon Tanner helped the Church to gain increased respect in the British community. The image some had entertained of the Mormons as a cult eroded considerably, partially as a result of the Tanner years in Britain. One small example will illustrate. During his tenure a large and important bank began to refuse to honor requests from individual missionaries for accounts at its branches. After a few well-placed telephone calls by Elder Tanner to top officials of the bank, the bankers reversed their decision. Within days, missionaries could be observed opening checking accounts at various branches of the bank all over the British Isles.

The missions of Western Europe continued to grow in number and strength and were so reported by Elder Tanner as he attended general conferences in Salt Lake City. During the October 1961 sessions he warmly praised the missionaries in his care. "We are baptizing enough new members every two months to create a stake of more than 2500 people," he reported. "I'm thrilled," he added, "with the attitude of our young people who come to the mission field. To hear them bear their testimonies is encouraging and an inspiration."[3] He returned to England renewed in spirit and enthusiasm after each occasion of meeting with his brethren as well as meeting with the parents of many of the missionaries who served under his direction.

After some eighteen months as an area supervisor, Elder Tanner began to see some of the results of policies he had been encouraging and supporting. Many stake and ward leaders had benefitted by his counsel to support each other as brethren, to be honest, and to stay close to the Lord. These new leaders observed an administrative style that was worthy of emulation. To Elder Tanner, people, not programs, mattered most. Although hard decisions often had to be made to implement policy and to release or call members to positions, he was always kindly and caring, never imperious or dictatorial. He realized the broad spectrum of ways individuals could contribute to the building of the Kingdom. The Saints were not expected to contribute equally in result or method, only in commitment and willingness to try. For N. Eldon Tanner, to do something was always better than to do nothing.

On July 8, 1962, the Scottish-Irish Mission, established some seventeen months before, was divided to create the Scottish and Irish missions. On August 26, 1962, Elder Tanner accompanied President David O. McKay to Scotland to organize the Glasgow Stake. President McKay was then eighty-nine years of age, and he had traveled all day and all night in order to organize the stake in the land of his paternal ancestors.

As Elder Tanner made his way to general conference in October 1962, his mind was full of plans for the future, for the Saints in Europe, and for a joyful reunion with his loved ones and associates. He prayed that the Lord's Spirit would attend his co-workers during the conference sessions. Yet, he was not fully prepared for the way his prayers were to be answered. On October 4, 1962, he responded to a call to visit President McKay. The visit produced an unexpected result, one that he confided in his diary as "the most outstanding day in my life." He was asked to become a member of the Council of the Twelve Apostles, to succeed the late Elder George Q. Morris, who had passed away the previous April. The answer could only be affirmative. To the audience in the Salt Lake Tabernacle Saturday, October 6, 1962, he responded with deep emotion:

> President McKay, brethren and sisters, in meekness and sobriety, and with a deep feeling of humility and inadequacy, I stand before you today in response to a call from a prophet of God to accept this honor and responsibility. Since he spoke to me I have slept little, but I have wept and prayed much. Because I know he is a prophet of God—our beloved President David O. McKay—of which I have borne testimony many times, I feel to accept this great call and responsibility, and I am prepared to dedicate myself and all that I have to this call. I shall continue to pray for the spirit and blessings of the Lord to attend me that I might have the wisdom and knowledge, the courage and strength, the desire and determination and ability to show my appreciation and prove worthy of the confidence of this, our prophet, these chosen men, the General Authorities, and you, my brethren and sisters, who raised your hands to sustain me in this calling.[4]

After expressing his love for his wife, his family, and colleagues, he made the following challenging statement; "I want to bear you my testimony, my brethren and sisters, that if every member of this Church would accept the call of our prophet today and live the gospel and keep the commandments of our Heavenly Father and become missionaries in very deed, we could contribute more to the cause of peace than all the power that might be gathered together by all the governments and all the men in uniform."[5]

Nathan Eldon Tanner was ordained by President David O. McKay, on Thursday, October 11, 1962, the seventy-sixth apostle to be placed in the Council of the Twelve. As a special witness of the Savior, the American-born Canadian's testimony was now to be heard and felt beyond Europe and England. It was to be borne in all the world where doors might be open. Elder Tanner returned to Leatherhead, Surrey, England, knowing that soon his mission there would end and another phase of life begin.

Before coming home, however, he and Sara were appointed to fill an important and delicate assignment to investigate in the African country of Nigeria the possibility of opening missionary work. A few years before, upon reading some Church literature, a number of Nigerians had become so interested in the restored gospel that they had organized study classes and group meetings and called themselves "The Church of Jesus Christ of Latter-day Saints." Numbers of them wished to learn more and to become official members of the Church.

To further investigate this matter, the Tanners flew to Lagos, Nigeria, over the Christmas holidays of 1962. During the next two weeks Elder Tanner met with American Consulate members and with some of those wishing to unite with the restored Church. It was perhaps the most unusual Christmas the Tanners had ever spent together. Their small hotel apartment, located in the steamy heat and humidity of West Africa, contrasted sharply with the cold Decembers experienced in Edmonton and England.

Few would have thought a few years before in what mysteri-

The Tanners during their visit to Nigeria, December 1962

ous way the Lord was furthering his work among the nations of the world. After some satisfactory and some less encouraging interviews with leaders in that new West African nation, Elder Tanner reported to the First Presidency that he recommended cautious optimism for the future. (It is now a matter of record that in October 1978, two couples, Elder and Sister Rendell N. Mabey and Elder and Sister Edwin Q. Cannon, Jr., were allowed to serve missions in West Africa and formally launch the work there.) Like Great Britain and Europe in the nineteenth century, Africa, Asia, and South America would become centers of fervent conversions in the closing decades of the twentieth century.

By the time Eldon and Sara Tanner were released from the West European Mission at the close of 1962, much had been accomplished. Through November of that year there had been 16,279 baptisms in the West European Mission. Many people had increased in ability to lead, preach, and testify of the truths of the gospel. Mission leaders looked forward to the creation of five or six new stakes as well as three new missions in 1963. Forty-three chapels had been completed in England in 1962, and forty-four buildings were under construction in 1963, with two more in the planning phase. Elder and Sister Tanner left Europe with mixed feelings—happy to be going home, but wistful toward leaving cherished new friends and co-workers. They were able to spend only a short time with their successors, Elder and Sister Mark E. Petersen, before they left the winterscape of England behind, filled with memories of the past two years, eager for the future.

In Salt Lake City, a new assignment awaited Elder Tanner. He was to assume the direction of the Genealogical Society of the Church during a time of much growth and expansion. He confided to his diary and to a few intimates that of all the tasks to which he could have been called, he felt least prepared for genealogical work. This call was definitely one he did not seek. But in characteristic fashion, he geared himself to meet the challenge. Through the next few months, he oversaw a restructuring of departments within the Society and helped to formulate new goals and procedures for that organization.

Although Elder Tanner traveled weekly on stake conference assignments, it was good for him and Sara to become more settled at Church headquarters. He had been a General Authority for more than two years, but because of his overseas assignment, there had been little opportunity to associate with his brethren. Now it was possible to meet and counsel with them on a regular basis. He savored the opportunity. As junior member of the

Twelve, he found few idle moments. But whenever he and Sara were able, they participated eagerly in social get-togethers with family and friends. The remark by the young Canadian missionary in Yorkshire so many years before appeared to be fulfilled.

Footnotes

[1]Conference Report, April 1960. See also *Seek Ye First*, pp. 285-86.
[2]J. Howard Dunn, interview by Gordon Irving, 1981, pp. 1-3. James Moyle Oral History Program, Church Archives.
[3]*Church News*, September 30, 1961, p. 3.
[4]Conference Report, October 5, 1962, p. 68.
[5]Ibid.

11

The Call to the First Presidency

On the morning of September 18, 1963, as Elder Tanner drove to work at the Church Administration Building, he heard on the radio news of the sudden death in Florida of President Henry D. Moyle, first counselor in the First Presidency. President Moyle and Elder Tanner were close friends, having had common experiences with the oil industry (Elder Moyle had been associated with Wasatch Oil Company, which later merged with Phillips Petroleum). Only a few days earlier the Moyles had been dinner guests of the Tanners. One of Elder Tanner's first actions upon arriving at his office that morning was to telegraph Alberta Moyle his sense of loss over her husband's death.[1]

During the following days Elder Tanner worked on his talk for general conference as well as a talk that he would give to a convention of the Genealogical Society October 4. He drove to Southern Utah for the dedication of the Zion Park Bowl, gave an address, then returned early the next morning for President Moyle's funeral. That evening he was back in southern Utah for a stake conference assignment at Cedar City. A visit to Idaho Falls for a conference followed the next weekend. Meetings of the Twelve and of the Church Coordinating Committee, an ad-

Note: Glen M. Leonard assisted in some of the research, documentation, and drafts of this chapter.

dress at a Bountiful Stake elders quorum dinner, review of a genealogical training film, and other activities filled the week.

On Tuesday, October 1, Elder Tanner put final touches on his conference talk, and Maureen, a secretary, worked on it during the afternoon. Conference visitors were arriving—acquaintances from the Western European Mission and Canada, stake presidents, family members. The following evening Elder Hugh B. Brown, who that weekend would fill the vacancy in the First Presidency left by President Moyle, telephoned his nephew and asked good-humoredly how Eldon's pulse was, adding that he hoped he had "slept well." This comment, dropped casually in a longer conversation, appeared to mean only one thing. But Eldon resisted the implication. "If this is it," he confided in his diary, "I feel most humble and most inadequate and really doubt seriously that the president would move in this direction as I have been a member of the Twelve for just one year, and during the two years that I was an Assistant to the Twelve, I spent only one month with the president and other members of the General Authorities here in Salt Lake City."

At 7:30 the next morning, October 3, just thirty minutes after Elder Tanner arrived at his office, he was invited to meet in President McKay's office. There he was told that he had been selected to serve as second counselor in the First Presidency. President McKay, in issuing the call, assured Elder Tanner that the Lord had made it known to him; he then expressed his own feelings about the qualities that made N. Eldon Tanner the right man for the office. Later that morning, in the meeting of the First Presidency and the Council of the Twelve, the names of the new counselors, Hugh B. Brown and N. Eldon Tanner, were presented and approved, along with the name of Thomas S. Monson as the new member of the Council of the Twleve.

"I feel that I have been in a state of shock all day," President Tanner wrote in his diary that evening. "I was just getting well established in the Genealogical Society where I felt that I would be able to do the work in a way that the Lord would have it done, and now to take over and try to replace President Moyle is a

President David O. McKay with counselors Hugh B. Brown and N. Eldon Tanner

much greater call with heavier responsibilities, and I feel that I am very incapable of doing this. I feel that it is the highest honor that can be bestowed upon a man by this Church and, therefore, the highest honor one could be offered in the whole world.

"I just hope and pray that the Lord will give me the vision and strength and courage along with determination and ability to do this work in a way that will be acceptable unto Him. I have told the Lord and President McKay that I have rededicated my life to this service and that all that I have will be dedicated to the work."

David O. McKay, ninth president of The Church of Jesus Christ of Latter-day Saints, was born in Huntsville, Utah, September 8, 1872. A large man—six feet one inch tall, nearly two hundred pounds—he always presented a stately, dignified, distinguished appearance. Indeed, it was said of him that he had a "kingly" look. Nonmembers said he "looked like a prophet." To his position as ninth president of the Church, he brought more extensive experience within the Church, combined with world travels, than any other president had previously brought to the office. Not only had he visited most of the stakes of the Church during long service as a member of the Council of the Twelve, but he was also the first of the presidents or of the Twelve to have traveled in so many lands: Canada, North America, Europe, the islands of the South Pacific, the Middle East, and portions of Asia. In 1921 he dedicated the land of China for the preaching of the gospel, and, of course, he was familiar with Europe, having served as a missionary in Scotland as a young man and as president of the European Mission from 1923 to 1925. Under his direction missions were opened in Hong Kong, Singapore, Spain, and other lands; a Church College and the Polynesian Cultural Center were completed and dedicated in Hawaii, and other Church-sponsored schools were built in South America, Mexico, and the South Pacific; temples were built and dedicated in Los Angeles and Oakland, California, and in England, New Zealand, and Switzerland; stakes were formed in Europe, Australia, Mexico, and South America; the Indian Placement Program was inaugurated; Regional Representatives of the Twelve were called; and the Church Correlation Program was instituted.

In the course of this ministry President McKay had become well acquainted with Eldon and Sara Tanner. In 1956 he and Sister McKay had traveled to Calgary, where he had dedicated the new stake center constructed under the leadership of Eldon Tanner. Under this impressive leader Eldon had been called into the circle of General Authorities. And now, on October 4, 1963, he became second counselor in the First Presidency, a position he would continue to hold until the death of President McKay January 18, 1970. These years with President McKay provided him with significant insight into the workings of the First Presidency. The years that followed brought forth much fruit. He witnessed at close range the actions and responsibilities of a remarkable president and prophet. The opportunity for training under a leader of long experience who was also a master teacher served the Church and Eldon Tanner well when he was called to continue as counselor to three subsequent presidents. The evidence of his influence is in the record of many lives, actions, and developments too numerous to be catalogued.

As a result of his new call, President Tanner rewrote his conference talk to convey his feelings of dedication. Humbled by the weight of the responsibility, he willingly committed his life and energies to the work. His name was submitted and sustained by the conference at the morning session on October 4. In responding to the call, he addressed the conference as follows:

My beloved President David O. McKay, President Brown, and brothers and sisters: It is with great difficulty and a feeling of deep humility that I stand before you in response to this high honor and heavy responsibility that has been bestowed upon me, one of the most humble servants, the weakest and least prepared of all. . . .

"I am sure that my call to this position must have been a shock to many of you," he said, adding that only because of their testimonies that "we are led by a prophet of God" could his colleagues sustain him in this position. He concluded:

I have not words to express my deep love for the Lord and my gratitude to him for his many blessings unto me and mine, and I sincerely pray for his continued guidance and strength, as I try to serve him. And I wish to pledge with you again that my life and all that I have will be completely devoted to the service of my Maker and to my fellow men, always with a prayer in my heart that he will give me wisdom and knowledge, courage and strength and inspiration and determination and ability to keep his commandments and serve in a way that will be acceptable to him.[2]

His eldest daughter, Ruth, saw that her father was keenly aware of his brief length of service as a General Authority. "He cried inside for days, and knows what it means to have a broken heart and a contrite spirit," she said. He told Ruth: "Others, like President Harold B. Lee and President Marion G. Romney, had twenty-five years of Church experience while I was out fighting the world all the time, in business or industry or government, trying to keep my head above water. I've expressed my love and appreciation for these men many times for the way they supported and helped me when there could have been great jealousy and opposition."[3]

That was President Tanner's view. Other informed opinions were that the years he had spent in the world equipped him to be the notable link with business, industry, and government that the Church needed, just as it had needed J. Reuben Clark, Jr., in 1933 when he became a counselor to President Heber J. Grant never having been a bishop, stake president, or apostle.

After N. Eldon Tanner was set apart on October 10 by President McKay, he wrote in his diary that the prophet "said that the Lord was pleased with my service, and particularly with everything that I did as with an eye single to the glory of God; that I had been able to lose myself in the service; and that this made it possible for me to accomplish the work the Lord had assigned."

The volume of congratulatory messages and well wishes of visitors surprised the new member of the First Presidency. There were bouquets from the Moyle family, President Tanner's brothers and sisters, an aunt, and neighbors. Letters, cards, telegrams, and visitors extended the feeling of support Church members as a body had expressed with uplifted hand.

After the tiring weekend of general conference, President Tanner arrived early at the office on Monday "ready and rarin' to go" in his new calling, though he was still somewhat shaken by the events of the preceding days and wondering how this new job would change his life. But his responsibilities had already begun, for on the evening of his call the preceding week, President Brown had invited Eldon to accompany him to a meeting with representatives of the National Association for the Advancement of Colored People to head off a planned demonstration conference weekend. Leaders of the Salt Lake Branch of the NAACP made it clear that civil rights and not the Church's restrictive policy on priesthood was their concern. A civil rights march in Washington, D.C., in August 1963 had heightened interest in Utah for the passage of state antidiscrimination laws, and now the NAACP was seeking Church backing for such proposed legislation. Apparently the leaders felt they could attract Church support with a peaceful march around Temple Square on conference weekend. When Dr. Sterling M. McMurrin, a University of Utah professor and former U.S. Commissioner of Education, learned of the planned demonstration, he proposed and arranged a meeting between the NAACP officials and the First Presidency. The discussion, held in President Brown's office, included as participants Albert Fritz, president of the Salt Lake NAACP chapter, and other chapter members. Presidents Brown and Tanner pledged to discuss the matter with President McKay and recommend to him that some kind of statement be made expressing the stand of the Church.[4]

Mr. Fritz carried this message back to local members, who agreed at a Friday evening meeting to delay their march. An NAACP committee of five drafted a statement of concerns, and the statement was presented to the First Presidency the following day. If the Church would make an acceptable response before October 12, the civil rights group said, there would be no picketing. In the meantime, and after further consultation with interested parties, the two counselors agreed upon a statement, which President McKay reviewed and approved with minor modifications. It was decided that President Brown would read the statement as part of his Sunday morning conference talk and not as a separate First Presidency announcement. The statement declared that "there is in this Church no doctrine, belief, or practice that is intended to deny the enjoyment of full civil rights by any person regardless of race, color or creed," and urged "all men everywhere, both within and outside of the Church, to commit themselves to the establishment of full civil equality for all of God's children." NAACP officials accepted the statement as a significant first step in helping to solve the problems of race relations in Utah and across the nation. Mr. Fritz urged civil rights supporters to cooperate with the Latter-day Saints "to build a stronger Utah" and asked that planned demonstrations and picketing be cancelled.[5]

The local and national press took immediate notice of the statement. President Tanner was one of those interviewed by *Time* magazine reporters about the Church's position on blacks. The media almost unanimously broadened their coverage beyond civil rights to include reportage on Mormon denial of priesthood to the blacks. But civil rights workers in Utah were not able to entice the governor to call the legislature into special session that winter, so the question of Church support for civil rights legislation was held over until the regular biennial session of January 1965.

Three measures proposed by Governor Calvin L. Rampton that year received NAACP backing. Once again, President Brown and Tanner met with NAACP officials to consider their request for active Church support of the legislation, but the First Presidency made no public comment beyond the 1963 conference statement. When some of the proposed legislation met resistance in the legislature, disappointed civil rights workers scheduled a downtown prayer march on Sunday, March 7, 1965, to demonstrate their belief that Mormon legislators were misinterpreting the Church statement to stymie fair employment legislation. Even though the First Presidency once again chose not to respond directly, the Church-owned *Deseret News* reprinted in an editorial the statement given officially by President Brown, concluding: "This statement is clear and unequivocal. How its principles are translated into law becomes a matter for the consciences of individual legislators." The Utah legislature subsequently passed civil rights measures on public accommodations and fair employment (the latter exempted wholly owned Church businesses) but one of fair housing died in committee.[6]

Just what Eldon Tanner's role as counselor would be was not immediately defined by President McKay. Only one by one were tasks formerly handled by predecessors in the First Presidency handed to him, along with some rearranging of duties between the counselors. Work days grew longer; retiring early was seldom possible any more, as an extra evening hour or two became an essential aid in dispensing the workload. Saturday mornings at the office became another means of dealing with the increased workload.

For some time, President Tanner continued as president of the Genealogical Society in addition to his many new duties. In mid-October the First Presidency decided to call Elder Theodore M. Burton, an Assistant to the Twelve, home from Europe to help. President Tanner would remain at the head of the Society, with Elder Burton as vice-president and managing director, to carry the day-to-day administrative responsibilities. Early in the New Year President Tanner was replaced by Elder Howard Hunter as Genealogical Society president.

One of Eldon Tanner's last official functions with the Genealogical Society was his tour of the newly finished Granite Mountain Records Vault in Little Cottonwood Canyon east of Salt Lake City. Afterward he outlined for a luncheon group the progress of the nearly $2 million facility carved six hundred feet into solid granite, from its original conception in 1956 to its completion seven years later. One week before his release as Society president, President Tanner directed his staff and the Church Building Committee to proceed immediately with proposed new Genealogical Society and Church Archives facilities, a ten-story building planned for a site on the northeast corner of North Temple and Main streets. A few months later, President Tanner informed the Society that the needs of the two Church departments might possibly be met in wings of the new Church Office Building. This, in fact, was the solution reached, and the need for separate buildings was postponed until 1980, when President Spencer W. Kimball announced the decision to build a Genealogical Library and a separate Museum of Church History and Art on the block west of Temple Square.

Before October 1963, Eldon Tanner had had few opportunities to become closely acquainted with President McKay or with the inner workings of the First Presidency's office. On November 12, 1963, while on a trip to Canada, he received word from President Hugh B. Brown that President McKay had been hospitalized with a slight stroke. During a steady recovery period of several weeks, the two counselors shared the workload and conferred with President McKay at frequent intervals, first at the hospital, then in his Hotel Utah apartment. President Tanner found the president always in good spirits and "full of determination" during these visits.

Such events meant that President Tanner was quickly initiated into the duties of the presiding quorum. He was not long in gaining a firm admiration for President McKay and a calm grasp of the business at hand. The prophet, seer, and revelator was accustomed to frank exchange and discussions in the councils of the Church, and his new counselor was permitted to observe his keen mentality in the intimate relations of the First Presidency.

President Tanner did continue to have misgivings about himself. The patterns of his Church experience prior to his call in 1960 as an Assistant to the Twelve had been confined to small towns of Canada, the branch in Edmonton, and the Calgary Stake. While he was visiting with the author in Arizona during his early days in the First Presidency, the conversation turned to events and names around Salt Lake City headquarters of the Church. The author was familiar with them from the days of his boyhood in Salt Lake City. "But you know," said President McKay's new counselor, "I feel greatly handicapped in my present position. I have no background, experience, or knowledge with the people that the others in Salt Lake City have had and to which you refer."

Whatever initial handicap Eldon Tanner felt was shortly overcome, for he rapidly cultivated and gained friends and associates in the headquarters community. Some years later at a general conference he included in his major address some fairly pointed observations and suggestions regarding some significant centers of influence in Salt Lake City that, in the opinion of many, had directed unwarranted criticism at the Church. The criticism was not unwelcome to Eldon Tanner, but he felt that the approach taken was somewhat less than constructive.

Wendell J. Ashton, later to be the president of the Salt Lake Chamber of Commerce, was at that time a leading advertising executive handling major accounts of large Salt Lake City business firms, and he understood both sides of the situation. He commented to a friend, "None of the other brethren would get away with that kind of statement in a conference talk. It would be misunderstood, reacted to, and resented. Not so with President Tanner. They have too much respect for him."

From the beginning, President Tanner's schedule was crowded with meetings, discussions, and consultations on matters related to Church business and financial interests. Initially there were monthly meetings of the boards of U & I Sugar, Beneficial Life Insurance, ZCMI, Hotel Utah, Zions Securities Corporation, Deseret News, and KSL. Added later were Consolidated Freightways, First Security Corporation, Bonneville International Corporation, and the Coleman Company.

To acquaint himself with the operations of Church-related businesses, President Tanner immediately met with key company officials. During these first few months he absorbed countless details to form an opinion on management policies. To get acquainted with operations and business methods of ZCMI, for example, he met with Harold H. Bennett, the general manager of long experience, and asked what stores were owned by the company, what property was owned, and what the program was for the future. Arch L. Madsen and others involved with four Church-owned broadcast units explained development proposals and agreed that a holding company (to be known as Bonneville International) should be formed to administer the entire Church radio-TV operations. In consultation with boards and managers of the Church farms, President Tanner helped reorganize and stabilize these operations and resolve conflicts that were hampering efficiency.[7]

His assignments in the First Presidency involved him directly with the internal financial operations of the Church as well, through meetings of the Budget Committee, the Committee on Expenditures, the Personnel Committee, the Financial Department, and banks where Church funds were deposited. He quickly assessed needs and recommended solutions in a number of these areas. He wrote in his diary results of a discussion with the head of one major bank that served as a depository for Church funds. "The principle I had adopted with regards to the depositing of money in banks . . . [was that] we had to get the best interest we could from the bank where our money was deposited. He agreed fully with this regardless of whether we continue to deposit with the banks that have had it for some years."

In early meetings with the Church Budget Committee, he raised basic questions about procedures that he felt would make easier the task of assessing requests and needs and matching them with available funds. In the early sixties, the postwar building program had so drained Church reserves that at one point financial officers wondered if they would be able to meet the payroll. When President Tanner assumed the role as overseer of the Financial Department, one of the first actions was to declare a moratorium on building. Investments also were halted until a buffer reserve could be built up. Until now the budget had been "a halfway thing," with many activities not even included. Now a strict, comprehensive budget was established requiring individual departments and the organization as a whole to live within its income. Later an investment committee, a missionary trust

The Tanners dine with Church of England and Roman Catholic leaders in Tonga

fund, and a new employee pension plan were developed. Step by step the Church was introduced to corporate financing.

Another of President Tanner's assignments was to set in motion a reorganization of the Church education program decided upon by General Authorities. Again needs were assessed early in his months with the Presidency. He firmly opposed the expansion of a Church junior college program in the United States and Canada, where educational facilities were widely available. The emphasis, he felt, should be on well-organized seminary and institute programs that could operate at a small fraction of the costs of a single science department or college library. "The money that would be spent for junior colleges," he said, "could be spent much better in such places where education facilities are not available to our youth in those countries." He helped guide the further development of a unified Church educational system, which absorbed the Pacific Board of Education in October 1964; the establishment in March 1967 of what became the Church's International Magazine, to replace numerous local mission magazines; the creation in September 1967 of a body of Regional Representatives to assist in ecclesiastical supervision; and refinements in the Twelve's management of the Church throughout mission areas.

Though Eldon Tanner had been called to a position for which he felt he had no previous training, once again he swiftly mastered the assignment. He brought to his new job a native genius in finances, well-practiced organizational skills, a talent for efficiency, and something more—warmth and humanness. To subordinates, he may at first have seemed reserved to the point of sternness. They soon discovered, however, that they always left his office feeling better about their jobs and about themselves. In board meetings he would say, "Let's hear the other side of this," and insisted on decisions that satisfied all parties. Tense discussions would often be eased by a wry aside from him. He brought great wisdom that helped in making decisions, and with this he brought a sensitivity and caring for the people with whom he worked. It took neither the Church nor the community very long to discover who and what they had gained in this new counselor.

On Thanksgiving Day 1963 President Tanner reflected in his diary on the dramatic changes that had occurred in his life that year. Modesty as well as love led him to see personal events through mutual eyes, his and Sara's. "We feel most fortunate and greatly blessed," he wrote. "Our family and our health have been fine, and we are most thankful for one another. Although we have suffered some financial reverses, we are greatly blessed financially and feel most grateful for it. During the past twelve months we have finished our mission in the West European Mission, visited Nigeria, made our report on that, returned to Salt Lake City, where I was made president of the Genealogical Society, and then in October I was called to be second counselor in the First Presidency of the Church. All of these experiences have been heavy and have required our very best efforts. I feel that we have done the best we could, and hope and pray that the Lord will make us worthy of the many blessings he has given us and the responsibilities placed upon us."

Footnotes

¹Unless otherwise noted, quotations and personal experiences are taken from N. Eldon Tanner, diary, 1963-64.

²*Improvement Era,* December 1963, pp. 1060-61. See also *Seek Ye First,* pp. 291-93.

³Walker, "My Father," p. 4.

⁴See Sterling M. McMurrin, "A Note on the 1963 Civil Rights Statement," *Dialogue: A Journal of Mormon Thought* 12 (Summer 1979): 60-63.

⁵Ibid. Also, Eugene E. Campbell and Richard D. Poll, *Hugh B. Brown: His Life and Thought* (Salt Lake City: Bookcraft, 1975), p. 256; *Improvement Era* 66 (December 1963): 1058; *Deseret News and Salt Lake Telegram,* October 5 and 7, 1963.

⁶*Time,* October 18, 1963, p. 40; *Daily Utah Chronicle* (University of Utah), March 8, 1965; *Deseret News,* March 8 and 9, 1965; Associated Press dispatch, March 11, 1965.

⁷Salt Lake *Tribune,* October 24 and 30, November 27, 1963; April 28, 1964; January 4, 1974; *Church News,* October 26, 1963; May 2, 1964.

12

The David O. McKay Years, 1963-1970

The first few years of Eldon Tanner's service in the First Presidency were a time of important change in Church administrative patterns. In the decade of the 1950s, worldwide membership had increased by fifty percent to nearly 1.7 million members by 1960. During the next ten years, a steady increase would push the total number of members close to the three million mark, with far-reaching implications for Church programs. Adjustments and changes occurred at all levels of Church administration. President McKay appointed additional counselors in the First Presidency, ordained an apostle who served outside the Council of the Twelve, and established ecclesiastical regions served by Regional Representatives. Church growth explained much of this change in leadership patterns. In an early orientation session for Regional Representatives following the theme "The Church Faces the Future," a printed program spotlighted a comment from President McKay: "Most earnestly do I hope that we shall never lose the great conviction that the world is our field of activity. Can you think of anything more potent in moving people to action? But what a responsibility this entails of lead-

---

Note: This chapter is based on extensive research and a draft by Glen M. Leonard, with additional information provided by Ronald J. Otteson and Dean Dannon.

ing good men and good women all over the world to know God, and to know what their mission is on earth."[1] The 1960s were years of adjusting to the growing challenge of a worldwide church.

Because of President McKay's impaired health, his counselors generally met with him in his Hotel Utah apartment to conduct the business of the First Presidency. The counselors could handle some matters themselves, but many items could not be delegated. At these sessions President Tanner found the prophet "as keen and alert as ever," but impatient with the physical limitations his stroke had imposed.

In August 1964, President McKay reentered the hospital. When doctors forecast an extended recuperation, he asked the General Authorities to participate in a special administration. "President McKay asked that I anoint him," Eldon Tanner noted in his diary, "and that President Joseph Fielding Smith seal the anointing. It is a very humbling experience to be called to anoint a Prophet of God, and it has made me feel very humble and serious all day." President Brown was with these counselors at the hospital; other General Authorities were gathered at the same time in the First Presidency room in the Church Administration Building, where they held a special prayer presided over by Elder Harold B. Lee.

A few days later, President Tanner carried President McKay's greetings and blessings to a group of Latter-day Saint youths at an Explorer conference at Brigham Young University. "President McKay is improving in health," he told them.

> He's had a stroke and two heart attacks, but the other day, he said, "You know, I think it's about time that I'm getting well. I'm going to do away with this oxygen thing I've had here." And he threw it away. He came to our meeting last Thursday and he was with us for two hours, and Friday morning he was with us for three hours and a half in meeting. He was weary when he left, but do you know what he said to us? . . . [He said,] "You know, I don't have any aches or pains whatever. I am something like the little boy who said to his mother, 'You know, I feels well, and I eats well, and I sleeps well but I just can't work.' The mother said, 'You feels

well?' 'Yes.' 'You sleeps well?' 'Yes.' 'And you eats well?' 'Yes.' 'And you just can't work?' 'Nope.' She said, 'Well, now, that's no disease. That's a gift.'"

That's President McKay. He has a great sense of humor. He has great determination. He has been a great Explorer in his day, and he's found so many interesting things in life that he doesn't want to leave this old life. He is determined to stay with us, and we are all so pleased that he has that determination and that good sense of humor.[2]

President Brown coordinated the activities of the Presidency when President McKay so directed, and conducted the Thursday meetings of the Presidency and the Twelve in his absence. When President McKay could participate, these meetings would be of long or short duration, depending upon his energy.

For N. Eldon Tanner, the personal adjustment to his First Presidency calling in 1963 was followed two years later by further realignments of duties with the addition of two more counselors, and in 1968 by a fifth. On October 28, 1965, President McKay called Thorpe B. Isaacson to be a counselor to the First Presidency, and on the following day he extended a similar call to Joseph Fielding Smith. President Isaacson had been a counselor in the Presiding Bishopric for fifteen years (December 1946-September 1961) and then an Assistant to the Council of the Twelve. President Smith, an apostle since 1910, was president of the Council of the Twelve at the time of his call to the First Presidency, and he continued to function in both roles.

The appointment of additional counselors was not without precedent in the Church. President Brown had served in such a role for nearly four months prior to the death of President J. Reuben Clark, Jr., in 1961. Brigham Young had been the last president before that time to add extra counselors to the presiding quorum. His appointments in the 1870s, like those made by President McKay, came at a time of increased work loads on the counselors occasioned by Church growth and the advancing age of the president. But despite the precedents, the calling of two additional counselors in October 1965 was, as the *Church News* expressed it, "a surprise announcement." The newspaper had already printed its weekend edition when word came of President McKay's decision. Page 3 of the *Church News* was remade and the section reprinted in an updated edition.[3]

The final counselor added to assist the First Presidency during the David O. McKay years was Alvin R. Dyer, whose call came on April 6, 1968. President Dyer had been called as an Assistant to the Twelve in October 1958. Nine years later, on October 5, 1967, President McKay ordained him to the apostleship. He was not called to the Twelve, however. His assignment in the First Presidency provided for a council of six, presided over by President McKay, with his first and second counselors, and with the three counselors "to the First Presidency."

President Tanner's work load was evidence enough of the appropriateness of the call of additional counselors. "It seems that every day is full of problems and a lot of work to be done," he wrote in his diary nine months after his own call to the First Presidency. "I just hope I can continue to stay on top of it."

With the added counselors in the Presidency, the means and methods of Church administration naturally were somewhat modified. President Isaacson, a vigorous man who had been a high school athletic coach in his young manhood, pursued his goals and objectives with both energy and tenacity. Such was also true of President Dyer. This was in some contrast to the quiet but analytical methods of President Tanner. One incident is reported when Eldon felt that one of the counselors in the Presidency was taking matters directly to President McKay that probably should be considered by the entire council of the First Presidency. Eldon took it upon himself to speak rather directly to President McKay about the matter. As a consequence, for a few hours he felt he might possibly be released because of the strong position he had taken. President McKay was making a valiant effort in his closing years to muster his strength and energy, to maintain direction and control of presidential matters. Eldon understood this, although his own circumspect methods gave him other thoughts for those few hours. The matter was resolved without incident, and the work continued to go forward.

215

President Isaacson's vigorous style was immediately evident in the assignments given him in the First Presidency. Besides his work in Salt Lake City, he traveled extensively, including a European tour in November 1965 that took him to Germany and the Holy Land to meet with servicemen, mission presidents, and Church members. But just three and one-half months after his call, his service was severely curtailed by a disabling illness. On Monday morning, February 7, 1966, he suffered a stroke, and for two days he lay in critical condition at LDS Hospital in Salt Lake City. Gradually his condition stabilized, and after several weeks, he was transferred to the University Hospital for special physical therapy. It was not until October that he was able to join with the General Authorities in a temple meeting and sit with the First Presidency for a group photo at conference time. Upon the death of President McKay in January 1970, President Isaacson and President Dyer resumed places as Assistants to the Twelve. President Isaacson died November 9, 1970. Alvin R. Dyer served as managing director of the Historical Department from 1972 to 1975. He was sustained as a member of the First Quorum of the Seventy October 1, 1976, when that quorum was created, and died March 6, 1977. Experiences with these leaders provided opportunity to observe important contributions made by personalities in Church affairs.

Eldon Tanner's role in Church administration has spanned the full scope of its agencies, departments, and programs, as well as other temporal and educational stewardships. It is not possible nor appropriate to chronicle the activities of each committee he has chaired, officer he has counseled, or program he has reviewed. But a sampling of his workday world as second counselor in the First Presidency is essential to understanding his leadership and influence.

As a member of the First Presidency, he shared the common responsibility of General Authorities to travel among the nations and regulate affairs of missions and stakes. Generally, his assignments were limited to special occasions, such as the reorganization of stakes, dedication of buildings, and the like. He made

President N. Eldon Tanner at the pulpit, adorned with lei

back-to-back visits to Canada and the eastern United States in May 1967. On the first of these, he dedicated a chapel at Regina in the Western Canadian Mission and spoke at a youth conference on the University of Calgary campus. He returned to Salt Lake City for two days, then visited Ottawa and Montreal in eastern Canada and concluded the tour at South Royalton, Vermont. There, more than five hundred fathers and sons of the New England Mission and Boston and Hartford stakes assembled for an Aaronic Priesthood restoration observance.

In 1968, two South Pacific tours were among the highlights of President Tanner's busy schedule. In February he and Elder Spencer W. Kimball and their wives attended three stake conferences in New Zealand, visited the Saints in Tahiti, and then visited the Polynesian Cultural Center in Hawaii. In November, he responded to the invitation of Tongan Mission president John H. Groberg to participate in the fiftieth anniversary of that mission. The week-long activities at the Church's Liahona High School included programs, displays, a dance, a music festival, conferences, and public meetings attended by government officials.

In his travels, he witnessed firsthand the expansion of Church membership in the 1960s. It was a time of rapid growth in Mexico and Latin America. The first stake in South America, at Sao Paulo, was organized in May 1966, and a branch was established that same year in Poland. Many priesthood holders called as stake leaders in fast-growing areas were relatively inexperienced in the Church. President Tanner called a member of only four years, thirty-four-year-old William Campbell, as stake president in Wellington, New Zealand. Selected as counselors were Iain McKay, twenty-eight, also four years a member, and Henry Randall, a twenty-five-year-old Maori lawyer. "'I told these brethren that their age should be no deterrent in their work,'" Eldon told the *Church News* in his report of the action. "The Prophet was only 25 when the Church was organized, and the Savior died when he was younger than President Campbell. . . . The work of the Lord must go on. It demands diligence on the part of all those called to service."[4]

His own efforts in supporting the Lord's work most often centered in the routine work of his office and in meetings at Church headquarters buildings. The regular schedule of these meetings soon locked him into a rigorous routine, broken only by the steady stream of visitors and telephone calls. Keeping track of appointments, handling correspondence, transcribing the daily diary, and performing the numerous other tasks required of a secretary was Maureen Newbold Fowlks, who served as his secretary for a time in Europe and until August 1964 in Salt Lake City. Maureen, described by Eldon Tanner as a "faithful, devoted, efficient secretary," was succeeded by LaRue Sneff, who was already experienced in First Presidency business, having worked with President Stephen L Richards and then with Elder Joseph Anderson in the First Presidency's office. A trusted and completely devoted secretary to President Tanner, she became a favorite also of the Tanner family, and was included from time to time in family excursions and activities.

One of President Tanner's regular duties was that of interviewing those being called as new mission presidents. He also did a considerable amount of personal counseling. It might be a friend or acquaintance seeking advice in business or marital problems, a departing missionary troubled by an unresolved personal matter, a faithful woman concerned about a nonmember husband, an immigrant Saint confused about citizenship. In those years before Regional Representatives or area supervisors (later executive administrators) furnished administrative assistance to stake and mission presidents, President Tanner would field his share of questions from local Church leaders.

When his schedule permitted, he would perform marriages in the Salt Lake Temple for friends and family. There were always opportunities to speak before church, school, and civic groups and invitations for a morning round of golf or an evening out with colleagues or family. He also made time, on behalf of the First Presidency, to meet with touring groups and visiting dignitaries from governments, businesses, and public life. He would refer job inquiries to appropriate Church departments, respond to inquiries about possible Church interest in investments, and consult with other General Authorities on matters of concern to them in their own committee assignments, and, of course, with department heads who reported to the First Presidency.

In some situations, he found himself counseling and advising General Authorities senior to him in length of service in the presiding councils. Just a few weeks after his call to the First Presidency—with President McKay hospitalized and President Brown in New York on Church assignment—President Tanner found himself conducting the weekly temple meeting of the First Presidency and the Twelve. "It is a very humbling experience, having been a member of the Twelve for only a year and a member of the First Presidency for a month and ten days, to go alone and preside over the meeting," he wrote in his diary. "However, all members of the Twelve were very gracious, and we proceeded satisfactorily and accomplished the work that was there to be done." A few months later, he gave Elder Mark E. Petersen of the Twelve a send-off interview as he left to preside over the West European Mission. He advised Elder Petersen "that he was in charge of all operations over there, and should take whatever action is necessary to see that the Church is put in order and kept moving in the right direction." On another occasion Elder Spencer W. Kimball discussed at length the Lamanite program and other matters of interest and sought advice on how to get more enthusiastic support from the Brethren for the Indian programs. "I encouraged him to go forward fearlessly, knowing that he was doing what the Prophet had approved," President Tanner noted in his diary.

One of the threads that tied President Tanner's First Presidency years to the earlier periods of his life was his concern for the youth of the Church. This was manifest particularly in his continuing support for the Scouting program, but in many other activities as well. In 1964, he helped General Authority advisers and auxiliary leaders form a committee to look after the welfare of working girls who had moved to Salt Lake City from out-of-town. As often as possible he responded to invitations to speak to youth groups at Church schools and stake firesides. When dedicating a building he would frequently make note of the facility's usefulness in building testimonies. At the Farr West Stake Center in Ogden, Utah, for example, he urged parents, "Here is a training center for your youth. Make it a training center by the way you live. Bear your testimony that they may know the truth."

At centennial activities of the Young Women's Mutual Improvement Association in 1969, N. Eldon Tanner was principal speaker at a sunrise service in the Salt Lake Tabernacle. "You cannot estimate the great influence you have on the lives of those with whom you labor," he said. "They cannot help but be better as a result of your influence."[5] As part of the YWMIA centennial, he attended the festive June Conference dance festival at the University of Utah stadium and a Centennial Ball at the Salt Palace. From time to time he was a speaker at MIA June Conference sessions, a participant in all-Church softball tournament devotionals, and a speaker at Scouting fetes.

President Tanner's commitment to the Scouting movement was noted in the citation awarding him the Silver Buffalo, the highest award of the Boy Scouts of America: "Always a champion of youth, it has been said of you that no leader has been more ardent in his support of the ideals of the Scout movement."[6] He was one of very few men to have received Scouting's highest honor in both the United States (Silver Buffalo) and Canada (Silver Wolf). To receive the Silver Buffalo award, he traveled to Boston for the annual meeting of the National Council on May 22, 1969. At the time he was serving as a member of the advisory committee of the Great Salt Lake Council's executive board. He was the seventh General Authority thus far to receive the award; others were Presidents Heber J. Grant, George Albert Smith, and David O. McKay; and Elders Harold B. Lee, Ezra Taft Benson, and Delbert L. Stapley of the Council of the Twelve.

Eldon Tanner could not forget the influence upon his life of his own Scoutmaster in Canada, a neighbor who exemplified through his life the Scout Promise and Scout Law. "He gave me ideals, helped me set goals, made me realize what it was to make a promise, and especially on my honor," he told a gathering of leaders, parents, and Scouts in the Salt Lake Tabernacle in 1964. "I know of no greater responsibility that can be given to any man

221

President Tanner being sworn in as a U.S. citizen by Third District Judge Joseph G. Jeppson at the Utah State Capitol rotunda

or woman than the responsibility of working with our youth while we are influencing their lives and preparing them, or failing to prepare them, for the future. . . . Let us always remember that boys will do what their dads and Scoutmasters do regardless of how often they tell them to do right."[7]

President Tanner's talks before Scout and civic groups often touched upon the theme of freedom and the need for Americans to "maintain our free agency, the right to choose, and the right to worship God, according to the dictates of our con-

222

science." These feelings took on new meaning when, on Law Day, May 2, 1966, he became a United States citizen with thirty-seven others. The ceremony was held in the Utah State Capitol rotunda, with Judge Joseph G. Jeppson of the Third Utah Judicial Court presiding. For five years, Eldon Tanner had been a registered resident of the United States. Though born in Salt Lake City, he had lived in Canada since shortly after his birth. He had not resided in the city of his birth until he was called as a General Authority. After the judicial proceedings, President Tanner was the speaker at the Law Day citizenship program arranged by the U.S. Immigration Service. As reported by the *Deseret News,* he said:

> Every American citizen should be sincerely concerned with the nation's efforts to advance freedom and individual opportunity, curb lawlessness, and achieve equal justice.
> The Constitution, together with the Bill of Rights, is meant to insure for each of us the rights to which people everywhere are entitled. It is through these principles and the principles of democracy and belief in God that the United States became the most powerful, prosperous, and freest country in the world.[8]

Two weeks later he reflected upon the meaning of American citizenship in an address at Brigham Young University. "One must never forget that vigilance is the price of liberty," he said. "I often think that we become indolent and careless and fail to appreciate what we have because we are just too comfortable and well taken care of."[9]

Describing her father as a life-long loyal Canadian, Isabelle Tanner Jensen explained why, in her opinion, he acquired American citizenship. Said she, "He's always maintained, and that's the way we have been raised, that if you are going to live in a country and you are going to make your living there, then you owe a loyalty to that country—it is now your country."[10]

In appearances before community groups, President Tanner did not hesitate to share his religious convictions, always in a manner that caused no offense but left no doubt of his beliefs. "Lip service is not sufficient," he told a joint luncheon meeting of the Salt Lake Rotary Club and Salvation Army. "People can only be Christians when they accept Christ as the Savior of the world and govern their lives by the plan of life and salvation He established. We are truly brothers only as we love one another and recognize our brothers as the children of God."[11] He admonished University of Utah graduates not to neglect the spiritual side of life and challenged them to accept individual responsibility for learning the truth independent of "the senseless emulation of the crowd. The world needs men with high ideals, who love their fellowmen and are prepared to contribute to a better community and a better world."[12]

Public appearances often found him representing the Church or sitting in for the First Presidency at groundbreakings, dedications, and other formal events. Through these activities he won many friends for the Church and demonstrated Church support for uplifting activities and community development. As a speaker at the groundbreaking for Valley Music Hall, then a music theater in North Salt Lake, he shared the speaker's platform with Hollywood radio and television personality Art Linkletter and told of the history of the theater in early Utah. On another occasion, he and Elder Delbert Stapley represented the Church at a special meeting of Sioux Indian tribal leaders at Pierre, South Dakota. The topic of the session, organized by President Grant R. Farmer of the Northern Indian Mission, was "How the Mormon People and the Indian People Can Work Together for the Spiritual, Social, Economic, and Physical Development of the Sioux Nation." Indian leaders were impressed with the explanation of Church programs, including Indian placement and auxiliary educational activities. When one of them asked, "Is it divine?," President Tanner took the opportunity to talk about the divinity of the Book of Mormon and the value of home training, living the Word of Wisdom, and clean moral living. One of the chiefs then asked how the miracle of getting the Indian peoples to adopt this program could be performed. President Tanner challenged him to "accept it and take it to your people." A few days later he was informed that one of the chiefs had accepted that challenge.

Often President Tanner's role was ministerial, that of offering a dedicatory prayer, as he did at the new Visitor's Center for the Golden Spike National Historic Site at Promontory, Utah; the Stephen L Richards Physical Education Building at Brigham Young University; and the newly completed Salt Lake City Public Library.

At times, these formal occasions could be fun. In 1968, he offered the dedicatory prayer at the new Deseret News editorial offices in Salt Lake City. During a tour afterwards, a group gathered in the lobby of the new building around the first Deseret News press. According to newspaper reports, President Tanner "donned the traditional 'printer's hat,' made from a folded newspaper, to serve as foreman on the original Ramage Press that turned out the first copy of the Deseret News in 1850. . . . Using the new type especially set for the purpose, President Tanner printed a replica of the front page of the first issue. 'I don't know if I can remember how to do this,' he smiled. 'I haven't done it for 100 years.'"[13]

Church public relations efforts were among the personal administrative responsibilities of the First Presidency. During the McKay years, three apostles—Elders Richard L. Evans, Mark E. Petersen, and Gordon B. Hinckley—served as General Authority advisors to the Church Information Service, organized in 1963 to centralize various public relations and press relations programs. These advisers would bring proposals, policy matters, and problems to President Brown or President Tanner. But even the new CIS didn't entirely resolve what President Tanner saw as a need to streamline the Church information and communications work. His assessment of the situation in 1964 was that too many committees were at work in overlapping jurisdictions, and that these committees and staff members were taking too much time of the advisers, including himself. It was another case of an administrative arrangement that could be improved, and he lent his administrative talents to help the work go forward with greater effectiveness. Many of his suggestions were implemented during the McKay years; others were put into effect with the reorganization of the department in July 1972, when the Church Information Service was renamed External Communications Department (later changed to Public Communications Department), with Wendell J. Ashton, Salt Lake advertising executive, named to the newly created position of managing director.

One of President Tanner's most visible involvements in the 1960s was his role in the transfer of some fragments of the Joseph Smith Papyri from the Metropolitan Museum of Art to the Church in November 1967. The sequence of events began quietly more than a year before public transfer of the manuscripts. Dr. Aziz S. Atiya had recently relinquished the directorship of the Middle East Center at the University of Utah to devote more time to his work as Distinguished Professor of History. He had been studying ancient Coptic papyri at the Metropolitan Museum as part of a continuing study of his own Coptic Orthodox Church. In one of the small parcels in the museum's collection, he accidentally discovered the papyri. Though not a Latter-day Saint, he had lived in Utah long enough to become acquainted with the Pearl of Great Price. He recognized among the pieces before him the original of Facsimile No. 1 from the Book of Abraham.

The Metropolitan had owned the pieces since 1947. Officials there had known of their existence since 1918. With the pieces was a letter attesting to Joseph Smith's ownership of the papyri; signed by Emma Smith Bidamon and Joseph Smith III, it was dated May 26, 1856. The family that bought the items from Emma retained them until they were left in the hands of a housekeeper, who passed them to her daughter, Alice Huesser of Brooklyn, from whom the museum obtained the collection.

Dr. Atiya notified Eldon Tanner of his find, and he in turn discussed it with the First Presidency. President McKay asked him to inform Dr. Atiya of the Church's interest in obtaining the manuscript. Dr. Atiya then began the inquiry that eventually led to a call from Dr. Henry G. Fischer, curator of the museum's Egyptian section, informing him that the museum's director, Dr. Thomas P. F. Hoving, had authorized transfer of the papyri as a gift to the Church.

The transfer took place at a press conference in New York City on November 27, 1967. The announcement set off an intense historical investigation and prompted numerous articles as well as several monographs and books. President Tanner met with the Council of the Twelve three days later and showed them the Emma Smith Bidamon letter and Facsimile No. 1, along with photos of other fragile papyrus pieces he and Dr. Atiya had brought to Salt Lake City. The Twelve left to President Tanner and Elder Howard W. Hunter the decision on how best to preserve the papyri, and after study by Dr. Hugh Nibley of the Department of Ancient Studies at Brigham Young University, they were delivered to the care of the Church.

In recording his experiences later, President Tanner recalled how, following the formal presentation at the Metropolitan, he had sat at a luncheon with museum director Hoving and vice-president Joseph V. Noble. The conversation turned to the Church and its origin, teachings, and organization. In explaining priesthood offices, he mentioned the patriarch, and Dr. Noble asked for a closer definition. President Tanner felt impressed to explain his own experience with patriarchal blessings. As a young man of fourteen, he said, he had received a blessing from his grandfather, who was serving as a patriarch. The blessing outlined some impressive possibilities, and Eldon Tanner admitted to thinking that his grandfather "was just a doting old man, telling his grandson what he would like him to be," and therefore he had difficulty accepting it as a patriarchal blessing. Ten years later he received a blessing from another patriarch. He was astonished, he said, to see how closely the two pronouncements paralleled each other. His grandfather's blessing stated that Eldon Tanner would be directing the priesthood of the Church throughout the world, but until he was called as a

General Authority, Eldon said, he had made no attempt to inter-
pret the blessing. The museum official, he reported, was impressed by the sharing of this spiritual experience.[14]

When Eldon Tanner joined the First Presidency, the work of
restoring a part of the old Mormon city of Nauvoo was just beginning under the auspices of Nauvoo Restoration, Inc. Soon
after his call to the First Presidency, President Tanner traveled
to Nauvoo to get acquainted with the officers and the purposes
of the Church-supported agency. Officers and members of the
board who attended included Dr. J. LeRoy Kimball, president;
Harold P. Fabian, vice-president; A. Hamer Reiser, secretary-
treasurer; A. Edwin Kendrew, J. Willard Marriott, and David M.
Kennedy, trustees. He was particularly pleased to see the interest
expressed in the project by Mr. Fabian, a long-time associate of
the restored Colonial Williamsburg and member of the National
Park Service's Citizen's Advisory Council, and by Mr. Kendrew,
an architect and senior vice-president of Colonial Williamsburg.
In conversations with these men and in presentations of others
involved in the project, President Tanner was distinctly impressed with the scope of the project and its potential. "It is a
great testimony to anyone who will look at it without prejudice,"
he concluded, "and a story that should be told to the whole nation." He advised the trustees to prepare for the First Presidency
an outline of their overall program, including options for a mini-
mum, alternative, and final program, together with estimates on
the costs of land acquisition, development, and operating costs.
This would supplement information he had gathered on his
fact-finding trip and allow him to be an informed participant in
decisions that would be required of the First Presidency.

Another assignment Eldon Tanner received as a member of
the Presidency was supervision of the Church data-processing
program. As he would do with other programs assigned to him,
he met often with those involved in the project, the Advance
Planning Committee, reviewed their responsibilities, and made
suggestions for improving the organization to accomplish its objectives more effectively. In 1969 Advance Planning became

Management Systems Corporation (MSC), a subsidiary of the Church-owned Deseret Management Corporation. MSC provided computer service and systems development for Church departments and Church-owned companies, and, with available free time, contracted for work with commercial firms. The corporation's first major assignments for the Church were in Church membership and financial records (computerized beginning in 1970) and in processing names for temple work for the Genealogical Society. By 1978, the Church was able to use all of the computer time, so MSC was sold and an Information Systems Department was created to handle Church needs. President Tanner's vision in developing a strong data-processing capability found it in place by the time the Church was ready to use its full potential.

Footnotes

[1]"The Church Faces the Future," printed program for a leadership dinner and program, Hotel Utah Lafayette Ballroom, Salt Lake City, September 28, 1967. Unless otherwise noted, other quotations in this chapter are taken from N. Eldon Tanner, diary.

[2]*Church News*, September 4, 1965.

[3]*Church News*, October 20, 1963.

[4]Newspaper clippings reporting these trips are preserved in N. Eldon Tanner, Scrapbook; *Church News*, February 18, May 20, and June 3, 1967, and November 30, 1968; *Millennial Star*, April 1967.

[5]*Deseret News*, June 27, 1969.

[6]*Church News*, May 24, 1969; Salt Lake *Tribune*, May 23, 1969.

[7]*Church News*, February 15, 1964.

[8]*Deseret News*, May 2, 1966, and *Church News*, May 7, 1966.

[9]Address delivered May 16, 1966, published in *BYU Speeches of the Year* (Provo: Brigham Young University, 1966), p. 5.

[10]Jensen, Oral History, 1981, p. 2.

[11]*Church News*, May 7, 1966.

[12]Salt Lake *Tribune*, August 17, 1969.

[13]*Deseret News*, September 21, 1968.

[14]A typewritten account related to the gift of the papyri is in N. Eldon Tanner's scrapbook, as well as a mimeographed copy of an Associated Press story by George Cornell dated November 26, 1967. See also *Deseret News*, November 27 and 30, 1967; Salt Lake *Tribune*, November 29, 1967.

Church Administrator, Citizen, and Community Leader

N. Eldon Tanner's role as a member of the First Presidency came increasingly to be viewed by observers over the years as that of a master administrator. Although Church members generally saw little of the detailed work he accomplished, he became known as one whose assignments centered on matters of administration. During the David O. McKay years, and in succeeding administrations, he was recognized publicly for this contribution. The University of Utah College of Business Outstanding Achievement Award, received in 1964, reflected principally upon accomplishments in Canada, but it foreshadowed similar recognition that would come as he involved himself in the promotion of Utah's commercial and industrial development and as he participated in Church administrative duties worldwide.

President Tanner's skills as an administrator have been described by Douglas H. Smith, president of Beneficial Life Insurance Company, who has been associated with him in various business assignments. In an interview for the James Moyle Oral History program of the Church, Brother Smith reports that in all the time President Tanner served as chairman of the board of Utah Home Fire Insurance Company and in similar capacities, his major concern was for the interests of minority stockholders and their protection and representation. He found the Tanner administrative qualities to include keen perception, outstanding judgment, an ability to put people at ease, and trust and confidence in others. "He had enough personal experience in managerial roles to know that management needed the support of the board that represented the owners." Douglas Smith could not recall President Tanner giving a directive to do a specific thing; instead, he would ask for the recommendation of management, which enabled the board to get the views of those close to the situation before they would accept, modify, or disapprove the recommendation. Another thing he observed was that the management philosophy of President Tanner was that management always had to be flexible, not tied to rigid concepts; able to meet changing times and conditions and to respond quickly to circumstances and situations.

These qualities proved invaluable in Church situations as well as business and community enterprises, and Eldon Tanner's ability to accomplish much within the strictures of his busy schedule, as well as give quality leadership in his many areas of responsibility, was felt far and wide.

One activity that fell under President Tanner's supervision was the Church Building Committee. The committee's staff carried out many of the functions later assigned to the Physical Facilities Department, including the acquisition of property and construction of Church buildings. During the late 1950s and early 1960s, the committee had developed an extensive labor missionary program to help hold down the costs of new meetinghouses. By the time President Tanner was assigned to supervise the committee, stresses related to the growth of the Church were creating problems. He met frequently with General Authority advisers and Wendell B. Mendenhall, chairman of the committee, to assess problems and needs. Policies were established and acceptable accounting procedures adopted to ensure that all work commissioned by the building committee was handled through written agreements and contracts to avoid misunderstandings.

During the following year a committee appointed by President McKay was charged with finding ways to reorganize the building program to keep pace with the expanding Church. Elder Delbert L. Stapley was chairman of the committee, assisted by Elders LeGrand Richards and Howard W. Hunter of the Council of the Twelve and Elders Thorpe B. Isaacson and Franklin D. Richards, Assistants to the Twelve. Following their recommendations, the Church Building Committee was reorganized effective July 1, 1965. The First Presidency appointed Mark B. Garff as chairman, and as committee members, Fred A. Baker, Julian S. Cannon, Victor Laughlin, Allan M. Acomb, Emil B. Fetzer, Horace A. Christiansen, and Ray Engebretsen. They brought to their assignment wide experience in construction, engineering, architecture, business management, and finance.[1]

Several temples were under construction during the 1960s, and President Tanner played a major role in their completion, both through his guidance of the Church Building Committee and through assignment from the president of the Church. The Oakland Temple was dedicated a year after he became a member of the First Presidency. Six sessions were held November 17-19, 1964. He spoke at one session and conducted three of the six sessions. President McKay presided and offered the dedicatory prayer. In the summer of 1967 President Tanner participated in the selection of sites for two temples in Utah—in Ogden and in Provo. In early August, he and President Brown met with stake presidencies in each community, and the temple plans were announced August 25. Groundbreaking ceremonies for the Ogden Temple were held on President McKay's ninety-sixth birthday, September 8, 1969. The president, at his home in Huntsville, was unable to attend, but President Tanner conducted, and President Brown spoke and turned the first soil. A week later, on September 15, similar ceremonies were held in Provo, and President Tanner both conducted and spoke. During the 1960s construction also began on the Washington Temple in the nation's capital.

Construction of the high-rise Church Office Building on the block behind the Church Administration Building commenced during the McKay presidency. In December 1964, President McKay cut a silver ribbon to the three-level parking plaza over which the high-rise would be built. President Tanner and Presiding Bishop John H. Vandenberg rode with the president in his car, the first to enter the plaza. Actual construction of the office building was delayed for several years. In April 1969, the First Presidency announced the decision to begin the work that summer. With completion of the twenty-eight-story office tower in 1972, Church departments and auxiliaries scattered in more than a dozen buildings in the Salt Lake Valley moved into the central headquarters structure.

During the planning stages for the Church Office Building, it appeared that the Lion House in the same block might be affected by the parking plaza. Happily, Brigham Young's historic home was preserved, and in February 1964, President Tanner met with YWMIA General President Florence S. Jacobsen and her second counselor, Dorothy Holt, to review their recommendation that the Lion House be refurbished for its continued use as a social center as it had been during the preceding three decades. He obtained President McKay's approval for the project, and the work began under the direction of architect George Cannon Young and the Church Building Committee, with Sister Jacobsen supervising the historical redecoration. In September 1968, President Tanner offered the dedicatory prayer for the refurbished social center.

Among other responsibilities, President Tanner was involved in Church schools. As a member of the First Presidency, he served on the Church Board of Education as second vice-president of Brigham Young University's Board of Trustees. Dr. Ernest L. Wilkinson was chancellor of the Church Education System and president of BYU during the 1960s, except for a leave of absence during 1964 for a try at a U.S. Senate seat from Utah. During his absence, his duties were divided between Harvey Taylor as acting chancellor and Earl C. Crockett as acting BYU president. President Tanner helped define the duties of these temporary officers to ensure a smooth interim administration. He was also involved in the regular business of the board, including reviewing budgets of the schools.

During 1964, the Church opened new schools in Chile and dedicated an elementary school at Papeete, Tahiti. Effective January 1, 1965, the First Presidency discontinued the Pacific Board of Education, and schools in New Zealand, Samoa, Tahiti, Tonga, and Hawaii were placed under the control of the Church Board of Education as part of the Unified Church School System.

To help meet financial needs of the growing Church school system, as well as relieve the increasing burden placed on tithing funds, President Tanner assisted in launching a long-range fund-raising effort at Brigham Young University. The campaign began with a development fund organizational meeting in his office on October 15, 1966. In attendance were David M. Kennedy, who headed the executive committee; Dr. Ernest L. Wilkinson, president of BYU; Raymond E. Beckham, BYU's development director; O. Leslie Stone, J. Willard Marriott, Ralph J. Hill, Kline D. Strong, Reed Callister, Morris Wright, Royden G. Derrick, and Guy Anderson, prominent businessmen who would head the program to develop operating funds from public supporters of the university. An advisory committee representing General Authorities included Elders Delbert L. Stapley and Howard W. Hunter of the Council of the Twelve and Elder Marion D. Hanks of the First Council of the Seventy. The mission of the development office soon expanded to serve other Church schools and eventually included selected general Church programs as well.

The 1960s were a period of rapid growth for the Church. New stakes and missions were springing up, and with the expansion, it became increasingly difficult for leaders and others who wanted to attend general conference sessions to find seating in the Salt Lake Tabernacle and adjoining buildings. Ways had to be found to reach the many Saints throughout the world who desired to share in the conference spirit. Radio and television afforded such means for parts of the United States as well as other countries. In 1962 the Church began expanding broadcasting services from its intermountain bases. A first step was to acquire WRUL, a shortwave station with studios in New York and five transmitters near Boston. At the time WRUL was the only advertiser-supported commercial shortwave station in the country. In the spring of 1964, the radio and television properties of KIRO in Seattle were acquired. President Tanner kept in touch with officials of these broadcasting outlets to become acquainted with development plans and financial needs. At a critical meeting in November 1963, Bonneville International, a holding company to give centralized support to Church radio-television efforts, was formed.

In addition, President McKay appointed a Church communications committee consisting of Presidents Brown and Tanner, Elders Richard L. Evans and Gordon B. Hinckley of the Council of the Twelve, and broadcasting executives Arch L. Madsen, Isaac M. Stewart, and James B. Conkling. President Tanner noted in his journal the purpose of the committee: ". . . to gradually take over the direction of all communications in the Church. At first we are working with the KSL, WRUL, and KIRO radio and television, which belong to the Church. Richard Maycock was appointed by President McKay to be the secretary or director of this activity and will be directed by the committee, with Paul Evans assisting him. Ted Cannon will continue as secretary of the Church Information Service, also under the committee."[2]

In September 1964, the First Presidency announced publicly the creation of Bonneville International Corporation as the parent organization for its broadcasting companies. Bonneville, the announcement said, would provide consolidated engineering, financing, promotion, purchasing, and other operational functions for these facilities, but leave to the local stations the establishment of policies and handling of ongoing operations. Despite his involvement in organizing the company, President Tanner was not able to hold a position in the firm under FCC regulations because he was at that time still a Canadian citizen. The initial roster of officers included David O. McKay as chairman of the board and Hugh B. Brown as vice-chairman, with N. Eldon Tanner as a consultant; Arch L. Madsen, president; Richard L. Evans, Gordon B. Hinckley, and Thomas S. Monson, vice-presidents; James B. Conkling, William F. Edwards, D. Lennox Murdock, David Lawrence McKay, Edward M. Grimm, and G. Stanley McAllister, directors; Robert W. Barker, secretary; and Blaine W. Whipple, assistant secretary and treasurer.

Bonneville International would soon become the parent firm to other broadcasting outlets. In May 1966, Bonneville acquired an FM radio station, WRFM, in New York City, and a year later added a pair of stations, KMBZ-AM and KMBR-FM, in Kansas City. The Bonneville umbrella extended to southern California in March 1969 with the addition of a pair of stations, KBIG and KBRT, in the Los Angeles area. In the mid-1970s, under President Spencer W. Kimball's administration, FM stations were purchased in Chicago (WCLR) and San Francisco (KOIT). With these additions, Bonneville reached the limit of seven FM stations permitted under single ownership. Accordingly, in order to serve the southwestern United States, Bonneville International sold KSL-FM and bought two Dallas radio stations, KSSM and KAFM. Equally important was the contribution the stations made in serving the needs of the separate communities with programming, and their availability for religious broadcasting, including Tabernacle Choir broadcasts and general conferences.[3]

By 1968, the General Authorities could stand at the pulpit in the century-old Salt Lake Tabernacle and address an audience reached through the cooperation of two hundred television and thirty radio stations in the United States and Canada; in Spanish over twenty stations in Mexico; in Spanish and Portuguese by shortwave to South America; and in English and German by shortwave to some parts of Europe. Conference talks could be heard in Hawaii by satellite transmission, and in Great Britain, Germany, Austria, Holland, and Denmark by transoceanic

Sara and Eldon Tanner on the day he became a U.S. citizen, 1966

cable. In addition, films of the addresses translated into ten languages would be distributed to thirty-nine countries. Even then, shortwave transmission was becoming outmoded technologically, so in 1974 Bonneville sold WNYW in order to concentrate its efforts in developing satellite transmission and increased use of telephone cables and videotapes. Church broadcasting efforts had come a long way from that day in May 1922 when President Heber J. Grant spoke the first words over KZN, predecessor to KSL radio.

Bonneville International became part of a larger management organization in February 1967, when the Church organized Deseret Management Corporation. President Tanner had a leading role in this step. The increasing necessity of separating commercial operations controlled by the Church from the Church's ecclesiastical mission had long been recognized, and Deseret Management was an important step in lightening the load of business management that had been borne by the First Presidency since 1847. Included within Deseret Management's purview were tax-paying entities that had grown up to help sustain what began as a pioneer, frontier economy. The Church had already divested itself of former bank properties, and Church-owned "academies" (junior colleges) had been given to the state of Utah thirty years before; the Church-owned hospitals in the intermountain area would be turned over to private operation in the 1970s.

Another means for extending Latter-day Saint values to the world under President McKay and his counselors was the Polynesian Cultural Center. After a decade or more of study, the First Presidency approved development of the ten-acre project at Laie, Hawaii, adjacent to the Church College. Construction began in 1962. President Hugh B. Brown dedicated the center October 12, 1963, just a few days after Eldon Tanner received his first briefing on the Polynesian village.

During President McKay's administration, his second counselor's concern over proper financial and personnel management in Church businesses revealed itself prominently in involvements with Church-owned ranches, particularly those in Florida and Georgia. The Church had earlier expanded its farming operations at widely scattered locations. Facing the future of a growing Church and world population, from 1950 to 1970 the Church acquired the Elberta Farms Corporation at Elberta, Utah; Deseret Ranches of Alberta, Canada, based at Lethbridge; Deseret Farms of Florida, at Deerpark; Deseret Farms of California, at Sacramento; and Deseret Farms of

Texas, near Pecos. Management was shifted in 1967 to Deseret Management Corporation, lessening the First Presidency's direct involvement. But for the first few years, President Tanner was directly participating at the request of President McKay, particularly in the management of Deseret Farms of Florida and Deseret Farms of Georgia. He visited and toured the Florida and Georgia properties four times in 1964 and 1965.

On his trips to the ranches, President Tanner enjoyed the southern hospitality of his hosts. He was welcomed with distinctly western flavor, since many of the principal officers of the Deseret Farms were experienced ranchers from the western United States. On his first trip to the Georgia Feedlots, he made note of the luncheon menu at Hunter's Lodge: quail, baking powder biscuits covered with milk gravy, tossed salad, a relish plate, pickled apples, and pickled peaches. Later in the evening, a social hour featured pecan and strawberry ice cream. The drive to the ranch from Orlando was through a beautiful country of small lakes encircled by citrus groves. "This is the first time we had seen oranges and blossoms growing on the trees at the same time," he noted in his diary. "The fragrance was very strong and delightful." The Church property in Florida was reclaimed rangeland formerly covered by wild palmetto, and managers of the ranch were constantly expanding the area of cultivated and pasture land. After one visit President Tanner observed, "The ranch certainly looks like a Garden of Eden. The cattle are in good shape."

Although the visits had their pleasant aspects, their major purpose was to allow President Tanner to get acquainted with the ranching activities, both out on the range and behind the scenes. He put in long days on these tours. Up early for a tour of the ranch—sometimes by truck, sometimes on horseback, once even by way of a flyover in a small plane—he would end the day with consultations with managers and accountants. His no-nonsense approach to business management was to gather the information needed for a rational decision that would lead to sound business practices and increased profits. "It is certainly a wonderful sight to see three or four thousand head of cattle feeding in one row of lots," he wrote of his first trip to Georgia, "and then to see the other 30,000 scattered out all over the other feed lots. The closer I get to this, the more important it seems that everything be run on a strictly business basis, and with very careful cost accounting of the whole operation, both in Georgia and in Florida." It was his nature to show exactly how much it cost to fatten each steer, and he wanted the managers to explain how they intended to keep that cost low enough to avoid loss and undue expense. He expected the size of the herd to be kept within manageable levels, and gauged according to available feed.

Old-timers in Florida believed that Brahma blood was necessary for a successful southern cattle ranch, but Church managers felt the Angus cattle were doing as well as, if not better than, other breeds. President Tanner assessed the situation and accepted the evidence of his managers' experience. He also carefully quizzed the Georgia ranch nutritionist to see if he "really knew what advantages there were to feeding the formulas which he prescribed" and where he got his information. Eldon Tanner was convinced that cottonseed meal, molasses, and hot rolled corn as supplements to hay were working well. The cattle looked healthy to him, but he recommended selling off the older ones. And he believed that some of the newly cleared land should be leased to outside interests for cane growing. When the land and cattle operations were separated, President Tanner recommended that all machinery and equipment associated with the Florida cattle business and all the livestock be transferred to the books of the Georgia Feedlot Company or sold to them so that costs could be assessed against the cattle operation instead of the Florida Land Development Company.

Elsewhere in the economic sphere, President Tanner contributed significantly to major community projects in the 1960s, including Utah's campaign to bring new business and industry to the state to strengthen and diversify its economic base, and the construction of a Salt Lake County civic center, later known as the Salt Palace.

His most visible role in encouraging industrial development in Utah came in 1967 and the early months of 1968. During this time Utah Governor Calvin L. Rampton's campaign to diversify the state's industrial base reached its widest public audience. Trusted and respected by both Latter-day Saints and non-Mormons, President Tanner successfully challenged opponents of the program by appeals to basic teachings and by his own business and government experience. In February 1967 he was a principal speaker at a Five County Organization Community Development and Planning Conference in Cedar City, Utah, held to encourage the cooperation of residents of Beaver, Iron, Washington, Kane, and Garfield counties in southwestern Utah. A month later he stressed the need for a united effort in a similar speech at the Utah Valley Industrial Development Association's first annual dinner meeting in Provo. In April he participated in a symposium in Salt Lake City as keynote speaker on "Bringing Successful Industry to Utah."

Soon afterward, Governor Rampton organized a State Coordinating Council of Development Services to supervise the administrative and budget matters of various development groups to avoid duplication of services. President Tanner, with President McKay's approval, accepted an appointment to a four-year term on the council. He later accompanied Governor and Mrs. Rampton on an industrial promotion tour to Los Angeles, San Francisco, and Seattle. At each site, prospective Utah businesses were informed of "The New Industrial Utah" and were hosted at luncheons and receptions. Supplementing the hard-sell facts of economic opportunity were performances by the Utah Symphony Orchestra. The Southern California Mormon Choir joined with the orchestra for concerts in the Hollywood Bowl; then the orchestra continued its Pacific Coast tour with performances in San Francisco and Seattle. Elder Howard W. Hunter of the Twelve joined President Tanner and the Ramptons for the Hollywood concert, which doubled as a "Family Night" concert for Church members in the Los Angeles area.

In his remarks to Utah business leaders, President Tanner challenged three assumptions. Despite oft-reported stories, he said, the Church did not oppose industrial development. It had been Church policy in Utah from the time of Brigham Young to encourage temporal as well as spiritual accomplishments, he explained. Second, people who would follow new industry to Utah should be welcomed for the contribution they could make. He calmed fears of undesirable influences from new industrial immigrants; they would have much to contribute, he said, in the way of new ideas, new points of view, and new perspectives. Local citizens could ensure a voice in this through active participation in development planning. Finally, he urged a united action by varied interest groups. "By all joining together it is possible to develop an atmosphere or climate where industry will feel inclined to come," he said. "By refusing to join forces and work together, we could greatly retard the very thing we are trying to accomplish."[4]

When officials sought use of a site on West Temple in Salt Lake City for the civic and convention center, President Tanner helped clear the way for the use of that site, which involved significant amounts of Church property. The Church had been buying property in the West Temple area for a proposed Church assembly hall to accommodate expanding general conference crowds. During the spring and early summer of 1964, Eldon Tanner met with civic and Church leaders to negotiate details on the site. It was agreed that the county would buy out all property owners except the Church on the two-block site. Church property in sixteen separate pieces would be consolidated into one parcel at the north end of the site and would be leased to the county for fifty years at one dollar per year. In return, the Church would have use of the auditorium for twenty-four days each year for general conference and other gatherings and activities. The county retained options to buy the property at any time during the lease. This arrangement satisfied Church members who felt the Church should not dispose of this valuable property; nonmembers who opposed expending public funds to buy the land; the Churchmen who felt the Church should have its own assembly hall. The Church saved the $12 million cost of a separate auditorium, and the leasing arrangement and use of the building were better for the Church than the continued use of the property by small businesses and parking lots.

In the groundbreaking ceremony March 10, 1967, President Tanner participated with Roman Catholic Bishop Joseph Lennox Federal, Governor Calvin L. Rampton, Mayor J. Bracken Lee, County Commission chairman McCown E. Hunt, and other commissioners. In the opening prayer, President Tanner appealed for realization of the hope for a concert hall for the complex; that feature, originally part of the planning, had been eliminated when costs exceeded original estimates. For many years the Salt Lake Tabernacle had been used for concerts of the Utah Symphony, and Church officials had assured Maestro Maurice Abravanel they would allow the orchestra to continue using the Tabernacle until a suitable concert hall could be built. Symphony scheduling involved a demanding client, but the Church would work around it.

Manwhile, O. C. Tanner, chairman of Utah's American Bicentennial Committee, met with President Tanner to discuss his committee's goals, which included establishment of an art center and concert hall. The Church, long a supporter of the arts in the community, pledged its support. To help bring the center to fruition, President Tanner arranged the lease of Church-owned property west of the Salt Palace for expanded parking, to replace parking that would be lost when the new cultural facilities were built. At the interfaith dedicatory services for the Salt Palace arena and exhibit hall, N. Eldon Tanner offered the dedicatory prayer, and the Mormon Youth Symphony and Chorus made its first public appearance, under the baton of Jay Welch. The Symphony Hall and Salt Lake Art Center were completed in the fall of 1979, and the Utah Symphony, after more than thirty years of concerts in the Salt Lake Tabernacle, finally had a permanent home built especially for its needs.

The Salt Palace and Symphony Hall complex served not only its own interests, including conventions, sports activities, and concerts, but was also a spur to other development in the area. President Tanner expressed the feeling that its success enabled ZCMI to move ahead with its downtown mall, and the hall's presence encouraged developers to build hotels and office buildings and to restore older properties in the blocks surrounding the complex. This was all a part of the program encouraged by civic as well as Church leaders to rejuvenate the central business district adjoining Temple Square and the Church's world headquarters.

Another visible contribution of N. Eldon Tanner during the 1960s was his service on the Utah Legislative Study Committee, chaired by Neal A. Maxwell, then an administrator at the University of Utah. The committee was appointed by the 1966 special session of the Utah Legislature to investigate ways to strengthen the lawmaking body. President Tanner's experience in Canada had demonstrated to him the wisdom of balancing the power of a strong executive branch with legislative influence. In Utah, the legislature met for biennial sixty-day sessions and for special sessions called by the governor. The committee recommended that annual sessions be held. Major employer groups in Utah challenged the recommendation, but the committee members stood firm. They believed that a sixty-day general session in odd-numbered years and a twenty-day budget session in even-numbered years would enhance Utah's legislative needs. The committee endorsed four constitutional amendments to accomplish this aim, and Eldon Tanner was listed as one who strongly supported the amendments. In a statement released to the media, he said that as a concerned citizen he was urging a "yes" vote on the measures. At the November 1966 election, Utah voters soundly rejected all four amendments, along with four other proposed changes in state government. The defeat was temporary, however, for after the more controversial items in the package were eliminated, voters in subsequent elections approved the four proposals that the legislative study committee had endorsed.

From time to time, President Tanner was involved in other matters of public concern at state and local levels. In June 1965, he joined with President McKay and President Brown in issuing a statement on efforts in the U.S. Congress to repeal section 14-B of the Taft-Hartley Law. Repeal would have made membership in a labor union a condition of employment where a union was recognized as the bargaining agent. The 1965 statement reiterated President McKay's earlier statement supporting voluntary unionism as a fundamental right under the Constitution.

In 1968 President Tanner spoke out in his April general conference talk against efforts to liberalize Utah's liquor laws. "We must take a stand against liquor by the drink and any and every other move that would make liquor easily available," he said. In his talk, he used examples of unnamed persons damaged by the effects of liquor. He was careful to point out that he was not attacking the character of any friends or business associates who used alcohol and cigarettes, but only pointing out the dangers and consequences of such use.[5] This ability to speak frankly to issues without offending friends was one of his special abilities. President McKay urged Utahns to vote against the measure as a moral issue, and Elder Gordon B. Hinckley of the Council of the Twelve outlined the reasons for the Church's position in an address over KSL Radio in June 1968. The liquor-by-the-drink measure was turned down by Utah voters.

On the national scene, President Tanner was the First Presidency's representative in January 1969 at the Richard M. Nixon inaugural, which was chaired by J. Willard Marriott. He brought home a raft of items for his scrapbook to remind him of the concert, inauguration, and other activities. A highlight was the performance of the Mormon Tabernacle Choir and Washington National Symphony in Constitution Hall.

A few years earlier, President Tanner had been given an opportunity to meet personally with President Lyndon B. Johnson at the White House. In January 1964, President Johnson invited President McKay to visit him in Washington. Eldon Tanner and President McKay's son Lawrence went along at President McKay's request. They were met at the airport by local members of the Church. On January 31, the three Utahns were introduced to the president in the Cabinet Room and then had lunch with him in a private dining room in the White House. President Tanner recounted the conversation in his diary and later used the experience in a Boy Scout talk:

> [President Johnson] told President McKay that he had met him on two or three occasions before and each time he had come away inspired. He said that he had many problems, such as the shooting down of the plane over Germany, the Panama dispute, the Viet Nam problems, and others of great magnitude. Sometimes he felt like a little boy who needed to lay his head on his mother's breast and ask for consolation. He said that the spiritual and moral tone of the country and the people should be built up, and he asked President McKay how this could be done. President McKay advised him that he had read where President Johnson had said that he was first a free man, second an American, third a public servant, and fourth, a Democrat, in the order named.
>
> President McKay said that he thought President Johnson was sincere in this, and that he was also sincere in wanting to improve the spiritual and moral tone of the country. He said, "My advice to you is to let your conscience be your guide. Let the people know that you are sincere in this and live so that they cannot question it. Be their example and their leader in it." It seemed to me that President McKay could have talked for an hour and said nothing more significant.[6]

The White House visit included the traditional tour and picture taking. Two Latter-day Saints working in the White House, Nancy Lou Larson of Salt Lake City and Connie Gerrard of Evanston, Wyoming, were invited in to be in the photos with Presidents McKay and Tanner, a gesture of President Johnson that Eldon Tanner thought "very thoughtful indeed." President McKay and his counselor were impressed with the opportunity they had had. As far as they knew, it was the first time in the history of the Church that a president of the Church had been called privately by the president of the United States for an interview. Although the trip was publicized by the media, neither side of the conference disclosed the reason for the meeting. One of the Mormon Congressmen involved in part of the discussion told a reporter the political and religious leaders had discussed the moral and spiritual health of the nation. The two Church leaders would not comment publicly on the conversation, and President McKay told inquiring newsmen to ask President Johnson.[7]

One other president affected President Tanner's life in the 1960s. On November 22, 1963, he heard the shocking news of John F. Kennedy's assassination at Dallas, Texas. "It is unbelievable that such an action could take place here in the United States," he wrote in his diary. "I don't know when I have ever seen such a pall of grief on the whole community and across the nation, and it seems throughout the world, as we have experienced today." The First Presidency met and decided that President Brown would represent them at the funeral services in Washington, D.C. On November 25, President Tanner conducted local memorial services in the Salt Lake Tabernacle. He spoke briefly, and eulogies were offered by Elders Howard W. Hunter and Harold B. Lee of the Council of the Twelve. "It was a very lovely service," President Tanner observed. "The (Tabernacle) Choir was in attendance and sang four appropriate songs."[8]

Just a few months after the visit with President Johnson, Eldon Tanner observed his sixty-sixth birthday. He was now past the current legal age for retirement, and that fact no doubt prompted a comment on his age and his recent calling to new service as a member of the First Presidency. One of his goals, a *Church News* reporter wrote, was that "through proper care of his health he could extend future birthdays to the 92-year-mark." He observed that his first seven months in the First Presidency had been "really a humbling experience and great blessing to be associated closely with the Prophet." Perhaps the recent

Washington visit suggested another question, and it forecast his own yet future involvement. "I am convinced," he said, "that more people, in fact all of us, should take a keen and active interest in community and public affairs." He would be doing that, but his heavy load of Church duties and civic activities would not impinge on another responsibility, that of his family.[9]

Throughout President Tanner's years in the First Presidency with President McKay, he made time to be with his wife and family. A quiet evening at home with Sara, visiting or reading, visits with the children and grandchildren, a movie or dinner out with friends, golfing—all continued to be a part of his schedule in the 1960s as far as possible.

"I am so proud of my wife as a wife and mother," he wrote in his diary on their forty-fourth wedding anniversary, December 20, 1963. "She has contributed greatly to what little success I have made in life and progress in different fields and has been responsible for directing the thinking and activities of our children, which has resulted in them being what I consider an outstanding family." That particular anniversary was a busy day. He performed two marriages, met with the Genealogical Society for its Christmas party, met with the Presiding Bishopric, interviewed a new mission president, and met with the KSL board of directors. At five o'clock he and Sara left for the airport. They flew to Calgary, arriving there at one in the morning. Meeting them at the airport were members of the family living in Canada, including their daughters Ruth, Isabelle, Zola, Beth, and Helen, and sons-in-law Cliff Walker and Willard Jensen. It was another two hours before the welcome was over. The Tanners finally retired at three o'clock for some much-needed sleep. Over the next few days they enjoyed family dinners and activities, especially those involving grandchildren, who participated with music, singing, reciting, and other talents. On December 23 Sara took the six oldest granddaughters and Eldon the six oldest grandsons to lunch at the Palace Hotel. So that the younger children wouldn't feel entirely left out, their grandfather presented each with a dollar.

Sara and Eldon Tanner shared many other memorable experiences during the 1960s. She contributed to community activities, including service as a member of the board of trustees of the Utah Civic Ballet. The couple's special contributions to the Church were recognized at the MIA June Conference of 1964, when they were named honorary Master M-Man and honorary Golder Gleaner. "We both consider this a great honor," President Tanner said of the occasion.

Among the special social occasions the Tanners looked forward to was an annual garden party they hosted for the General Authorities and their wives in July. At other times during the year, they enjoyed dinners at their home with smaller groups of colleagues from among the Church leaders. And from time to time President Tanner's brothers and sister would spend an evening at the Tanner home, with visiting and light refreshments. He and Sara would also look back with a chuckle to an experience with the Howard W. Hunters and Spencer W. Kimballs at a borrowed cabin in Big Cottonwood Canyon. The three couples enjoyed a leisurely picnic dinner and evening, but sometime during the evening, while all were outside enjoying the cool canyon atmosphere, they found themselves locked out of the cabin, with the key inside. It took an hour to get back inside, after a call to the owner to locate an extra key.

Another memorable family activity involved a visit from three grandsons in July 1964. Their grandfather took the boys golfing and swimming. They watched the Days of '47 Parade on television on July 24. Later that day grandfather and grandsons enjoyed a movie, followed by a pioneer pageant at the Salt Lake Tabernacle. The next day they traveled to Idaho, where fishing, horseback riding, and a campfire program were Saturday's events, and attendance at the local priesthood and other church meetings marked Sunday's schedule.

December 20, 1969, was Eldon and Sara's fiftieth wedding anniversary. As the time drew near for effective planning, Eldon asked Sara what she would like for the occasion. She replied she would like to take the family to Hawaii. That is exactly what they

To celebrate the Tanners' fiftieth wedding anniversary in December 1969, thirty-eight members of the family went to Hawaii

did. Thirty-eight members of the Tanner family went. Travel schedules were carefully coordinated, and the party all gathered in Seattle for the flight to the islands, some coming from Calgary and Edmonton, others from Wisconsin and Salt Lake City. During their layover in Seattle, Eldon arranged for a bus and guide to take the party on a tour of Seattle. Isabelle describes the glorious family experience in Hawaii:

> Our time in Hawaii was exciting from start to finish: competitive sports, surfing, swimming, early morning strolls along the beach looking for glass balls, banquets, and tours to every point of interest. Three separate parties were held to celebrate. A Chinese friend arranged a ten-course meal for all the adults and invited guests. The Polynesian Cultural Center was visited with a tour of each village, where we were all greeted as VIP's and given gifts. A luau was served for dinner, and then we all went to the Polynesian show. At intermission big Hawaiian ice cream sundaes were served to the whole group.[10]

These, indeed, were memories the Tanners and their family would remember, activities that would reinforce their love and understanding of one another. President Tanner viewed these involvements with his family as a requirement of living. There must always be room for Sara and the family, no matter what load he carried as administrator and counselor in the Church.

Footnotes

[1]*Church News,* July 3, 1965.

[2]Unless otherwise noted, quotations in this chapter are from N. Eldon Tanner's diary.

[3]For information on the Church's involvement in broadcasting, see Fred C. Esplin, "The Church as Broadcaster," *Dialogue: A Journal of Mormon Thought* 10 (Spring 1977): 26ff.; Herbert F. Murray, "A Half Century of Broadcasting in the Church," *Ensign* 2 (August 1972): 48-51; *Church News,* October 20, 1962, and April 20, 1968.

[4]Salt Lake *Tribune,* February 4 and March 26, 1967; *Deseret News,* editorial, January 10, 1968.

[5]*Deseret News*, April 8, 1968.
[6]*Church News*, February 15, 1964.
[7]*Deseret News*, January 30 and 31, 1964; Salt Lake *Tribune*, February 1, 1964.
[8]*Deseret News*, November 25, 1963.
[9]*Church News*, May 9, 1964.
[10]Isabelle T. Jensen to G. Homer Durham, August 4, 1981.

14

The Joseph Fielding Smith Years, 1970-1972

Sunday, January 18, 1970, was a cold, wet day in Salt Lake City—snowflakes and sleet mixed with rain. As people prepared for Sunday activities, many had radio or television sets on. The Sunday morning *Tribune* had been delivered without any announcement of what television and radio would declare shortly before 9 A.M.: President David O. McKay had passed away at the age of ninety-six. Despite some of the difficulties resulting from his advanced years, his first counselor, Hugh B. Brown, told his son Charles Manley Brown, "David O. McKay has done more for me than any other man in my life."[1]

At his home on East Thirteenth South Street, Bishop Joseph Fielding Smith, Jr., of the Yale Ward, Bonneville Stake, had earlier been awakened with a telephone call from the New York *Times*. The caller had the impression that Joseph Fielding Smith, Jr., was the successor to President McKay. Instead, of course, it was his ninety-three-year-old father, President Joseph Fielding Smith of the Council of the Twelve, who had been serving as counselor to the First Presidency since October 29, 1965.

Before the morning was over, President Smith and his wife, Jessie Evans Smith, appeared on television for an interview, which took place on Temple Square near the Assembly Hall. The new president responded to the reporters' questions, ably seconded by Sister Smith, who said, as the questions flew, "President Smith will assume his responsibilities in the normal course of events in accordance with Church procedure."

Thus came to an end the distinguished career of David Oman McKay, an outstanding leader. Succeeding him was the premier theologian and doctrinal teacher of the Church. The true personality of this kindly, fatherly, benevolent man soon became apparent.

President Smith was born July 19, 1876, in Salt Lake City, a son of Joseph F. Smith, sixth president of the Church, and Julina Lambson Smith. Following a mission to Great Britain (1899-1901), he obtained employment as a clerk in the Church Historian's Office, beginning October 4, 1901. He became the librarian January 1, 1904, and at the April 1906 general conference, he was sustained as Assistant Church Historian, a position he held until March 17, 1921, when he became Church Historian. On April 6, 1910, at the age of thirty-three, he was called to the Council of the Twelve Apostles.[2] President Smith had served as acting president and then president of the Twelve for ten years when he was sustained as President of the Church on January 23, 1970. He therefore brought to that position sixty years of experience in the stakes and missions of the Church, as well as expertise in the Church's history and theology.

Elder Harold B. Lee stood next to President Smith in seniority among the Twelve; they had sat side by side in the Council for more than thirty years. It was therefore natural and appropriate for Elder Lee to be selected as first counselor in the First Presidency, with N. Eldon Tanner as second counselor. Elder Boyd K. Packer, an Assistant to the Twelve, was called to membership in the Council of the Twelve, filling the vacancy created by the death of President McKay.

Hugh B. Brown, who had served as President McKay's first counselor, resumed his seat as an apostle. A few months later he would confide in his nephew, N. Eldon Tanner, that he missed the intense involvement of the First Presidency. In failing health, he could attend meetings of the Twelve only infrequently, so Eldon became one of his few regular contacts with General Au-

President Joseph Fielding Smith, center, with counselors Harold B. Lee and N. Eldon Tanner

thorities. Following one visit, President Tanner wrote in his diary, "I am sure it is difficult to adjust after being in the First Presidency." He added an experience related by his uncle that had helped President Brown adjust to these years of declining responsibility.

"He said it was not a vision, but the Lord appeared to him, very informal, the same as I was sitting talking to him. The Lord said, 'You have had some difficult times in your life.' Uncle Hugh responded, 'Yes, and your life was more difficult than any of us have had.' In the conversation Uncle Hugh asked when he would be finished here, and the Lord said, 'I don't know and I wouldn't tell you if I did.' Then He said, 'Remain faithful to the end, and everything will be all right.'"

President Lee had long been associated with the correlation program of the Church. His leadership, experience, and energetic abilities breathed new vigor into the expanding church. In the months ahead there would be reorganizations of the Church magazines, the Sunday School, and the Social Services Department; the development of a new teacher training program and meetinghouse libraries; and the establishment of a Public Communications office. The first area conference was held in Manchester, England, and plans were made for the second one, to be held in Mexico City. Eighty-two new stakes were organized during President Smith's thirty months as president, and fourteen new missions were created, bringing the total number of stakes to 581 and of missions to 101. Some thirty-five additional Regional Representatives were called, and seventy new regions were created.

Under President Smith, meetings of the First Presidency continued each morning, often in conference with associates and aides. Members of the First Presidency also functioned individually within their assignments. If policy questions arose outside his jurisdiction or warranted consideration by the entire Presidency, President Tanner would invite the party involved to write a brief proposal for presentation at a meeting of the First Presidency. Some proposals were personally unacceptable to him, but if he had promised to do so, he would refer the matter to the Presidency.

President Smith's counselors carried heavy responsibilities, with President Lee especially conducting many of the council and committee meetings. One member of the Presidency would often fill in for another, such as when President Tanner remained in Salt Lake City while President Smith and President Lee attended the Manchester area conference in August 1971.

As an administrator, President Tanner had long since

·learned when to make a decision and when to refer the matter to the Presidency, the Twelve, or an appropriate staff member. Often when inquiries were brought to him, he deferred to the Commissioner of Education or the finance, legal, or other department. His philosophy was, "In the operation of anything, you first gather around you the very best people available to do the job. Then you define their responsibilities and bounds beyond which they should not go, let them know they're expected to give you a report—and leave it to them to perform."

His door was never closed to anyone, employee or visitor. He never appeared to overstep his own bounds, nor did he ever run away from a problem.

In observing transactions at Church headquarters, he sometimes asked Elder Joseph Anderson, who had been secretary to the First Presidency nearly half a century, "Now, why do we do it this way?" Elder Anderson would reply, "Well, we have just always done it this way." And President Tanner would respond, "Well, that's no reason." As his secretary, LaRue Sneff, discovered, he wanted changes instituted because there were better reasons than that things had always been done in a certain way.

In his office President Tanner used a big, red leather chair as a comfortable means to help those who came into his office feel at ease. "I always like my visitors to sit in that chair," he once remarked. Through the years many men were invited to sit in that big red chair while they were interviewed and asked to serve as mission president or in other positions.

As before, when he had served in the First Presidency under President McKay, Eldon Tanner referred major questions to the First Presidency and worked closely with President Lee.

President Tanner assisted greatly during President Smith's short term, and decisions were made that affected Church employees, members, and the community at large. One of his responsibilities was to oversee operational expenditures of the Church. He was noted for being the guiding genius behind Church investments and finances, and he was often questioned about what the Church was doing with its resources and what involvement he had in Church finances. He would never hedge on his commitment toward the Church's conserving its means so that its worldwide Christian commission could be fulfilled. He felt that "the whole purpose of the Mormon financial organization is to provide the funds necessary to maintain the Church and to provide employment and assistance to its membership."

J. Alan Blodgett, who was managing director of the Church Financial Department from 1969 to 1981, found that President Tanner's style in financial administration was to insist that all expenditures be kept within income, with a reasonable reserve, and that no activity should take place outside the budget. In administration, his decisions were consistent and logical, coupled with a deep commitment to integrity. Brother Blodgett found President Tanner to be very sensitive to people's feelings, showing a highly cultivated sense of right and wrong. He said that President Tanner had unusual talent for formulating ideas, giving reasons for his decisions, and never forcing his will on people; one of his administrative skills was his flair for building organizations that could do the job assigned effectively and creating an environment that "lets things happen."[3]

Brother Blodgett also learned that President Tanner had "a great encyclopedia of wisdom" that he had formulated over many years that helped him make judgments. He knew by experience which business locations succeeded and which didn't, which types of businesses were feasible and which weren't. When a difficult financial problem came to his attention, he would break it down to its fundamental elements, examine it systematically and logically, and come to sound conclusions.

Finally, Brother Blodgett learned that behind President Tanner's quiet wisdom and organizational genius was an overriding sensitivity to the people involved. If staff changes were to be made, he wanted them done with the least distress to individuals. Business agreements should be equitable to all parties involved; each should leave the table satisfied. Eldon Tanner did not believe that whatever benefitted the Church was justifiable; rather, that actions must be taken justly and considerately, and that how something was done was as important as what was done.[4]

In addition to overseeing the financial interests of the Church, President Tanner was responsible for supervising the legal affairs. Not many days passed without his seeing Wilford W. Kirton, the general counsel of the Church.

When Ernest L. Wilkinson resigned from the presidency of Brigham Young University in March 1971, President Tanner was a member of the committee to select his successor. He approached this assignment with his usual care, interviewing many leading authorities in higher education along with President Lee and Elder Marion G. Romney. As a result, Dallin H. Oaks, professor of law at the University of Chicago, was named to head the university.

President Tanner was always interested in activities at Brigham Young University, particularly athletics. Chris Apostol, an assistant football coach at BYU, would sometimes bring in a prospective football player to meet some of the General Authorities. President Tanner enjoyed this, recalling his own experiences in working with young men in Cardston. He also attended games when his busy schedule would allow the time. When BYU played New Mexico in basketball one season, he recorded in his diary that it was "well-played, exciting competition." Later that year he watched the BYU-Long Beach State game on television. BYU, which had led by thirteen points at one time, lost in overtime. He commented, "It is another example of the tortoise and the hare and of enduring to the end."

As a member of the First Presidency, with Presidents Smith and Lee he attended meetings with visiting dignitaries. He was present to greet President Richard M. Nixon; Carl Albert, Speaker of the U.S. House of Representatives; and Senator Henry M. Jackson of Washington.

During Joseph Fielding Smith's administration, work continued on the 28-story Church Office Building, atop the previously opened three-story underground parking facility. Financing and finishing this structure and working with architects and contractors were among President Tanner's assignments. His concern about the design of the plaza was characteristic of his involvement. A private donor had submitted a design proposal for the open area between the Church Administration Building and the new office building, along with a pledge to pay part of the costs. President Tanner obtained the First Presidency's approval of the plan, then approached Glen Nielson, president of Big Horn Stake in Wyoming and president of Husky Oil Company. President Nielson, a native of Canada, agreed to donate the sum to complete the plaza with its gardens and fountains.

President Tanner was influential in revitalizing Church communications. In June 1970 he met with Elders Mark E. Petersen, Richard L. Evans, and Thomas S. Monson, and with Lee Bickmore, chief executive officer of the National Biscuit Company, to discuss communications problems. With Brother Bickmore's help, the management consulting firm of Cresap, Paget and McCormick was asked to do a study for the Church. On their recommendation, the Public Communications Department was organized to handle communications with news media, and a Department of Internal Communications, with J. Thomas Fyans as director, was formed to help improve communications and publications within the Church.

A professional consulting firm was also brought in to consider the potential of the *Deseret News*. Frank M. Magid, of Frank M. Magid Associates, presented the report to President Tanner. He noted that the *Deseret News* was declining as a metropolitan daily in the wake of a general decline of evening newspapers throughout the country. Part of the problem was that readers believed they obtained fresher, more thorough news from the competing Salt Lake *Tribune*, a morning newspaper. Another factor was competition from television news. A third factor was that the local public viewed the *Deseret News* as a Church organ. One implication was that the Church should disassociate itself from the newspaper, but this would leave the paper financially and administratively vulnerable in view of the *Tribune's* wide circulation and locally attractive dailies in other Utah cities. The decision was made that the Church would retain ownership of the paper, and the *Church News* would continue publication as a major Church news organ.

In February 1972 the First Presidency met with Henry Maschal, a hotel consultant, to discuss prospects for the Hotel Utah in the face of increasing competition from large new hotels in the southern part of downtown Salt Lake City. Hotel Utah was a landmark, with windows overlooking the city and Temple Square and an elegant top-floor dining room, the Roof Garden. Without improvements, Mr. Maschal argued, the hotel would depreciate in value. He recommended that the hotel be expanded and remodeled by the addition of 180 rooms, convention facilities, and the remodeling of kitchens and the Roof Garden. The First Presidency agreed and recommended the expansion to the hotel's board of directors.

Other Church departments and Church-owned businesses continued to benefit from President Tanner's expertise and concern. The organization of the Management Systems Corporation, the computer arm of the Church, was now completed. A more or less uniform nomenclature was established for many of the Church headquarters departments. The Historian's Office, for example, became the Historical Department under a managing director.

In November 1971 Richard L. Evans, long-time announcer for the Tabernacle Choir's national Sunday morning radio broadcast and a member of the Council of the Twelve, died. President Tanner had been very close to Elder Evans, and the passing of this man of stature touched him deeply. Now began the task of replacing the irreplaceable. Interviews were held, recommendations received, and auditions heard. J. Spencer Kinard, a local newscaster and President Tanner's first choice, was finally recommended. A suggestion was considered but rejected that Brother Kinard deliver sermonettes written by selected General Authorities. President Tanner felt that this might be wrongly interpreted, and that the Richard L. Evans tradition of "The Spoken Word," with its more personal authorship and appeal, should be continued.

Another development to which President Tanner contributed was the concept of a Church "ambassador," an emissary who would be available to represent the Church in developing contacts with foreign governments to try to improve the situations of Church missions and potential missions. David M. Kennedy, who was then U.S. Secretary of the Treasury, had connections worldwide as a result of his former position as chairman and chief executive officer of the Continental Illinois Bank, one of the world's larger financial institutions. The idea of a special Church representative would reach fruition a few years later when, under President Spencer W. Kimball, Brother Kennedy was appointed to the position.

In 1972, it became evident that expansion of the Church's physical facilities and temporal affairs warranted a reorganization of the Presiding Bishopric. President Lee and President Tanner submitted their recommendations to President Smith. They concluded that John H. Vandenberg, the Presiding Bishop, and his first counselor, Robert L. Simpson, should be called to serve as Assistants to the Twelve. Bishop Vandenberg's talents were especially needed as managing director for Physical Facilities and the worldwide building program, and Elder Simpson was needed in the expanding ecclesiastical programs. Two weeks later President Tanner discussed with President Lee recommendations submitted by the Council of the Twelve for a new Presiding Bishop. Victor L. Brown, a cousin with whom Eldon Tanner had had little contact for some thirty-two years, was to be called to the position, and President Tanner was given the responsibility of interviewing him and extending the call.[5] Bishop Brown selected as his counselors H. Burke Peterson and Vaughn J. Featherstone.

In March 1972 President Tanner met with President Lee to be advised about the heart condition of President Spencer W. Kimball, who was then serving as acting president of the Twelve.

Dr. Russell M. Nelson, the noted LDS heart surgeon, told them that President Kimball needed a complicated operation. Without the operation, he possibly had one year to eighteen months of service, but considerable risk was attached to the procedure. In the discussion, President Lee emphasized that Elder Kimball had received a sacred call to the apostleship, and that a person with such a call should do all he could to continue to live and perform his duty. It was up to Elder Kimball, however, to decide whether or not to have the operation.

Elder Kimball decided to consent, and the operation was planned after the April 1972 general conference. The First Presidency scheduled him to speak on the first day of conference in order to relieve tension prior to the operation. On April 19, 1972, Presidents Lee and Tanner administered to Elder Kimball at his request. The success of the subsequent operation has been dramatically demonstrated. When Eldon Tanner visited him in the hospital, Elder Kimball was impatient at taking so long to recuperate, the impatience with inactivity so characteristic of that great leader. His return to reinvigorated service is now history.

A summary of President Tanner's service in the First Presidency under President Joseph Fielding Smith may be found in his journal entry for January 1, 1972. He wrote: "I have worked very hard this year in my position in the Church, and feel I have made some contributions, and I am satisfied that we are making real progress. We have introduced some new programs and reorganized some of the departments, which I am sure will contribute to the growth and well-being of the Church. It has been a great privilege and blessing for me to work so closely with President Joseph Fielding Smith and President Harold B. Lee." Like the Church at large, he had come to know President Smith for his warm, affectionate ways and gentle courtesy.

Six months after this journal entry was made, on Friday afternoon, June 30, 1972, President Smith left his office and, with his son, Joseph Fielding Smith, Jr., walked across the lobby to the elevator and rode to the third floor. Since 1917, when the building opened, President Smith had occupied the third floor suite of the Church Historian's Office, now the Historical Department. As he entered the area, a new employee looked up from her desk and was surprised to see the Prophet entering. She immediately arose and went toward him, extending her hand. He nodded a greeting and, with a smile, reached out his own hand and shook hers. She recorded later that his hand seemed frail and white, but the thrill of meeting with a Prophet of God only two days before he passed through the veil into eternity was a rich and stabilizing memory.

On Sunday, President Smith attended fast and testimony meeting at the Eighteenth Ward of the Ensign Stake, his home ward, and rose with the congregation to sing the closing song, "The Star-Spangled Banner." Afterwards, his daughter Amelia McConkie, wife of Elder Bruce R. McConkie, drove him to the home of another daughter in Bountiful, where he visited briefly and enjoyed refreshments. He then returned to the McConkie home and was about to retire for the evening when, without suffering, he was taken into eternity. "He was here one minute, and gone the next. It was very peaceful," said a family member. The feeling was one of peaceful benediction.

Footnotes

[1] Campbell and Poll, *Hugh B. Brown*, p. 277.

[2] Albert L. Zobell, Jr., "President Joseph Fielding Smith," *Improvement Era*, March 1970, pp. 5-6.

[3] J. Alan Blodgett, interview by Gordon Irving, 1981, pp. 8-10. James Moyle Oral History Program, Church Archives.

[4] Ibid.

[5] Victor L. Brown, in a talk at Brigham Young University January 29, 1980, said: "I first became acquainted with him . . . as a child and teenager and knew him as 'Uncle Eldon' even though we are cousins. . . . During the next thirty-two years my exposure to him was practically nil. He lived in Canada and I lived much of the time in the eastern United States."

15

The Harold B. Lee Years,
1972-1973

On Sunday, July 2, 1972, N. Eldon Tanner was still fighting a severe cold that had hung on for several days. He followed the usual prescription of bed rest until midday; then, after meeting with family members, he was planning to retire early. About 9:40 P.M. he received a telephone call from President Harold B. Lee informing him that President Smith had passed away. He immediately dressed, drove with Sister Tanner to the Lee home on Penrose Drive, picked up President and Sister Lee, and drove to the Bruce R. McConkie home on Capitol Hill, where the Smith family had gathered.

Later President Tanner noted in his journal: "I think it is wonderful that [President Smith] was able to pass the way he did. He has lived a good full life and has contributed much to the building of the Kingdom. I consider it a great privilege and blessing to have been so closely associated with him. During the time that President Lee and I have worked so closely together as counselors to President Smith, there has been a bond of friendship, love, and confidence, and I have real admiration for President Lee. He will make a great President of the Church."[1]

The next day Eldon met with President Lee and told him that as the new president of the Church, he should feel perfectly free to choose anyone he wished as his counselors, and not feel obligated to call him. But if President Lee should call both him and a member of the Twelve who was senior to him, Eldon expressed the feeling that the other man should be named first counselor.

On Thursday, July 6, President Lee came to Eldon's office and told him that he felt sure he should call him as one of hi_ counselors, a feeling that had been confirmed for him in the temple. President Tanner wrote in his journal, "He was very complimentary on the service I had given ever since being called by President McKay. He said that he and all members of the Twelve and other General Authorities had realized the heavy load I carried and felt the strength and security of my being there and had great admiration for me. I expressed my love and admiration for him and appreciation of his confidence and pledged my full support. I recognized the fact that the Lord had prepared him in every way for this important call."

The funeral for President Smith was held in the Salt Lake Tabernacle at noon that day. The next morning, Friday, July 7, the Twelve met in the Salt Lake Temple to appoint the new president, Harold B. Lee. He named N. Eldon Tanner as first counselor and Marion G. Romney, his long-time associate in the Church's welfare plan, as second counselor. A press conference followed. In dictating his diary entry for the day, President Tanner was reminded of an earlier entry, made April 2, 1971, after he had met with the committee that would select a new president for Brigham Young University. At that time he wrote: "At the meeting President Lee occupied President Smith's chair, with Marion G. Romney on his right and me on the left, which made me think of the expression, 'Coming events cast their shadows before.'"

At age seventy-three, Harold Bingham Lee was a man of tremendous physical and spiritual energy, which he had freely spent in the service of the Church for many years. Few who heard his voice would forget its ringing, inspirational quality, nor would those who were recipients of his sympathetic and understanding counsel forget him. A steady stream of people had come to his office through the years. Those who he discerned were carrying heavy loads and who needed a place to unburden

President and Sister Tanner lead a delegation of Church officials at area general conference. Behind them are President Ezra Taft Benson, Elder Howard W. Hunter, and Elder Marvin J. Ashton

were told that his door was always open. Before he was ordained an apostle April 10, 1941, by President Heber J. Grant, he had served as managing director of the welfare program. Marion G.

Romney, who was then president of the Bonneville Stake, had served nearly from the beginning as assistant managing director of welfare, and at the same conference that sustained Harold B. Lee as an apostle, Brother Romney was sustained as the first of five original Assistants to the Twelve, April 6, 1941.

As counselor to President Smith, then as president of the Church, Harold B. Lee attacked the problems of Church organizations with renewed vigor. He viewed the world as a whole. A great teacher and practitioner of the art of delegation, he carefully outlined the work of the First Presidency both as a presiding council and with respect to the individual responsibilities of each member. As president he maintained the routine of daily sessions of the First Presidency; weekly meetings of the First Presidency and the Twelve; regular meetings with the Presiding Bishopric; monthly meetings of all the General Authorities; meetings of the Committee on Expenditures, the Council on the Disposition of Tithes, the Church Board of Education, and others. President Tanner's particular assignments included the Committee on Expenditures, Council on the Disposition of Tithes, Data Processing Committee, Purchasing Committee, and the boards of Church-owned companies.

During the eighteen-month presidency of Harold B. Lee, the correlation program, conceived to make order out of the needs of a rapidly growing church, was solidified. Events seemed to pour forth like a torrent, but a well-managed torrent, for behind each decision lay much prayer, consultation, discernment of means, and the most careful deliberation of the presidency as a whole and individually.

Almost immediately after President Lee became president of the Church, announcement was made July 8, 1972, that Wendell J. Ashton had been named to head the Public Communications Department. On July 22 W. Lowell Castleton was named president of the Oakland Temple, and two days later, President Lee and President Tanner and their wives rode in the Days of '47 Parade in downtown Salt Lake City. Other events that summer included a genealogical seminar at Brigham Young University;

funeral services for Earl Hawkes, publisher and general manager of the *Deseret News;* and dedication of the Promised Valley Playhouse, the former Lyric Theater on State Street in Salt Lake City, which had been extensively remodeled and refurbished to serve as a Church-sponsored community theater. An area conference was held in Mexico City August 25-27, with members of the First Presidency and the Tabernacle Choir participating. That month a new president of the Swiss Temple was announced, and the First Presidency met with workers of the Salt Lake Temple and introduced two new counselors to serve with President John K. Edmunds in the temple presidency.

During September Presidents Tanner and Romney managed the office while President Lee devoted three weeks to touring stakes and missions of Europe, climaxed by a visit to the Holy Land with Sister Lee, Elder Gordon B. Hinckley, and Sister Hinckley. On September 28, Lee S. Bickmore, chief executive officer of Nabisco, Inc., was named as a special consultant to the First Presidency in the areas of Church business operations, finance, building activities, the welfare program, and related matters.

When general conference convened October 6, the opening session was a solemn assembly at which Harold B. Lee was sustained as prophet, seer, and revelator, and president of The Church of Jesus Christ of Latter-day Saints, with Nathan Eldon Tanner and Marion G. Romney as counselors. Elder Bruce R. McConkie was called to fill the vacancy in the Council of the Twelve created by the death of his father-in-law, President Joseph Fielding Smith. O. Leslie Stone, James E. Faust, and L. Tom Perry were called as Assistants to the Twelve, and Rex D. Pinegar was named to succeed Elder McConkie as a member of the First Council of the Seventy.

Major additions and alterations to five existing temples—Idaho Falls, Arizona, Hawaii, Logan, and St. George—were announced October 28. Then on November 11 came a significant statement from the First Presidency announcing a fundamental revision and new leaders for the century-old Young Men's and

President Harold B. Lee, seated, with counselors N. Eldon Tanner and Marion G. Romney

Young Women's Mutual Improvement Associations. A Melchizedek Priesthood MIA was announced with important activities for single adults of all ages. That same day the Historical Department began to move into the east wing of the Church Office Building, the first department to occupy space in the new structure.

On October 18 the first area information office of the Department of Public Communications was established in New York City. The Santiago Chile Stake was organized November

19, 1972, the first of many South American stakes. When a severe earthquake shook Managua, Nicaragua, December 23, the Church, guided by President Lee with his long experience in the welfare program, quickly responded in assisting members as well as nonmembers. The year ended with the organization of an International Mission, established to provide Church services to members living in countries where organized missions and stakes did not exist. Bernard P. Brockbank, Assistant to the Twelve, was called to preside over the mission.

During 1973, decisions and events continued to flow thick and fast. On January 22 and 27 public statements were issued: the first, on abortion in response to a U.S. Supreme Court decision, and the second, on the long-awaited cease-fire in Vietnam. On February 4, 1973, the Marriott Center at BYU was dedicated with President Tanner as speaker. The Seoul Korea Stake, the first stake on the mainland of Asia, was organized March 8. President Tanner was active in negotiations for the sale of the McCune Mansion on North Main Street in which a school of music and art had flourished for many years. The mansion had originally been given to the Church in the administration of Heber J. Grant (1918-1945) as an official residence for presidents of the Church. President Grant, however, preferred to live in his own home on Eighth Avenue and A Street, and so, with the consent of the donors, the LDS-McCune School of Music and Art had been established.

That winter President Tanner participated in the search for a person to replace retiring ZCMI president Harold H. Bennett. Oakley S. Evans, a former J.C. Penney Company executive, was selected for the position. Later in the year the Hotel Utah management was reorganized, and Stuart G. Cross was named as executive vice-president.

At the general conference of April 1973, creation of a new Welfare Services Department was announced, unifying in one organization the Church's three basic welfare responsibilities: health, social services, and welfare. That year also, the LDS Hospital and the Primary Children's Hospital were merged under a single administration, encouraged by President Tanner's administrative skill. And in August an area conference was held in Munich, Germany. These are only a few of the events that illustrate the many activities in which President Tanner was involved during the brief but action-filled administration of Harold B. Lee. President Lee had begun his professional life as a schoolteacher, and his impact as teacher-prophet was great, whether from the Tabernacle pulpit or with those who served under him, one to one. After sharing one such moment at a meeting of all the General Authorities in the Salt Lake Temple, President Tanner wrote in his diary:

> In my testimony I referred to the comment made to me by President Lee on the way over to the temple, when he referred to the presents, letters, and congratulations he received on his birthday, and also the way people treat you when you are in that office. He said it was because of the office you hold, and not the individual, to which I replied that it is easier to respond to some people in the office than it is to others. My message to the General Authorities, after repeating his conversation, was that practically every time I have stopped at an airport, from one to a half dozen people have come up to shake hands and express their pleasure and satisfaction in meeting me, and I'm sure it is because of my office. My message [to the General Authorities], therefore, was that this being the case, where people do honor the office and show great respect for one holding office, he should do all in his power as an individual to be worthy of the honor being shown. I told them it was my greatest concern, and I pray always that I might live worthy of that.

For Eldon and Sara Tanner, 1973 had been another eventful year in which the pace constantly had accelerated. They looked forward to the Christmas holidays with their daughter Helen Beaton and her husband, Jack, in Phoenix, Arizona. They flew from Salt Lake City to Phoenix, grateful for the blessings and opportunities that had come to them and for the Lord's work, to which they were both so thoroughly devoted.

Footnote

[1]Quotations in this chapter are from N. Eldon Tanner's diary unless otherwise noted in the text.

16

The Spencer W. Kimball Years

Eldon and Sara Tanner had anticipated the 1973 Christmas holidays in Phoenix as a time of joy, especially since they would be spending time with their daughter Helen. There, on the evening of December 26, President Tanner received an urgent long distance call from President Harold B. Lee's personal secretary, D. Arthur Haycock. Brother Haycock, with more than ordinary emotion, told President Tanner that President Lee was very ill and that he should return home as soon as possible. As President Tanner was making arrangements to return to Salt Lake City, the telephone rang again. It was Brother Haycock. He said, "The Lord has spoken. President Lee has been called home."

The days following were difficult for those who loved Harold B. Lee. Accustomed to older prophets in recent years, Church members had looked forward to a long, stable term under the comparatively young President Lee. Only a few had known how close to empty were his stores of physical and emotional energy.

Following the funeral in the Salt Lake Tabernacle on December 30, Spencer W. Kimball, who was president of the Twelve Apostles, called a meeting of the Twelve for three o'clock that afternoon in the Salt Lake Temple. As the quorum met together,

Note: This chapter is based on contributions by Ronald O. Barney. Major sources were materials in the Journal History of the Church.

Elder Tanner was asked to conduct the prayer circle. In the historic constitutional procedure that followed, Spencer W. Kimball was sustained as the twelfth president of the Church. He retained N. Eldon Tanner and Marion G. Romney as his counselors.

President Tanner's renewed call to the First Presidency marked the first time that one counselor had served four presidents of the Church. The day following the solemn meeting in the temple, the new First Presidency held a news conference in which President Tanner said, "Although I was shocked beyond any expression at the sudden passing of President Lee, and experienced great sorrow, I feel honored to be a counselor to President Kimball. He has been prepared as well as a man could be prepared. Besides his natural abilities, he has had the Spirit of the Lord to direct him. And I'm sure that the work of the Lord will go forward under his direction as it has done in the past."[1]

This last sentence proved to be a profound understatement, for the work under President Kimball went forward with almost electrifying momentum. President Kimball called upon all members of the Church to "lengthen your stride." N. Eldon Tanner responded, determined to follow the president's call not only to lengthen his stride, but to quicken his pace as well. He would later say that his greatest challenge from the beginning of the Kimball administration was simply "to keep up" with President Kimball.

Born in Salt Lake City in 1895 and reared in the Mormon community of Thatcher, Arizona, Spencer W. Kimball was seventy-eight when he succeeded to the presidency of the Church, but he was tireless in carrying out his responsibilities as president. Warm and sparkling, compassionate and kind, conscientious and alert, he was a person whom Eldon Tanner could emulate and enjoy working for.

President Tanner now assumed even more public functions to relieve the demanding schedule that President Kimball made for himself. There were such duties as dedicating a bust of Brigham Young at the private Brigham Young cemetery in Salt

President Spencer W. Kimball with counselors N. Eldon Tanner and Marion G. Romney

Lake City and dedicating a special laboratory at the Primary Children's Medical Center. His lifelong involvement with the Boy Scouts received attention as well. When the first tickets for a Scout Camporee at Expo '74, Spokane, Washington, were sold, President Tanner bought them. He also served on the Western Region Executive Committee of the Boy Scouts of America and as a National Council representative. Another highlight of the year was a meeting in October 1975 in San Francisco, where, along with Elder Hartman Rector, Jr., of the First Council of the Seventy, and David M. Kennedy, the Church's special ambassador, he exchanged personal greetings with the Emperor and Empress of Japan.

In the summer of 1976 President Tanner represented the Church in his beloved land of Canada, where a Church exhibition was opened. Following the U.S. national elections that year, he and Sister Tanner represented the Church in Washington, D.C., at the inauguration of President Jimmy Carter and sat in a special section directly behind the new president of the United States.

Area conferences, initiated under President Joseph Fielding Smith, accelerated, beginning in Stockholm in August 1974 and ending in Jackson, Mississippi, in May 1980. In 1976 seventeen were held—in the South Pacific, Australia, New Zealand, the British Isles (London, Manchester, and Glasgow), and continental Europe (Paris, Copenhagen, Helsinki, Amsterdam, and Dortmund, Germany). President Tanner accompanied President Kimball on most of these occasions without any lessening of administrative duties at home.

President Kimball also led out in conducting an extensive series of solemn assemblies. In 1976, for example, twenty-one were held—in addition to the seventeen area conferences. This meant extensive weekend travel in addition to monthly world travels.

During 1977 President Tanner represented the First Presidency at headquarters while President Romney accompanied President Kimball to Mexico, Guatemala, Costa Rica, Peru,

Chile, Bolivia, and Columbia. In June 1978 the entire presidency was in Honolulu for the rededication of the Hawaii Temple and an area conference in Honolulu. October and early November of 1978 found the Tanners with President and Sister Kimball at area conferences in Johannesburg, South Africa; Montevideo, Uruguay; and Sao Paulo, Brazil, where the Sao Paulo Temple was also dedicated.

President Kimball was unable to attend eight of ten area conferences conducted in 1979. President Tanner conducted those that were held in Wisconsin, Washington, D.C., and Atlanta; he also later accompanied President Kimball to Toronto for the first area conference held in Canada. On that occasion Eldon Tanner's background served the President well in meetings with Canada's prime minister and governor general. On November 24, 1979, the Tanners found themselves in Auckland, New Zealand, beginning five of the ten area conferences held that year in the South Pacific and Australia. These also were conducted in the absence of President Kimball, who was recuperating from an operation. Additional conferences were held in Wellington, New Zealand, and in Melbourne, Adelaide, and Sydney, Australia. On December 6, 1979, President Tanner noted with satisfaction in his journal the warm welcome he and Sister Tanner received from President Kimball upon their return. All this illustrates the remarkable tempo set by Spencer W. Kimball as he "lengthened his stride" and counseled others to do likewise. It is a great tribute to his first counselor's skill, efficiency, and devotion that he did indeed "keep up."

Until 1977 the Financial Department was accountable to President Tanner, but in that year the Presiding Bishopric was reorganized to direct temporal aspects of Church administration. President Tanner was not afraid to give heads of departments assigned to him great responsibility and autonomy, though he followed events in detail and made himself available for frequent consultations. He also continued to be involved as chairman of the budget, financial, and personnel committees. In meetings he wanted to hear all sides of a matter, and he would listen thoughtfully, with little comment, but subordinates knew that any decision he made would be a fair and selfless one. At each meeting they gained from him new perspective about the demands on Church resources and the Church's growth outside the United States and Canada.

On March 29, 1978, N. Eldon Tanner became the sixth recipient of the annual "Giant in Our City" award, presented by the Salt Lake Area Chamber of Commerce. Nearly 1,500 people, including forty-six General Authorities and sixty members of President Tanner's family, attended the special occasion in the Hotel Utah. Feature speaker for the evening was William Ross-Mogg, editor of the *Times* of London. A bust by noted sculptor Edward Fraughton was presented, and a closed-circuit televised documentary of President Tanner's life was shown. The civic award, as presented by B. Z. (Bud) Kastler for the Chamber, was for

> the noteworthy achievements he has made in the community, especially for his efforts in helping to bring many new important buildings to downtown Salt Lake City during the past fifteen years. There has been more construction of major buildings in the heart of Salt Lake City in that period than in the previous 100 years, and President Tanner has been an influential factor in much of this activity. He is also being saluted as a man of superior character, a successful businessman with deep spirituality, a great leader esteemed by millions of people around the world.[2]

In perhaps the finest tribute of the evening, President Kimball described Eldon Tanner in these terms: "As approachable as a child, as wise as a father, and as loving as a gentle brother. This is a man of rare makeup. He has not shunned any obligation of which he was aware as a father, friend or brother, or as a businessman, citizen or civic leader, or as an Apostle of the Lord Jesus Christ. Certainly Nathan Eldon Tanner is a man to match our mountains: tall, rugged, unyielding, immeasurable."[3]

In the late 1970s a health condition of President Tanner was diagnosed as Parkinson's disease, and his rigorous and demanding schedule had to be curtailed somewhat. He was not able to attend some of the area conferences held in 1980 while his medication was being adjusted. But, like President Kimball, he continued to function effectively in his calling despite the disease and diminished vision. So many key staff members trooped to his home that Sister Tanner one day said, "It's like living in Grand Central Station."

Despite the impact of the disease, President Tanner was in remarkable health for a man of eighty. When he celebrated his eightieth birthday on May 9, 1978, he planned the daytime hours as just another working day. He was at the office and in a meeting by 7:30 A.M. This was followed by the meeting of the First Presidency at 8:00 A.M. Later in the morning he attended the annual meeting of a major firm on whose board he served. But by mid-afternoon he yielded to the affection of associates, expressed in the form of an informal reception. His secretaries, LaRue Sneff and Shanna Knight, presented him with a book of remembrance with a picture and note from every General Authority then serving. President Kimball wrote this tribute to his first counselor: "When I was a member of the Twelve Apostles and he was a member of the First Presidency, I went very often to his office and plunked myself down in his big, red leather chair, unloaded some of my problems, and he was always of great help to me." Later that evening the Tanner family gathered to pay tribute to and express love for their devoted husband, father, and grandfather.

A few days later the youth of the Eden Utah Ward sponsored a celebration that included a turkey dinner, party, dance, and program in President Tanner's honor. The Tanners had purchased a summer home at nearby Patio Springs, and when they were in the area, they attended Sabbath meetings in the Eden Ward. A year earlier President Tanner had helped the ward celebrate its centennial. Those who knew him there expressed a kinship and love for him that always made him feel at home in the little northern Utah community, nestled in a mountain valley near Huntsville, the birthplace of President David O. McKay.

During the fall of 1978 a regional periodical surveyed fifty

During visit to Egypt, President Tanner rode a camel

leading citizens of Utah and asked them to list the ten most influential people in the Mountain West. The list included four public officials, two newspaper executives, two businessmen, and two churchmen: Spencer W. Kimball and N. Eldon Tanner. The recognition was real and not a token gesture.

In the spring of 1979, an interfaith conference was organized and held by Westminster College in Salt Lake City. The event was co-sponsored by the Presbyterian Synods of the Pacific, the Rocky Mountains, and the American Southwest. More than two hundred clergymen and religious leaders attended, including ministers from all over the West and a number of invited Latter-day Saints. A good share of President Tanner's life had been spent in the company of non-Mormon friends. This conference allowed him to share his feelings of warmth toward those who were not members of his church but who mutually shared many of the same Christian goals. He told the participants that the feelings of brotherhood experienced at the conference ought to be encouraged and that he hoped that much good would come of the exchange of ideas, beliefs, and concerns among conference participants. "We are all children of God, engaged in His work. We are all under the Christian mandate to love our neighbors," he said. Elder Boyd K. Packer of the Council of the Twelve and Professor Truman G. Madsen from Brigham Young University also addressed the conference.

During the fall of 1979 President and Sister Tanner were able to participate in one of the more important international efforts of the Church when the Orson Hyde Memorial Garden was dedicated in Jerusalem. The Tanners were invited to accompany President and Sister Kimball, President Ezra Taft Benson, and Elders LeGrand Richards and Howard W. Hunter on a journey that took them to several countries of the Mediterranean.

A month later, President Tanner attended the cornerstone laying at the Seattle Temple. He was the concluding speaker and offered a special prayer immediately before the cornerstone was formally placed.

On December 19, 1979, President and Sister Tanner celebrated their sixtieth wedding anniversary. All during his life Eldon gave constant praise to his beloved Sally for any success he had achieved. He gave her full credit for their successful marriage, for the excellent manner in which their children had been raised, and for the support that allowed him to involve himself in the many projects that place strain upon a family.

On January 29, 1980, the Brigham Young University School of Management gave its "Executive of the Year" award to President Tanner. Normally he had been the one who recommended the final approval for this annual award, but final approval for this award was made while he was out of town. Presiding Bishop Victor L. Brown delivered the speech commending Eldon Tanner for his life and described the ten outstanding qualities of his character:

1. *Integrity.* In my observations, President Tanner is the personification of integrity as expressed by C. Simmons and also by

The Tanners with President and Sister Kimball en route to Israel for the dedication of the Orson Hyde Gardens, 1979

Shakespeare: "Integrity is the first step to true greatness. Men love to praise, but are slow to practice it. To maintain it in high places costs self-denial; in all places it is liable to opposition, but its end is glorious, and the universe will yet do it homage." And from *Hamlet:* "This above all, to thine own self be true, and it must follow as the night the day, thou canst not then be false to any man."

2. *The art of listening.* President Tanner is an expert listener even though generally his mind is leagues ahead of the one he is listening to. He shows the utmost respect by careful listening. Anyone who has sat through a meeting with him has observed this important trait. His intent listening is evidenced as he, in a very few words, summarizes what he has heard. Through this rare trait he impresses those of us with whom he works with his warm, supportive, kind personality.

3. *Considered decisions.* President Tanner never "shoots from the hip." He is most interested in all of the facts pertaining to a question and only makes a decision after weighing both the pros and the cons.

4. *Objectivity.* Those of you who have worked with President Tanner have heard him say this many times: "It isn't important

who is right. What is important is what is right." He has also said that he would rather be a part of the solution to the problem than a part of the problem. He has an uncanny knack of excluding bias and prejudice from his decisions. I have never seen him allow his ego to get in the way of good judgment.

5. *An unusual mind.* Some of us had an experience with President Tanner sometime ago which exemplifies his unusually sharp intellect. We were making a very concentrated, important presentation involving more than the normal amount of detail. The presentation lasted over two hours. There was very little discussion during this period. At the conclusion, President Tanner said something like this: "Recommendations one and two can be implemented with little difficulty. Recommendation number three needs some more study and your chart covering this portion of the presentation needs to be redone for the following reasons. . . . Recommendation number four will require much more study and appears to be untimely at the moment."

6. *He treats all men with respect.* He has an innate respect for his fellowman. He never indulges in speaking down to people. If he has a difference of opinion, he expresses it objectively, showing respect for the other person's point of view. He never tries to overshadow those about him.

7. *He unhesitatingly will acknowledge an error and does not dwell on the errors of others.* Nor does he bear grudges.

8. *He is an outstanding citizen of his community.* Through his being actively involved as a citizen wherever he has lived, he has earned the highest respect of leaders in industry and government in Canada, the United States, and many foreign lands.

9. *Honor of parents.* President Tanner has always shown the greatest respect for his parents and has honored them by the life he has led as he has honored his Sally and daughters.

10. *He is loyal to his leader.* It has been my blessing to observe his relationships as a counselor to four different presidents of the Church over the past sixteen years. During this period, many important things have happened. Some of these years have not been easy ones. I have never seen a more outstanding example of loyalty and fidelity to one's file leader than I have seen in President Tanner. This loyalty extends to all of his associates. He is the personification of the admonition of the Lord that we should be one. Even during his outstanding business and political career, his loyalty to his family and church came first..[4]

Soon after the "Executive of the Year" award was given, President Dallin H. Oaks of Brigham Young University announced that the new Management School building at BYU was to be named the Nathan Eldon Tanner Building. The seven-story building houses the academic offices and programs of the College of Business and Graduate School of Management. President Oaks said, "With the naming of the N. Eldon Tanner Building, we memorialize the name of a great businessman and public servant in our School of Management, just as we have already memorialized the name of a great lawyer in our J. Reuben Clark Law School." Later in the year President Tanner pressed the button that set off three separate charges that broke ground for the new building.

The many awards given to President Tanner continued apace thereafter. In January 1981 the University of Utah established a $1 million endowment fund, contributed by business leaders for the College of Business under his name. An N. Eldon Tanner Chair of Business Administration resulted, along with several graduate-level scholarships and research fellowships for the faculty. B. Z. Kastler, a member of the endowment committee, expressed the feeling of the committee and university. He said: "The intent of the endowment fund is to imbue future business leaders with the vision, honor, determination, self-reliance and high ideals that led President Tanner to contribute so unselfishly to a better community and world. Friends and admirers of President Tanner, including local, state and national business leaders, have been most enthusiastic and generous in their support of the fund."

In February 1981 President Tanner received an honorary Doctorate of Humane Letters from Westminster College in Salt Lake City. He had led and encouraged a fund-raising drive to keep Westminster College alive as an effective institution of higher learning. The award was conferred by President David Cornell for Eldon Tanner's "long years of support and personal interest" in Westminster College.

A month later the University of Utah honored him with its annual Honorary Alumnus Award, conferred by David P. Gardner, president of the university, and the Alumni Association. This award is given annually to a non-alumnus who has displayed unusual dedication to the university and contributed significantly to its advancement.

Other awards included the Distinguished Service Award of Utah Technical College for his "involvement in education, in particular his involvement in vocational technical education and his concern for employable skills for youth"; a plaque from the Salt Lake Golden Eagles hockey team for supporting hockey as well as other sports in Salt Lake City; and recognition from ZCMI upon his relinquishing his role as member of the board of directors for seventeen years and chairman of the board for six years.

President Tanner in 1981 dedicated several important buildings, including the Monte Bean Life Science Museum and the renovated David O. McKay building at BYU; buildings on the Southern Utah State College campus; and a building at Stevens Henager College in Provo. He also participated in the dedication of several sculptures depicting the ideals of family life as part of the downtown Salt Lake City beautification project.

On April 21, 1981, President Tanner presided at a general budget planning meeting of General Authorities and other department heads in the Church Office Building. His particular role in that meeting included chairmanship of the Personnel Committee as well as leadership of the Budget Committee and the Financial Department. There President Spencer W. Kimball's first counselor related how he had had four brothers, each with his own ambitious needs and desires for acquiring things beyond his income, the normal human condition. On one occasion the boys went to their father and asked why such desirable things couldn't be purchased. Said the wise father, "Boys, I can give you three reasons. The first is, we can't afford it. The other two don't matter."

The meeting then proceeded under President Tanner's direction with a detailed discussion of a computerized budgeting system for Church headquarters, essential wisdom in seeking efficient departmental management, other budget matters, and personnel policy. The tone and character of the meeting were visibly and profoundly affected as the men and women present related President Tanner's quietly told story to the growing demands on the resources of the expanding world Church. New perspective was added to the thinking of each who had responsibility for submitting the next annual request to the Budget Committee.

In 1982 President Tanner's address "Constancy amid Change," delivered in 1979, was recirculated to assist the Saints in coping with economic adversity. To illustrate the importance of budgeting and financial management, he told the story of an immigrant father who kept his accounts payable in a shoe box, his accounts receivable on a spindle, and his cash in the cash register.

"I don't see how you can run your business this way," said the man's son. "How do you know what your profit is?"

"Son," replied the businessman, "when I got off the boat, I had only the pants I was wearing. Today your sister is an art teacher, your brother is a doctor, and you're an accountant. I have a car, a home, and a good business. Everything is paid for. So you add it all up, subtract the pants, and there's my profit."[5]

Although President Tanner was given credit for fostering much of the revitalization of downtown Salt Lake City, he nevertheless was very careful about such growth at the expense of losing the beauties and the environment God gave to the earth. Speaking to a group of developers he once said, "The First Presidency of The Church of Jesus Christ of Latter-day Saints encourages expansion of good, wholesome industry in the state. Expanding industry is necessary to provide jobs, but we should be mindful of protecting nature's beauties around us."

On May 12, 1981, it was announced that the resignation of N. Eldon Tanner as a member of the board of Mountain Fuel Supply Company had been accepted "with regret." The extent and sincerity of those regrets were eloquently expressed by B. Z. Kastler on behalf of the board. A personal friend of Eldon and Sara Tanner, he particularly appreciated President Tanner's wit and wisdom as well as his extensive knowledge of the oil and gas busi-

B. Z. Kastler with Eldon and Sara Tanner at the "Giant of Our City" dinner at Hotel Utah. Bust of President Tanner was sculpted by Edward Fraughton

ness. In an interview for the Church Archives, Mr. Kastler said, "If I were to characterize one single thing, it would be (Eldon Tanner's) positive approach to things . . . and his basic humanity. . . . Some people don't think he's outgoing . . . but this man is tremendously outgoing, and anybody who's ever invested a few moments of time to get to know him feels that. He's a constructive, outgoing, very human individual."[6]

In January 1981 the First Presidency appointed a committee of members of the Church Coordinating Council to review and make recommendations on what organizations and activities being performed by the First Presidency could be assigned to the

The First Presidency, 1982: President Spencer W. Kimball, top left, with counselors N. Eldon Tanner, Marion G. Romney, Gordon B. Hinckley

Council of the Twelve, the First Quorum of the Seventy, and the Presiding Bishopric. This was part of a continuing effort to adjust headquarters functions in order that the presiding quorums, particularly the First Presidency, could fulfill their responsibilities as the Church grew and expanded. An ongoing result announced April 12, 1982, was the formation of three executive councils, each with assigned responsibilities for certain departments at Church headquarters and world areas. In 1981 President Kimball announced plans for nine new temples, to be constructed in Chicago, Dallas, Guatemala City, Lima, Frankfurt, Stockholm, Seoul, Manila, and Johannesburg. On March 31, 1982, Boise, Idaho; Denver, Colorado; Guayaquil, Ecuador; and Taipai, Taiwan, were added to the list, bringing the total number of temples to forty-one. These latest groups feature a new, effective design that opens the way for an increasing number of temples. It has become increasingly evident that the former practices of groundbreaking by the president or a counselor in the First Presidency, cornerstone laying, and other ceremonies attached to temple construction and administration require increased attention, inasmuch as temples are central to the responsibilities of the Presidency.

On Thursday, July 23, 1981, Elder Gordon B. Hinckley of the Council of the Twelve was named a counselor to the First Presidency. Elder Neal A. Maxwell, who had been serving as a president of the First Quorum of the Seventy, was called to fill the vacancy in the Twelve. President Hinckley had had a close relationship with President Tanner in connection with a number of assignments, including the Public Communications Committee and Bonneville International. President Tanner joined other members in the Presidency in welcoming this strong, experienced leader to serve with them. The call demonstrated that the tremendous momentum that characterized the Kimball presidency would in no way diminish, despite the advancing years of the prophet and his counselors.

Elder Marvin J. Ashton once told a devotional audience at Brigham Young University: "President N. Eldon Tanner will go down in history as one of the greatest counselors ever to serve in the First Presidency of the Church. He is a man of few words and much performance. I have never heard him make a cheap or shabby remark. I have never seen him when he was not a gentleman, when he was not the personification of integrity. A tireless, dedicated leader, he is about his Father's business early and late. I say without reservation that I have never met a man with greater judgment or superior wisdom."

As the foregoing judgment is recorded here, one must recall that we stand much too close to the administration of President Spencer W. Kimball to comprehend its importance in the history of the restored Church. Measured only by temples constructed or announced during his administration, one could say that the Kimball years have been the most remarkable since April 6, 1930. "And more temples are contemplated," said the Prophet, who understands their eternal significance and their earthly value possibly better than any other person. Undoubtedly much more has been contemplated that will yet be unfolded!

Throughout this remarkable period of prophetic leadership, at the Prophet's side has stood his first counselor, President N. Eldon Tanner. His apparent service has been, for some observers, to have been weighted on the financial-administrative side. Certainly this talent, together with his unique ability to conceptualize organization patterns, has been outstanding. When President Kimball reconstituted the First Quorum of the Seventy in 1976, no one gave it more heart-felt support than President Tanner. When in 1977 the Quorum was expanded and reorganized with the addition of the former Assistants to the Twelve, it was evident that this significant event provided additional help to the First Presidency and Twelve in administering the world Church. But the full record of the administration of President Kimball must necessarily await proper perspective in the light of these important developments and what follows in the future.

Great as his service may have been in discharging his assignments, apparent as its outward manifestations may appear, it is safe to say that the spiritual strength and insight of N. Eldon Tanner will prove in time to outrun the other aspects of his remarkable support for President Spencer W. Kimball and President Kimball's three immediate predecessors. Nathan William Tanner taught his son well. Four presidents of the Church and many others have learned they can depend on the man from the log cabin of Aetna, Alberta, Canada.

Footnotes

[1] Unless otherwise noted, quotations in this chapter are from N. Eldon Tanner's diary.

[2] *Deseret News,* March 30, 1978.

[3] Ibid.

[4] Victor L. Brown, remarks at presentation of BYU's "Executive of the Year" award to N. Eldon Tanner, January 29, 1980.

[5] "Constancy amid Change," address delivered at the 149th Semiannual General Conference welfare session, October 6, 1979.

[6] B. Z. Kastler, interview with Gordon Irving, February 6, 1981. James Moyle Oral History Program, Church Archives.

17

The Tanners: Salt Lake City Neighbors and Friends

In 1967, Eldon and Sara Tanner moved to the Aztec, a new high-rise condominium in Salt Lake City on the brow of ancient Lake Bonneville. They immediately endeared themselves to their new neighbors, who knew them as friends of great warmth and dignity. The top two stories were being sold unfinished so that buyers could complete them to their own specifications. The Tanners acquired number 1001, occupying about one-fourth of the southwest corner of that floor, on the thirteenth level of the building. Their neighbors in 1002 were the O. Leslie Stones, who had left their comfortable home in Oakland, California, to come to Salt Lake City to preside over the Salt Lake Temple.

While their apartment was being finished, the Tanners rented an apartment from Colonel and Mrs. M. M. Layton, five floors below at 501. Later, Colonel Layton would ask President Tanner to ordain him a high priest in their ward, the 33rd Ward of what was then the Bonneville Stake.

Dr. Russell M. Nelson was serving as president of the stake at that time. He came to appreciate President and Sister Tanner as two of the most loyal supporters of ward and stake activities. He wrote of them:

> They had a way of making their bishopric and stake presidency feel as though they considered that they lived in the choicest ward and stake in the Church. Not only were they always

genuinely complimentary and encouraging in their remarks pertaining to our efforts; they sought ways to reinforce those thoughts with actions of love.

On January 2, 1968, President and Sister Tanner invited their home teachers, bishop, and stake president, and their wives, to their lovely home for a delicious brunch to celebrate New Year's day. Sister Tanner's delectable cooking was matched only by their gracious and generous expressions of support and love. As we left their home that day, we all stood taller than ever before.

When trouble struck in September 1971, as my mother was hospitalized with a stroke, President Tanner quickly came to help. He knew I was in Leningrad, Russia. The doctors told him she possibly would not live long enough for my return. He and my counselor, Joseph B. Wirthlin, gave Mother a blessing, that her life would be sustained. She began to rally, and then recovered, to sweeten the lives of her husband and family, as she does daily now about a decade since that blessing.

Among the many names honored in our home and among our family, none are revered more than those of President N. Eldon Tanner and his sweet Sara. We know we are better than we otherwise could have been because of their support, encouragement and love.[1]

The bishop of the 33rd Ward was Don B. Hales, a Ph.D. in electrical engineering, a big man with a diminutive wife of very sweet nature. President Tanner took an interest in the Hales children, especially Kyle, the oldest son, then a lad of about fourteen, and his younger brother, Bart. When Bart became a teacher in the Aaronic Priesthood, he was assigned as President Tanner's home teaching companion. The influence Eldon Tanner had had with young men as a bishop and as a school principal in Canada came to envelop these two young men, albeit in different ways from the activities that had characterized Eldon's younger days. Both young men were to fill missions and to be happily married in the temple.

Members of the ward looked forward to seeing President Tanner in his familiar seat on the right end of the front row on the stand. There he sat quietly and attentively during meetings whenever he was in Salt Lake City on a Sunday. Sister Tanner was a mainstay participant in the ward Relief Society. Bordering the University of Utah, the 33rd Ward contained a large number of young married couples with small children. Though those who were university students were eligible for membership in the married student wards maintained by the Church for students attending the University of Utah, increasing numbers exercised the option to attend the 33rd Ward. The presence and quiet influence of Eldon and Sara Tanner had a great deal to do with this. A feature of a December sacrament meeting was to hear their annual Christmas message and reminder that "this is the Church of Jesus Christ. We ought to remember it and conduct ourselves as such."

To see and be greeted by either or both of the Tanners at the ward or on the elevator at the Aztec was always an inspirational and encouraging experience. The greeting would be accompanied by some short-sentence humor spoken quietly by President Tanner, or an editorial remark on an event of the day that carried more than ordinary editorial impact. When Neal A. Maxwell was called from his post as executive vice-president of the University of Utah to head the widely expanding Church Education System, one such occasion arose. President Tanner turned to the author, at that time State Commissioner of Higher Education, and said, "Now we have two fine trustworthy men involved in the education of our people both in the state and throughout the Church."

It is doubtful that ward members realized the weight and complexity of the administrative duties carried by this able counselor to four presidents of the Church, let alone the marvelous background of his life and labors. The 1960s and the decade of the 1970s had seen these tasks increase as the Church grew toward the five million membership mark. Neighbors driving home late in the evening would often see a light burning in the tenth-floor study of the apartment. Only the knowledgeable could guess at the heavy concentration that was being applied to significant matters at those late hours. And if one were on the elevator a few minutes before seven the next morning, there would be President Tanner en route to the office.

When the Bonneville Stake was realigned in 1972, President

and Sister Tanner found themselves in the University West Stake, later renamed the Salt Lake Central Stake. Then the familiar figure of President Tanner graced the Assembly Hall on Temple Square, where the stake held quarterly stake conferences. Sister Tanner would be in her usual place on the right aisle about one-third of the way back, where she would have a clear view of her husband and the platform, unblocked by the stately pillars that held up the balcony of that historic building. President Tanner's quiet, thoughtfully penetrating messages on those occasions added a dimension that conveyed much to the thoughtful listeners, particularly the young people, who sat in rapt attention.

After the stake realignment, the general stake priesthood meeting was held monthly in the 11th Ward at 8 A.M. on Sunday morning, in lieu of priesthood meeting that week in the various wards. On one occasion, President Tanner's extensive absences on First Presidency assignments interfered with his understanding of the meeting schedule. Finding himself in the city that morning, he proceeded to his ward for priesthood meeting, but found the building empty. He continued to walk down Eleventh East to First South, where the general priesthood meeting of the stake was in session. The stake president was at the pulpit expounding with enthusiasm some of the newer programs being emphasized by the Church, and so intent was he that he failed to notice President Tanner walking quietly up the aisle and taking his accustomed seat. When the stake president finished his talk, he was chagrined to have failed to notice and acknowledge President Tanner's arrival. President Tanner immediately soothed his anxiety, and the meeting proceeded with the member of the First Presidency giving his usual intensive attention.

One of his more remarkable observable traits was the absence of any restraints exercised on discussions in Sunday School or priesthood classes he attended. The high priests' class instructor during much of that time was John Cordery, a skilled printer and Englishman, rich with memories of his mission in Hawaii as a younger man. Brother Cordery, an avid student of the gospel, prepared the lessons so as to encourage extensive discussion, with one or two provocative questions to bring the group into active participation. Furthermore, he always came armed with books and documents. President Tanner would sit behind a table with the group leaders, while the secretary sat in the corner keeping careful minutes. The discussion never got lost in byways or paths of speculative mystery, although their boundaries may have been explored, and discussions were often intense. It was a deep tribute to President Tanner that he sat attentively through such excursions into experience, observation, and high priestly expression. He evidently liked the discussion to run its course, for the brethren to have their proper say. Then, toward the end, Brother Cordery often turned to him and said, "President Tanner, could we have your comments on this point?" Those comments would always be given quietly and concisely.

The 33rd Ward membership included a number of widows in advanced years. On one occasion, a sister expressed concern in fast meeting for a recent illness and said how lonely she had become. The next thing anyone knew, she was a guest at the table of Eldon and Sara Tanner on several occasions. Likewise, when a funeral was held in a distant meetinghouse, who quietly took a place on the stand on a busy weekday, to pay his respects to a friend and neighbor, but President N. Eldon Tanner. At his side as he entered the chapel to greet the family was his devoted Sara.

While for many years their brief summer vacations took them to Waterton Lakes and their cabin, the Christmas and New Year's season usually found the Tanners in Salt Lake City. For many years the residents of the Aztec arranged a Christmas social, often a dinner, to bring occupants of the condominium into closer communication and friendship. The large Aztec room on the main floor served this and other useful purposes to build friendships. It was always impressive to see the way in which President and Sister Tanner would go around the room, finding opportunity to greet nearly everyone, including those with whom they were not well acquainted, usually newcomers. Particularly did this demonstrate their ability to establish rapport with some of the outstanding people who were not members of the Church but who respected the individuality, friendship, and warmth of their neighbors.

Occasionally the Tanners would hold open house on New Year's day. Present would be family members who were in the vicinity, close friends in the community, and neighbors in the building. Everyone felt at home. The hosts' welcome was genuine. Their expression when one left—"Do you have to go so soon?"—was sincere. They loved these occasions, and the neighbors loved them.

As neighbors, Eldon and Sara Tanner have moved in and out of delicate situations unobtrusively, always leaving a feeling of uplift and peace. As disciples of Jesus Christ, the Prince of Peace, they have established a legacy of His peace among family, friends, and fellowmen. President Tanner, often in the public eye as well as before the Church, has associated with those who have been involved with important events and people. His demeanor on such occasions has been no different from times with family or friends.

President Spencer W. Kimball remembers one example of President Tanner's influence displayed at a Labor Day weekend gathering of the Tanner family at Bear Lake in northern Utah. This was a holiday weekend when people were not especially careful about their dress, Sabbath observance, and public example. As described by President Kimball: "Sunday evening one of the members in the area came up to President Tanner and asked to shake his hand and say a word to him. She said that earlier in the day she and her husband had been discussing the proper observance of the Sabbath day. They decided to watch the Tanner clan during that day. They saw all the men and boys get ready and go to priesthood meeting in the morning . Then the whole group went to Sunday School and later to testimony meeting. She said that after seeing this, her husband remarked, 'Well, I think I had better go in the house and put on my suit and tie.' At

President Tanner in his office at 47 East South Temple

all of the meetings during the day, all sixty-one members of the Tanner family had been well-groomed, well-dressed, and in their Sunday best."

President Tanner has continually supported his family. His

wife, Sara, has always been the number one priority in his life. He has recorded time and time again how delightful she was. In the past he often went golfing with her. He made sure that one or both of them were at important family gatherings. He sent her to their daughter's doctoral graduation from the University of Wisconsin when it was impossible for both of them to go. She also attended their daughter Helen's second marriage when he could not attend, and he instructed her to take the entire family to dinner and charge the bill to him. He once guaranteed a bank loan for a son-in-law. At another time he called the bishop of a university ward in Edmonton and encouraged him to help a grandson in whatever way possible.

Through the years President Tanner enjoyed occasional golf games whenever possible with Elders Franklin D. Richards and Delbert L. Stapley, with a fourth added to made a foursome. Such opportunities to get out into the open air became less frequent and more appreciated.

President Tanner has been publicly recognized for his support of a variety of sports. This, he has found, has been a good way to cultivate civic development. He and Sara have particularly enjoyed professional hockey, an interest that stems from their early contact with the sport in Canada. They have supported university athletic programs and the Church's softball, basketball, volleyball, and golf activities. His support of sports programs reflects the personal values that may be derived from them. He has long recognized the qualities to be gained from active participation in athletics under the right auspices, but he has never developed "spectatoritis." As the years have sped by, he has attended generally as a civic duty, less frequently watching athletic contests on television. He has preferred golf and fishing, because they allow one an opportunity to be involved personally in the sport, with people, fresh air, and the natural environment.

During their Salt Lake City years, it has been evident to keen observers that the Tanners strongly support the cultural organizations of the community and state. They have supported the Utah Symphony, the Pioneer Memorial Theater, and Promised

Valley Playhouse. They have enjoyed the educational and artistic value of the fine arts, and have played a key role in efforts to enrich the culture of the city as the headquarters of the Church. "Let Zion in Her Beauty Rise" is more than a song in the hymnal to them; it is an obligation to contribute to such an ideal.

Eldon and Sara Tanner have long enjoyed dinner parties, casual or formal. Nearly weekly during the time they lived in Canada, and frequently since, they have attended or hosted such gatherings. The more casual or informal gatherings, particularly those with family and close friends, have usually involved games, such as table tennis, Rook, rummy, cribbage, and charades. If they have gone out to eat, they have preferred good restaurants over fast-food places. They have not been, however, above stopping for a hot dog, if that is all time allows, or picking up some fried chicken, a frequent take-home favorite, especially for short-notice meals.

People have always been comfortable with Eldon and Sara Tanner. A striking example of hospitality occurred in the summer months of 1981 when Sister Tanner personally invited the wives of the General Authorities—more than sixty in all—to happy, intimate luncheons at intervals in groups of twelve. "Eldon wants me to do it," she said to one of the sisters. So, too, did she want to do it. Whether it is newly arrived Maria Abrea from Buenos Aires, Jutta Busche from Dortmund, Germany, or a longtime friend like Helen Richards, all feel instantly at ease with Sara Tanner. If President Tanner cannot be there personally to add his warmth, all feel his influence and know it bespeaks an effort to promote love and friendship among people. It has been like that always, whether in Cardston, Edmonton, Calgary, or Leatherhead, Surrey, England, or Salt Lake City.

Many similar, though perhaps less unusual, family gatherings followed in the years after the Golden Wedding anniversary trip with the family to Hawaii. Each occasion is etched deep in the minds of those who have gathered and participated. On July 24, 1981, President and Sister Tanner held a family reunion attended by eighty-five of their direct descendants. A cursory analysis of the group by one of their daughters showed the following, in addition to family members' temple marriages and church and civic activities: College degrees are plentiful. Five are lawyers. One is in medicine, one in dentistry. A dozen or more are outstanding business men and women. One is an engineer. Eighteen of the grandchildren present had served full-time missions. And so it goes. The story of their posterity goes on and on, demonstrating that the ultimate record of an eternal family, its nature and extensions, can never be fully written. But the record to date would indicate that the love, devotion, and example of a father who whistled while making fires to heat the little home on cold Alberta mornings is remembered and emulated.

There is an old saying from former, more aristocratic times that no man can be a hero to his valet. Whether this is translatable to contemporary executives and their secetaries may be irrelevant. But certainly Mary C. Livingstone in Canada and LaRue Sneff at Church headquarters enjoyed vantage points of observation not open to everyone. Miss Livingstone's judgment has been recorded earlier in these pages. What about LaRue Sneff at 47 East South Temple in Salt Lake City?

LaRue began work as President Tanner's secretary in January 1964. Her previous employment with the telephone company and as secretary and reporter for the *Church News* gave her valuable background for her appointment with N. Eldon Tanner. She began Church employment in 1951 in the Office of the First Presidency, working under Joseph Anderson. In 1954 she moved to the office of Stephen L Richards when he became a counselor to President David O. McKay, and continued working there until President Richards's death in 1959. When Henry D. Moyle succeeded President Richards, she became his secretary and also continued doing some work for the Office of the First Presidency. When she was first interviewed by President Tanner for the post of secretary, she was told that he desired to have a friendly atmosphere in his office so that "everyone who came in . . . felt better when they left than when they came in."² She pictured him sitting at his desk thinking, as an appointment would arrive, "Now what can I do or say to make this person feel better?" This consideration has extended to employees. He is always courteous and forgiving. "There is nothing dictatorial about anything he does. He is a firm believer in the idea that it's *how* a thing is done that matters."

President Tanner likes his correspondence to be taken care of promptly. He dictates by means of the Nyematic system, so that at home he can dial a number on the telephone and his dictation will enter the tape in the office. At the office he can sit at his desk and dictate while a secretary sits at her desk and types as the message comes through. He has always labored strenuously on conference talks, usually dictating many drafts. "I have seen him many times in general conference, even, with a completed talk, and he would be sitting there ready to give it and still going over it, making changes just before delivering it," said Sister Sneff.

An astute observer, Sister Sneff described President Tanner as a financial genius, although, she noted, he does not like to be known as such. She also viewed him as a great "people" man. With pride, she added, "It isn't everyone who gets a dinosaur named after him!" This, after Dr. James Jensen of BYU discovered a new species and named it "Torvosaurus Tanneri."

Some have felt that President Tanner's public image is stern. Sister Sneff says, "He is very misunderstood in that regard. I have people tell me all the time that they are almost afraid of him, and yet if they spend just a few minutes in his presence, they feel at ease." On occasion she has told him frankly, "People have told me that you should try to smile a little more while you are giving your talks." The counselor in the Presidency replies wryly, "I'm not going to stand up there and grin like a Cheshire cat. This is serious business we are engaged in."

President Tanner's daughter Ruth commented in an address at Brigham Young University in June 1980, "My father has often had the reputation of not smiling very much. . . . Yet, he did have a good sense of humor and didn't take himself too seriously. . . . Many times people would say to him, 'How do you accomplish so much? How do you do so many things?' He usually replied, 'Not very well.'"[3]

Ernest C. Manning, former premier of Alberta, finds Eldon Tanner's influence to stem from a keen analytical mind, capable of penetrating complicated issues and reducing the central issue or issues to the essentials. In government, when the basic elements were made apparent, Eldon's judgment, whether on personal, financial, or other policy issues, "was unerringly good," said Mr. Manning of his former colleague.[4]

Such qualities have been increasingly visible during Eldon Tanner's service as Church leader and member of the First Presidency. President Kimball, in an address to General Authorities, Church officers, and Regional Representatives, said, in effect, "My first counselor is a man of few words. But when he speaks, one had better listen." He then commended similar depth of thought and economy of language as the desirable model for all Church officials.

The quality and quantity of administrative talent developed by N. Eldon Tanner, if given to an individual of ordinary (not to mention excess) ambition and coupled with a Machiavellian front of piety, could take advantage of most leaders in most councils. But the disciplined restraints Eldon learned from boyhood, his sense of being trusted and dependable, combined with a stern but quiet acceptance of his accountability to his Maker, have always assured those to whom he has been responsible that he would never let personal considerations enter into the equation. Members of the Twelve at Church headquarters might on occasion, when advising staff members, say, "You (or we) had better take this up with President Tanner." Such a remark has always been made with the knowledge that (1) the matter fell properly within his realm of responsibility; (2) the judgment, advice, or counsel that was needed warranted his attention; and (3) if there was the slightest scintilla that the matter required consideration of the First Presidency, it would be so referred. Furthermore, if it was so referred, the party or parties involved would be invited to be present when the matter was to be considered, to clarify any further questions of fact.

Eldon Tanner, a quiet man, has never sought the limelight—and he has never backed away from making a decision when he has had the responsibility. Sister Sneff has said, "His efficiency and ability to handle with dispatch those matters needing his attention always amaze me." Keenly perceptive, President Tanner is known as a gracious man, moderate in his outlook. Elder A. Theodore Tuttle of the First Quorum of the Seventy once remarked after he left President Tanner's office, "That man is as common as an old shoe, and noble as a prince."

Dr. McCown E. Hunt, a non-LDS friend, recalls one occasion when, as chairman of the Salt Lake County Salt Palace Board, he was discussing a matter with President Tanner. Dr. Hunt persisted in addressing him as "President Tanner" throughout the conference. Suddenly the member of the First Presidency, who was so active in making Church property available for the Salt Palace, said, "Ed, we're getting too old for this sort of thing, titles and all that. Please, just call me Eldon."[5]

Eldon Tanner has always been a man of activity as well as thought, and his diary continually shows how many human contacts he has daily had during his busy years of involvement in government, industry, the community, and the Church. Able to dispatch a large amount of correspondence and to see numbers of important people in a day, he has still found the time to make a phone call to an acquaintance or to visit someone in the hospital.

In February 1972, in a talk at a leadership banquet in one of the Salt Lake stakes, he outlined his personal goals and methods. He emphasized four points: (1) anything that is worth doing is worth doing well; (2) one must always keep one's name good; (3) one must always be dependable; and (4) one must always seek first the kingdom of God. Dating back to lessons learned from his father, these have been the guiding principles of Eldon Tanner's life. Corollaries are found in his diaries. For example, he believes that projects should pay for themselves. When someone would come and invite his own or Church investment of time or resources, he always wanted to know if the project would pay for itself. He realizes that debt is necessary for business ventures, but one must not rush too quickly to borrow.

President Tanner has also felt that the Church as an institution should not be involved in politics. He advised Sunday School general board members against endorsing a candidate for mayor of Salt Lake City. He advised a stake president not to use his Church position to support any politicial candidate or party. He once declined to offer the invocation at the Republican State Convention because he did not want to favor any political party. In fact, it is difficult to ascertain his U.S. political leanings, and impossible to know how he has voted, from the entries in his diary. He has simply chosen not to record that type of information. Personal involvement as an obligation of citizenship is something else. He was evidently pleased when George Romney, who served as U.S. Secretary of Housing and Urban Development (1969-73), told him that he was going to resign from President Richard M. Nixon's cabinet and organize a bipartisan group to inform people about politics.

Another principle President Tanner has emphasized is support for authority. When a friend came to him and said he was having trouble with his bishop, President Tanner told him he should humble himself and work it out with his bishop. He once told a woman to refrain from criticizing her local authorities. When there were problems in a Church-owned company, he encouraged the employees to support and help the president of the company.

In 1981 an analytical psychologist of the University of Chicago faculty, Professor Suzanne C. Kasabor, completed a survey of stress experienced in the legal profession by Utah lawyers. She outlined three major elements helpful to an individual in successfully surmounting pressures: (1) commitment to one's values, (2) control of one's responses, and (3) challenge to respond successfully to the situation or situations.

N. Eldon Tanner has absorbed a lot of stress in his more than eight decades. Instead of diminishing, that stress has continued to accelerate in his later years. But his *commitment* to follow the Master's injunction, "Seek ye first the kingdom of God" (Matthew 6:33), has been for him not only a goal encasing a set of values, but also an overriding source of inner peace, strength, and security. His *control* of himself and his personal environment, despite calendar demands, dimming eyesight, and Parkinson's disease, has been manifest hourly. His *challenges* may often have been to learn patience in such a context, to listen long, hear much, assess the facts, then speak little but act wisely. A constantly recurring phrase heard in his uttered prayers or statements of hopeful concern, seeking guidance as a general Church leader, has been "We pray that our labors may be acceptable to Thee." His daughter Helen has said, "His life is like a testimony reaffirming that the Church is true."[6] Always there have been heard from this disciple of the Savior, this special witness, these words, spoken softly as if uttered in reminder to himself:

"This is the Church of Jesus Christ."

Footnotes

[1]Letter of Russell M. Nelson to G. Homer Durham, July 10, 1981.
[2]LaRue Sneff, interview with Gordon Irving, 1981. James Moyle Oral History Program, Church Archives.
[3]Walker, "My Father."
[4]Letter of Ernest C. Manning to G. Homer Durham, May 29, 1981.
[5]McCown E. "Ed" Hunt, conference with G. Homer Durham, August 4, 1981.
[6]Beaton, "My Father: N. Eldon Tanner."

Appendix I

"Nathan Eldon Tanner"*
by McCown E. Hunt, Ph.D.

My first knowledge of Nathan Eldon Tanner occurred in January of 1943. I was at that time a major in the Corps of Engineers assigned as chief of operations and construction in the Dawson Creek, Canada, district. This office had responsibility for the construction of the lower half of the Alaskan Highway. We were also concerned with forwarding supplies and personnel for Canol, the related oil procurement project of the Northwest Division of the Corps of Engineers.

Mr. Stewart McRae, an officer of Imperial Oil Limited, was assigned as special representative to the Alaskan Highway Division and as such, stayed with my unit for some weeks. During this period, we had numerous discussions on the oil production potential of Canada and Alaska. He mentioned a number of times the name of Nathan E. Tanner, a member of the provincial government who had very far-reaching and progressive ideas with respect to the development of oil and other natural resources of western Canada.

My next information with respect to President Tanner occurred around 1959. I was interested in the legal concept of libel and had been referred to a book, then current, about a famous libel trial in New York. During the course of the trial, the question was posed as to the relative truthfulness of the average individual. It was asked if anyone could cite an individual of perfect probity. The name of Bishop Nathan E. Tanner of western Canada was put forth on the court records as such an individual.

---

*This essay by Dr. McCown E. Hunt, former chairman of the Salt Palace complex in Salt Lake City, is included as an appendix to illustrate, from an informed and non-Church point of view, further insight into the civic activities and personal influence of N. Eldon Tanner.

From 1959 to 1962, the groundwork was being done to obtain a civic auditorium for Salt Lake County. President David O. McKay was a strong backer of this project, and in 1963, he asked President Tanner to do anything he felt necessary to make this project a success. My personal acquaintance with President Tanner began at this time.

The site selection committee of the Salt Lake County Civic Auditorium board of directors had presented four potential sites to the board for final selection. One of these sites was the one on which the Salt Palace now stands. The County Commission finally chose this site over much opposition from different segments of the community. One of the objections was related to the fact that The Church of Jesus Christ of Latter-day Saints owned approximately seven acres of the property concerned.

The LDS Church had been considering the construction of a large assembly hall for use during conferences and other events, but had put aside these plans to support the Salt Palace. Many LDS Church members felt that the Church should not dispose of this valuable property and also should have its own assembly hall. Many outside the Church felt that the acquisition of the property would be an excessive expense to the public treasury.

Negotiations were begun with the LDS Church through President Tanner. His primary concern from the first was the overall well-being of the community, but he also recognized the need of the growing church for a larger meeting place. The agreement as finally made showed President Tanner's concern for the community and his ability to solve problems. It was agreed that the Church would lease the land to the county and in turn the county would allow the Church to use the facility for up to twenty-four days a year for different events. The county could acquire the property at any time, under several different options, and deduct the time the Church had used the property from the purchase price. This agreement allowed the county to spend at least $3.5 million more on capital facilities than would have been possible if they bought the property.

The civic auditorium concept had been attacked from many quarters, by some of Utah's most prominent public officials and business executives. They stated it would be a "white elephant" and a major burden on the community. President Tanner, however, felt just the opposite. He foresaw the civic auditorium as the catalyst for downtown Salt Lake development. As early as 1964, he visualized the major changes needed to rehabilitate the city, and felt that a change in the area west of West Temple and south of South Temple was the key to further development of the entire city. He later advised that the success of the Salt Palace project was a spur to the building of the ZCMI Center and the subsequent building spurt of office and hotel buildings.

Throughout the development phase of the Salt Palace, when it was being sold to the community, President Tanner constantly used his influence to counteract attacks on the project from all quarters and continually reaffirmed his own belief that it would be a success. His own extremely successful business and political record carried great weight during this time, and the great respect all segments of the community had for his personal integrity more than counterbalanced the opposition to the project.

Subsequent to the construction of the Salt Palace, there was a great spurt of general construction in Salt Lake City, which included offices and hotel buildings. After a time, opposition to a certain amount of this construction arose both within and outside the LDS Church. The general theme of the opposition was that too many offices and hotels were being built, and low occupancy rates would cause extreme competition and loss of money to all.

President Tanner stated that because of Utah's stable work force and general quality of living, it was attracting the head offices and plants of major business firms. Their auxiliary enterprises and spin-off expenditures would generate a need for this additional office and hotel space. Since President Tanner was a key factor in the attraction of these businesses, his knowledge of the plans of these companies has proven him correct about the need for the additional buildings. He also advised that no legal concept existed to prevent anyone from building and that the market automatically took care of unsuccessful enterprises.

An interesting aside to the construction of the civic auditorium occurred at the time bids were taken for its construction. The bids received were over $5 million more than the funds immediately available for construction. After consultation with public and private individuals and agencies, the Salt Lake County Commission and civic auditorium board of directors decided to proceed with the construction, with the additional funds to come from the county's capital improvement funds as they accumulated.

Mayor J. Bracken Lee and his assistant Jennings Phillips, Jr., both of whom had strongly opposed the civic auditorium, immediately entered suit to prevent the county from proceeding with the project on the ground that a municipality could not obligate itself in this case for other than available funds. A judge was brought from central Utah to try the case, and he ruled for the mayor.

After a study of the plans and interviewing as many interested groups as possible, the civic auditorium board of directors decided to eliminate the concert hall and retain the arena and exhibit hall. This was done strictly on the basis of economics. The arena and exhibit hall would make money, while the concert hall would consume money.

Prior to this time, the conductor of the Utah Symphony, Maurice Abravanel, had shown little apparent interest in the civic auditorium. Although he had been invited to meet with the board of directors to discuss the concert hall, he had not taken the occasion to do so and seemed uninterested in the specifics of the project. He did meet with the architects, but not often. However, when it was announced that construction of the concert hall must be postponed, Maestro Abravanel immediately announced he would force the board of directors and the county to build the concert hall instead of the arena. He was assured that every effort would be made to add the concert hall to the complex as soon as possible, but he stated that it had to be done now.

The history of the arts shows that the artistic type of performer has a major attraction for mature ladies. Symphony conductors are certainly not among the least attractive of artists, and Mr. Abravanel was able to arouse a major disturbance in certain influential circles. The opponents of the civic auditorium joined the outcry, and for a time it appeared that the existence of the civic auditorium itself was threatened.

One of the major reasons for construction of a concert hall was to give the symphony a permanent home, thus relieving the Salt Lake Tabernacle of a periodic use that had become more difficult to schedule as the LDS Church increased in numbers. The Tabernacle was needed for Church functions at many times when the symphony was scheduled, and the Church frequently subjugated its own needs to the symphony's.

In this case, although it would appear to be in the interest of the LDS Church to have the concert hall built, President Tanner met with Mr. Abravanel and symphony board personnel and assured them they could continue to use the Tabernacle. He also assured them that he would make every effort to obtain the promised concert hall as soon as possible. The heads of the news agencies also informed Mr. Abravanel that economic factors must be considered and that they would also support efforts in the near future to obtain a concert hall.

This occasion arose in 1972. Preparations were being made for the bicentennial celebration of the American Revolution of 1776. An interim organizing committee for this event was appointed by Governor Calvin L. Rampton, with Obert C. Tanner designated as chairman. Mr. Tanner and the committee's interim executive director, Oakley S.

Evans, met with President Tanner for advice on planning their organization and goals.

Since one of the bicentennial committee's major goals was the establishment of an art center, including a concert hall, President Tanner advised them to meet with the directors of the Salt Palace for mutual assistance in meeting this goal. The committee was furnished office and meeting space in the Salt Palace as well as secretarial assistance. After appropriate legislation was passed and the permanent Utah American Revolution Bicentennial Commission was appointed in 1973, much of the necessary preliminary work had been done, and it was comparatively easy to establish that the major goal of the commission was the Bicentennial Center for the Arts.

As is usually the case, there was some opposition to this project, based on the need for a bond issue and the feeling in other parts of the state that Salt Lake County was unjustly receiving too large a share of bicentennial money. Again President Tanner alleviated the opposition of many of these groups.

An additional problem was the parking situation. One of the major sources of revenue of the Salt Palace was and is parking fees. If a concert hall and art center were built on the north parking lot of the Salt Palace, a major source of parking revenue would be eliminated.

President Tanner again was instrumental in overcoming this obstacle. The LDS Church owned property immediately west of the Salt Palace at South Temple and Second West. President Tanner recommended that this area also be leased to Salt Lake County at one dollar per year to replace the parking area to be covered by the concert hall and art center. This action was taken, and another desirable group of public facilities was constructed with President Tanner's able assistance.

President Tanner's guiding philosophy can probably be best summed up by thinking of the philosophy expressed in the poem "Abou Ben Adhem." He truly loves his fellowman. He, however, is no visionary. He believes that you must take action to better yourself and your fellowman, and his entire life is an illustrated lesson of this fact. Salt Lake City and the state of Utah have blossomed through the kindness of his heart, his spiritual perception, and his strong mental and physical drive.

Appendix II

"Tannerisms"*

"One of the bad things about a build-up is trying to live up to it."

"We are fishers of men, so we must make sure we have the right tackle."

"We can't be judged by how we feel, but how we act."

"Let children honor their parents, and let parents be worthy of that honor."

"The things that discourage Satan most are testimony and prayer."

"Rivet your mind to the task at hand."

"There is no greater power in all the world than a missionary of the Church of Jesus Christ holding the priesthood who is prepared and will go out and bear his testimony."

"The most important part of this missionary program is to love one another."

"Elder: 'If the Lord's willing, we'll have four baptisms.' President Tanner: 'Don't worry, son, the Lord's willing.'"

"If you want your dreams to come true, wake up."

---

*Excerpted from "Tannerisms," teachings of President N. Eldon Tanner in the West European Mission, compiled by missionaries in the Northeast British Mission, Grant S. Thorn, president, 1962-65, and edited by Doris D. Smith. Copy in Church Library, lithograph.

312

"It isn't the mountain that is hard to climb; it is the sand that gets into your shoes."

"Discipline—to progress, to become what you want to be, and to serve the Lord the way you should—requires that you discipline yourself constantly, discipline yourself while in your youth so that it will become a habit that will sustain you in later years."

"Think big and never underestimate yourself."

"Repentance is changing your ways."

"Every problem is another step upwards. It is a privilege and opportunity to overcome these problems and move upward."

"Do what you have at hand, realizing that it is the thing which will bring you happiness and success in the future."

"It isn't what you say; it's the spirit of it that counts."

"If you want to be happy, do what the Lord asks you to do."

"Prepare yourself to dwell with God."

"The people who object to rules are people who don't obey the rules."

"Thinking big is thinking about that which is important."

"The boiling point is 212, not just 208, or even 211 degrees."

"We need to be prepared or we can't get the job done. When you get a fish on the hook, it's usually your fault if you lose him."

"You should take home the very best person your suit will hold."

"It is not the easy things that build us."

"We're not honest when we waste our time, knowing our parents are sacrificing to send us on our missions."

"Don't depreciate yourself. The Lord will make you equal to your calling, no matter who you are, if you will put yourself in His hands."

"How can missionaries bear testimonies of Christ and then go out and do nothing about it?"

"If you want to be a leader, just lead."

"When we teach Christ and Him crucified, we should stop and think what that implies."

"How many of you would be willing to let others go and speak in your name? That is what Christ has allowed us to do."

"We have the spark of divinity that enables us to reach unlimitable heights."

"If you grow an inch a day, you grow 730 inches a mission—spiritual growth."

"Your children at best are only investigators, so live your lives in order that they may be converted."

"You cannot live right and think wrong, any more than you can plant weeds and harvest grain."

"As leaders you must begin where you are, use what you have, and start the journey."

"Some of us ask for big blessings but never take anything to receive those blessings in."

"The greatest thing that stops the Lord's work is our fear of what other people think."

"Concentration—be always conscious and aware of the job at hand."

"Think yourself into success."

"The Lord said he would make you a fisher of men. Take him at his word and fish for men."

"When we are in tune with the Lord, we have great spiritual experiences."

"Young man, the world is divided into two groups—you and the rest of the world; and of the two, you are the most important because it is you who works out your salvation, your exaltation, and your eternal life."

"Teach with enthusiasm."

"Walk humbly but with conviction."

Appendix II: "Tannerisms"

"If you follow the authorities' advice in the Church, you will never go wrong."

"Overcome fear by doing what you are afraid to do."

"If you want to win, you've got to work."

"Those doing their duty are enjoying their work; those not doing their duty criticize."

"Discouragement and fear are tools of the devil."

"Learn how to give up as much as you take."

"In the judgment you'll be you—a product of everything you have done and thought."

"Keep the pledges you make with yourself."

"It's the plan of salvation that will bring peace to the world."

"It's a great honor to be a missionary. Don't shirk!"

"Be where you should be doing what you should be doing."

"Live the standards you are teaching."

"The price of possession is the discipline of preparation."

"Don't worry about finding the perfect wife or husband. Make yourself perfect for the wife or husband you do find."

"It doesn't matter which one of you is right—the important thing is to do that which is right."

"Determination—your guide to success. Set goals for yourself, and through determination strive to reach those goals."

"If I'm close to the Lord, he's always there to help me."

"Have you ever seen a tomorrow? Today's the only day you have to work with."

"Ask the Lord to lead you today, and tell Him you will report to Him tonight."

"I've never seen a full tithe payer criticize how the tithes are used."

"There is no disciplinarian in the world like work."

"If I were to meet you at your digs at 6:00 A.M., would you be up?"

"Prepare yourself, and the Lord will tell you where to cast your net."

"The blessings we get are greater than the services we give."

"Don't embarrass the Lord."

"It's better to understand a little than to misunderstand a lot."

"Let's quit blocking the Lord's progress."

"Don't preach sermons—live them."

"Look back from ahead, not back from behind."

"Be loyal to each other—but not to dishonor."

"You are the most important thing in the world."

"Have a good opinion of yourself, but have a reason for it."

"Your children are deserving of the best father or mother possible. You're preparing for it now."

"When you bear testimony that you know that Jesus is the Christ, that the gospel's true, then if you don't go out and do something about it and don't put yourself into the work, you're dishonest."

"Remember who you are wherever you are."

"We're facing the same situation today in the world with anti-christs as we did with Satan in the preexistence."

"It is no handicap to meet trouble."

"I would rather follow the prophet blindly than my own judgment without the prophet."

"Our goal should be the highest degree of the celestial kingdom. Every problem is a challenge, and when it is overcome we are one step higher."

"We are not happy when we are not doing what we are supposed to do."

"Obtain knowledge, and the Lord will guide your thoughts."

"Be the kind of missionary everyone expects."

"Keep close to God, and nothing will hurt you."

"Every person baptized should be converted as well."

"Be unselfish. Do not work for credit."

"A man can't be successful unless he follows the rules."

"The definition of sacrifice is giving up something that you are doing or that you would like to do for something that is more important."

"If you lose yourself in the work, you'll be successful all your life."

"Some people have to make a decision on the same thing three or four different times."

"The glory of the present is to make the future free."

"It's better to aim at the moon and miss it than to aim at nothing and hit it, but while you are aiming, don't forget to pull the trigger."

"People place too much emphasis on the nonessentials of life."

"There is this that is good about looking at things with a critical eye, and that's to look into the mirror and improve yourself."

Gems of Thought*
By President N. Eldon Tanner

Belief in God

Many who argue that Christianity has failed excuse themselves for their actions by saying that men who profess God and Jesus Christ are hypocrites and do not live the teachings that they profess. Too often men waste their time questioning even the existence of God instead of accepting his teachings and enjoying his blessings. It is something like those who try to prove Shakespeare never lived, that he was not the author of the Shakespearian plays, some of the choicest of all literature. While they waste their time arguing, others are enjoying the beauty and philosophy of his works. (139.)

Some years ago, while traveling with Lord Rowallan, Chief Scout of the British Commonwealth, I was thrilled with his comment as he led in the Scout promise. As he said, "On my honor I promise to do my duty to God," he stopped and said to the Scouters who were present, "As I make this promise I think of a God who can hear and answer prayers, who is interested in what we are doing, and who will guide us and bless us according to our needs and our faith." And then he said, "If any of you do not believe in such a God, you can serve better someplace else." (210-11.)

---

*Excerpted from N. Eldon Tanner, *Seek Ye First the Kingdom of God,* comp. LaRue Sneff (Salt Lake City: Deseret Book, 1973). Page references are indicated following each excerpt.

The Power of Prayer

I often wonder if we really realize the power of prayer, if we appreciate what a great blessing it is to be able to call on our Father in heaven in humble prayer, knowing that he is interested in us and that he wants us to succeed. (154.)

We must not be misled by the doctrines of men. All the studies of science and philosophy will never answer the question: "What is man and why is he here?" But it is answered clearly and simply in the gospel of Jesus Christ, and we are instructed: "If any of you lack wisdom, let him ask of God. . . ." (157-58.)

We are as astronauts, sent out by God to fill our missions here upon the earth. He wants us to succeed. He stands ready to answer our prayers and assures us a safe landing as we return if we will but keep in touch with him through prayer and do as we are bid. (158-59.)

Men pray for different reasons. Many are driven to their knees out of fear, and then only do they pray. Others go to the Lord when in dire need of immediate direction for which they know of no other place to go. Nations are called by their governments in case of a national tragedy, drought, or plague, famine or war, to call upon God for his blessings, for his protection, and for his direction. Some people ask to be healed, others to be strengthened. They ask for the blessings of the Lord to attend their families, their loved ones, and themselves in all their righteous endeavors. This, I am sure, is all good in the sight of the Lord. It is most important, however, that we take time to express our gratitude to our Father in heaven for the many blessings we receive. (159.)

When we pray, it is important that we set about to do all in our power to make it possible for the Lord to answer our prayers. As my father said to me when I was just a boy, "My son, if you want your prayers to be answered, you must get on your feet and do your part." (160-61.)

I have never found it embarrassing to kneel down and pray in the presence of other men. More than once I have seen men kneel down when I knelt down, or when I got up, I have found them kneeling down offering prayer. I am sure that every man, wherever he may be, though he doesn't pray regularly, would, if he found himself in very great danger or emergency, be glad to call upon God. We need not apologize for being one who calls on the Lord and knows he stands ready to answer our prayers. (225.)

Revelation

Without modern revelation the world would be left in complete darkness regarding, first, the Book of Mormon, which is a new witness for Christ and contains the gospel in its fulness; second, the purpose and importance of temple work; third, vicarious work for the dead; and many other things pertaining to the kingdom of God. (134-35.)

Prophets: A Blessing from the Lord

Our Heavenly Father, knowing our weaknesses and our need for constant direction, sends us prophets to continually teach us and keep us reminded of this plan of life and salvation. Our salvation, and that of our loved ones, depends upon our listening to and heeding the words of the prophets, realizing that we must believe all that God has revealed, all that he does now reveal, and that he will yet reveal many great and important things pertaining to the kingdom of God. (171.)

As we look back over the history of God's dealings with his people and read the revelations that he gave to his prophets to guide and direct them and prepare them for the future, we cannot help marveling at the continued interest he has shown in his people and the patience he has shown and the care that he has taken to see that they were continually directed in the paths of truth and righteousness, if they would but listen to his holy prophet through whom he was speaking. (129-30.)

Joseph Smith the Prophet

No greater man other than Jesus Christ himself has ever lived upon this earth or contributed more to man's welfare and the spiritual side of life, and whose influence has been and will be felt throughout the world, than Joseph Smith the Prophet. (243.)

Now I have a very close, tender feeling about the Prophet Joseph Smith. You know, he lived in this dispensation. He isn't somebody who lived in an earlier dispensation. His influence has been felt in my family ever since the Church was organized. (243-44.)

To me, the story of Joseph Smith and the restoration of the gospel is the greatest story of modern times. If the world knew these truths and would accept them, then the purpose of Christ's mission would be fulfilled, because he said, ". . . this is my work and my glory—to bring to pass the immortality and eternal life of man." (Moses 1:39.) And through our prophet today the Lord has asked us each to be a missionary to help the world realize that this is the gospel of Jesus Christ, the plan of life and salvation, which, if accepted, will bring peace to the world, joy to mankind, and make it possible for us to enjoy immortality and eternal life. (252-53.)

The Priesthood

I am always thrilled and inspired when I meet with the priesthood of The Church of Jesus Christ of Latter-day Saints, which is the priesthood of God. I often feel to ask the question: Do you really believe and appreciate the fact that the priesthood is the power of God, delegated to you to act in his name in the things which you are directed to do when you are ordained to the priesthood you hold and the office therein? If we did nothing more than answer that question and renew our determination to keep the covenants we make when we are ordained to the priesthood and let our lives be lives of example to our children, to one another, and to the world, our gathering would be very, very profitable indeed. (174.)

You cannot realize and appreciate the influence of the priesthood in this church could have on the whole world if every man would magnify his priesthood. Brethren, the priesthood, if magnified, is a stabilizing influence and strength. It should be. Every wife and mother has a perfect right and responsibility to look to her husband who holds the priesthood for guidance, for strength, and for direction. And he has the responsibility of magnifying his priesthood so he might be able to give this direction, this security, this strength that is needed in the home. And he can do this. If he will magnify his priesthood, he will be magnified by the Lord in the eyes of his family, and his influence will be felt for good.

Boys, we have a responsibility to our sisters. Every sister should look to a brother who holds the priesthood, whether he is twelve years of age or older, and she has a right to expect in him a living example of what the priesthood should be, and to look to him for strength and counsel and direction and to feel safe with him. Every sweetheart should be able to feel he would do anything, even to the giving of his life, to protect her womanhood and her virtue, and would never think of depriving her of it, if he is magnifying his priesthood; and he will not be tempted if he is thinking of the priesthood that he holds and responsibility that he has. (177.)

321

Value of the Scriptures

We learn from the teachings as recorded in the Book of Mormon, the Doctrine and Covenants, and the Pearl of Great Price about man's relationship to God, our preexistence, the council in heaven when every one of us was there and in which all of us took part. All of us voted for Jesus Christ as the leader. This knowledge is available to the world only through the revelations of Joseph Smith. We are taught about the resurrection. Read Alma in the Book of Mormon and learn about the resurrection. No other place in the world do we find such clear teachings of this important event, nor does the world understand it as we understand it as a result of these teachings.

We are taught also how we can work for our dead, thereby making available the blessings of the gospel to millions of our ancestors who died without a knowledge of it. We have the principle of celestial marriage and eternal progression. What a wonderful thing it is to know that I can be sealed to my wife for time and all eternity, and she to me, and that we can carry on as a family unit throughout eternity and continue in eternal progression. (250-51.)

In spite of all of the opposition they [Joseph Smith and Oliver Cowdery] received, the Book of Mormon was translated in just a little over two years. No one has been able to prove it wrong. The Book of Mormon is not in conflict in any way with the Bible, but is a new witness for Christ. The Jewish people—those who accept the Bible—accept the Old Testament as the word of God. The Catholics and the Protestants accept the Old Testament and the New Testament as the word of God. The Latter-day Saints accept the Old Testament and the New Testament as the word of God as literally as, if not more so than, any other church, but they also accept the Book of Mormon as the word of God, the gospel in its fullness as taught by Jesus Christ on the American continent. And all those who have tried to prove the Book of Mormon wrong—its religious teachings or its history—have failed to do so. (248.)

Immortality

We mortals have never experienced death and the resurrection, nor do we remember our preexistence. Therefore, it is not commonly believed or understood that we had a premortal existence, that we are the spirit children of God, the Eternal Father, and that when we have finished our life here upon the earth we will enjoy a literal resurrection and may continue on in eternal progression. (165.)

I appeal to each member of the Church to ask himself: Where am I? Am I ashamed so that I want to hide, or am I where I should be, doing what I should be doing, and preparing to meet God? Let each of us determine to humble ourselves and repent, and prove ourselves worthy of the great promise that those who keep their second estate shall have glory added upon their heads forever and ever. (153.)

Personal Testimony of N. Eldon Tanner

To our young people today I should like to bear my own personal testimony that by the power of the Holy Ghost I know as I know I live that God lives; that Jesus is the Christ, the Redeemer of the world; that he came and dwelt among men; that he willingly gave his life for you and me; that he was literally resurrected; that he and God the Eternal Father did actually appear to Joseph Smith in answer to his prayer; that Joseph Smith and all who have succeeded him as President of the Church are indeed prophets of God.

If people throughout the world would accept Jesus Christ as the Son of God and keep his commandments, there would be no more war, but peace and good will would reign in the world, and we would be assured of immortality and eternal life. (30-31.)

Let us never be ashamed of the gospel of Jesus Christ, for it is the power of God unto salvation (see Romans 1:16), and let us never hesitate to call upon the Lord. Let us be obedient to the Lord; let us be obedient to the priesthood. Let us magnify our callings so that they can magnify us. Let us not cheat as we go along and try to do it halfway, or serve in our way; but let us serve in his. (5.)

Freedom of Choice

One of God's greatest gifts to man is freedom of choice. At an early period in the journey through life, man finds himself at a crossroad where he must choose one of two great highways—the right, leading to progress and happiness; and the wrong, leading to retardation and sorrow. There exists this eternal law that each human soul, through the choices he makes, will shape his own destiny. Our success or failure, peace or discontent, happiness or misery, depends on the choices we make each day. (83.)

Self-discipline is essential in helping us make proper choices. It is much easier to drift than to row, to slide downhill than to climb up. Satan is constantly at work to drag us down by placing temptations in our way in the form of alcohol, tobacco, drugs, pornography, deceit, dishonesty, and flattery, always waiting to catch us in our misdeeds. (86.)

People who argue that they have constitutional rights and want to use what they call their free agency to accomplish unrighteous ends abuse the idea of free agency and deprive others of their constitutional rights. While many of our problems are caused by those who are deliberately trying to further their own selfish and devilish interests, there is also a vocal, misled minority which is responsible for other problems as they exist in our country and in our communities. We must be equally vocal and firm in our efforts to maintain the quality of our surroundings, where we can enjoy family solidarity, which is the strength of any nation. We must take a firm stand against the concerted efforts in many areas to destroy the family unit. (89.)

Free agency is the prime purpose of man's mortal existence, for it affords him the opportunity to choose between good and evil, virtue and vice, life and death. Imagine our state of existence if we should lose the right to choose. Today, however, we are being threatened with the loss of this most precious gift. In fact, as a result of their lack of appreciation and understanding of the value of free agency, many people in countries that are dominated by dictators have practically lost their freedom. At all costs, we must maintain our free agency—the right to choose. (93-94.)

We are all concerned about conditions in the world today, and are searching for answers to the many problems that are affecting our personal lives, our communities, and countries throughout the world. Though it is true that the trend in the world today is toward lawlessness, rioting, and rebellion, we are sick and tired of having it played up so much both in conversation and in news media. We, with our positive approach, need to center our efforts on living and teaching the gospel, thereby eliminating the cause and improving conditions. Every man, including the rebellious, who is honest with himself must admit that what he is ultimately seeking is happiness and a better way of life.

Recently I was talking to a young man who said, in effect, "I am fed up and tired of being told, 'You *have* to do this,' or 'You *have* to do that.' I want to be free to decide for myself what I want to do."

My response was: "You *are* free to choose *exactly* what you want to do, as long as it does not restrict or impose on the rights or liberties of others, but you must be responsible for your acts and prepared to take the consequences." (116.)

Guarding Against Social Evils

It is trite but true to say that never before in the history of the world have we or our young people been faced with more evil, serious problems, and challenges than we are today. Wherever we go, and regardless of whatever news media we pick up or listen to, or whatever company we may be in, we hear discussed and have forced upon our minds the importance of such questions as divorce and family disintegration, new morality, new freedom, new security, the "God is dead" theory, war and strife, murders, riots, burglaries, and all kinds of crime and deception.

It is most important that we be acquainted with the evils of the day and realize how insidious they are and accept our responsibility to guard against them. We should realize that the new morality is nothing more than the old immorality, that the new freedom is nothing more than disrespect for law and the rights of others and will lead to anarchy. The new security gives one the idea that the world owes him a living; it destroys individual initiative and infringes on his liberty and freedom.

I am convinced that the only way to guard successfully against these evils is to accept the gospel of Jesus Christ, which offers not only a better way of life but the solution to these and all other problems facing us today. (136.)

If we are to stop the onslaught of immorality, divorce and family disintegration, lawlessness, strife, riots, burglaries, murders, crime, and deception, we must not ask what are *they* doing about it. We must ask and answer the question, "What am *I* doing?" Let us examine ourselves, acknowledge our faults, and repent where we should. (142.)

How can we combat the evil that surrounds us and which is so prevalent in the world today? Satan is trying harder than ever before to claim souls for his own domain. We must and we can thwart him, but only by choosing to follow the teachings of Jesus Christ and making our influence an active and positive force. As leaders, as parents, as teachers, and as neighbors, all good people everywhere who are striving for liberty and freedom, peace, success, happiness, and for eternal life with our Father in heaven must by example and precept be actively engaged in fighting against those forces which are threatening us and endangering our well-being and that of our children. (86.)

Is there danger that our whole civilization is like white-washed tombs? We have marvelous machines, towering buildings, and thousands of signs of what we call progress; but within we have unrest, strife between men and nations, and unrelieved burden of the poor, and the dead men's bones of wholesale wars. Someone has said: "Still we try to safeguard ourselves by calcimining the tomb."

With all the crime, changing of population from rural to urban, loosened morals, pornographic movies and literature, etc., we must stand firm in the cause of right. How can persons for selfish reasons be hypocrites enough to urge the opening or widening of the liquor laws when they know that where consumption of liquor is greatly increased, there is a similar increase in multitudes of social problems?

How can a newspaper which records the highway accidents, the deaths, the health problems, and broken homes as a result of drinking advocate making liquor more easily available in order to attract more tourists and industry? The cost to communities and individuals far outweighs any benefits. (65-66.)

To meet the serious issues facing us in our respective communities today, we must be examples of virtue and righteousness ourselves and choose today to take our stand on the moral issues which threaten us. We do not want our civilization to decay and fall because we failed to keep it on a high spiritual plane and allowed it to sink to the level where the animal instincts and passions dominate. (87-88.)

All the laws of God and the laws of nature and the laws of the land are made for the benefit of man, for his comfort, enjoyment, safety, and well-being; and it is up to the individual to learn these laws and to determine whether or not he will enjoy these benefits by obeying the law and by keeping the commandments. Laws do exist for our benefit, and to be successful and happy, we must obey the laws and regulations pertaining to our activities; and these laws will function either to our joy and well-being or to our detriment and sorrow, according to our actions. (117-18.)

Evils of Alcohol, Drugs, and Tobacco

It is an established fact that much sex delinquency begins when one is under the influence of alcohol. Also, alcohol is the cause of more broken homes, frustrated and disappointed children, warped personalities, and dulling of minds than any other single cause. No one needs to question the inspiration of the instruction "wine or strong drink is not good." (D&C 89:5.)

In a similar way, mounting pressure continues to pile up against the use of tobacco. At first, isolated studies linked cigarette smoking with an increased risk of death from lung cancer. Then in 1962 the British Royal College of Physicians reported that some 500 Britons were dying each week from lung cancer and that 80 percent of these deaths were caused by cigarettes.

Besides being connected with lung cancer and pulmonary diseases, tobacco is also associated with deaths from peptic ulcers, stroke, and cancer of the larynx, mouth, pharynx, esophagus, and bladder, as well as other diseases. It is reported that each year tobacco is responsible for more than 11 million cases of chronic illness in the United States and 77 million days lost from work.

It is little wonder, then, that the Lord has said, "And again, tobacco is not for the body, neither for the belly, and is not good for man." (D&C 89:8.) (186-87.)

I would like to refer to a story that I have often mentioned about the father who was called to the scene of a car accident in which his young daughter was killed. The group had been drinking, and the father in his anguish exclaimed: "I'll kill the man who provided the whiskey!" On returning home he found a note in his daughter's own handwriting in his liquor cabinet. It read: "Dad, I hope you don't mind our taking your whiskey tonight." (185.)

I am convinced that our youth do not want to be bad. They do not set out to be alcoholics, nor to be drug addicts, nor to suffer and die with cancer of the lungs or some other pulmonary disease.

However, they see people drinking all around them—men and women who are leading citizens. They see it in their homes with no evident ill effects. They see it advertised in all the popular magazines, in the daily press, on every television set, in many movies, and on the billboards; and they hear it over radio. Yes, and these advertisements are shown with well-dressed, healthy-looking, successful businessmen, with big cars and fine offices, with young men and women engaged in all kinds of sports, attending socials where people are standing around with a cigarette in one hand and a glass in the other, all seeming to have a good time.

How can our youth resist without our help? These high-power advertising media never show a man or woman nursing a bad headache the morning after, nor do they show the crumpled cars, the mangled bodies, or the broken homes, or men lying in the gutter. Nor do they show a man facing a doctor who has just told him that he has cancer of the throat or lungs, or patients in a hospital being fed with a tube through the nostril because they cannot swallow.

I am sure that many will say, "Why all this gory stuff?" No, I have omitted much of the gory stuff, the many, many really sad and heartbreaking experiences happening to families every day. We must face the facts; we must do our part. (195.)

On behalf of the First Presidency, and with their approval, I appeal to every member of the Church to keep the Word of Wisdom strictly, and to all responsible citizens to accept their responsibilities, to guard and protect our youth against the evils and designs of conspiring men who are determined by every available means to lead them to destruction. We cannot stand by and let our youth be destroyed because of our neglect. We must lead them not into temptation, but deliver them from evil.

There are those who argue that in the interests of tourism, liquor should be made more easily available. Surely every mother, father, and worthy citizen can see the folly of this and what it would do to our youth. We must not sell our heritage for a mess of pottage. There are better ways to encourage tourists.

I cannot imagine any father or neighbor wanting to contribute in any way to his or his neighbor's boy's becoming an alcoholic in order to get tourists into our area. Example is the greatest of all teachers. In the interests of our youth, I pray that we may all heed the warning of the Lord that alcohol is not good for man. We must take a stand against liquor by the drink and any and every other move that would make liquor more easily available. (196.)

The Wages of Sin

We must remember that Satan is always on the job, determined to destroy the work of the Lord and to destroy mankind, and as soon as we deviate from the path of righteousness, we are in great danger of being destroyed. The scriptures and history give us many examples of men in high places who, when they turned from and despised the teachings of the Lord, or in any way deviated from the path of righteousness, suffered much sorrow, loss of position, loss of friends and even family. (151.)

A Philosophy of Happiness

We are all like Adam in that when we partake of "forbidden fruits" or do the things we are commanded not to do, we are ashamed, and we draw away from the Church and from God and hide ourselves, and if we continue in sin, the Spirit of God withdraws from us. There is no

happiness in disobedience or sin. We have all learned from our childhood that we are happier when we are doing right. (147.)

The greatest achievement in life is not the acquisition of money,
position, or power. In my opinion, it is to come to the end of one's day
having been true and loyal to his ideals. I can think of no achievement
greater than that. (98.)

Life here and hereafter is one continual existence, premortal to
postmortal, without a break in this endless chain. As we go from one
stage to another, we must realize that all we can take with us is ourselves—that is, our intelligence, character, and experience. (98.)

To enjoy life to the full, one cannot neglect the spiritual side. We
must acknowledge God as the giver of all things, as the Creator of the
earth and the universe, and as the Father of our spirits, and realize that
he has given a plan of life that will lead us to salvation. (112.)

Lessons in Church Administration

As I speak to groups of Saints throughout the world, I often think
and wonder about those out there who are not with us, who are not a
part of the group because they think they are not wanted, understood,
or loved.

There are in every ward and branch persons of all ages who,
though they would deny it, are hungry for attention, for fellowship, for
an active life in the Church.

Let us all—as leaders and as disciples of Christ—always remember
and never forget that everyone is looking for happiness. Everyone
wants to be happy. It is our great privilege and responsibility to show
them the way to happiness and success. Often some little thing—some
slight or misunderstanding—causes one to become inactive. There are
those who are discouraged and inactive because they have felt neglected or have been offended; or they are guilty of some transgression
of their own and, as a result, feel that they are outcasts or that there is
no place for them, that they are not worthy or wanted. They feel that
they are lost and cannot be forgiven. We must let them know and make
them know that we love them, and we must help them to understand
that the Lord loves them and that he will forgive them if they will truly
repent. (48.)

When I was a stake president, we had a very able young man who had been trained in agriculture, and we needed an agricultural adviser on our welfare committee. He wasn't active in the Church. I knew that he wasn't keeping the Word of Wisdom, but I called and asked him to go to lunch with me one day; and as we sat and talked, I told him what I wanted of him. I said, "You are the best prepared, most able young man to do this job. We need you and you need activity."

We talked for some time, and he said "Well, President Tanner, you know that I don't keep the Word of Wisdom."

I said, "Well, you can, can't you?"

And he said, "President, that is a different approach. My bishop came to me last month and asked me if I would take a job in the ward. I told him that I wasn't keeping the Word of Wisdom. And he said, 'Well, then, we will get somebody else.'"

So I talked with him for a little while longer, and I said, "Listen, brother, you need activity in the Church, but we also need you—we really need you."

After we had talked a little while he said, "Do you mean that if I took a position like this I couldn't even have a cup of coffee?"

I said, "Yes, that is exactly what I mean. Any leader must be a leader, and you must be an example. If you are taken into a stake committee, we would expect you to live the gospel the way a man should live it."

He said, "Well, then, I shall have to think it over."

I said, "You think it over. But remember, you need activity, and we need you."

He said, "I will let you know."

He didn't call me the next day, nor the next day, nor the day after that. By the sixth day I thought, well, he doesn't want to admit that he can't keep the Word of Wisdom.

On the eighth day he called. He said, "President Tanner, do you still want me for that job?"

I said, "Yes, that is the reason I called you and talked to you about it the other day."

He said, "Then I will do it, and on your terms."

And he did it, and he did it on my terms. He was a single man, thirty-some years of age. He came into activity, and there was a young woman who was stake MIA president, a very fine young woman. He met her and became very well acquainted with her and fell in love with her and married her.

And then he became a bishop, and then a high councilor, and then a member of the stake presidency. You know, it has given me a great deal of satisfaction to know that that young man became active, and he now has children who are also active. (50-51.)

I would like to challenge every leader in the Church to determine that he or she will begin actively to bring some young person or older person into activity. There is nothing more important in our whole lives than to save souls. We have programs and we have planning outlines for teachers, and we give them teacher development training and all those things to take care of those who are attending, but I fear too often we are forgetting and neglecting and ignoring those who are not always there, satisfied to say we had 50 percent or 60 percent in attendance.

I don't care at all for percentages or statistics, but I do care for the individual, that person who is outside. I appeal to every person in the Church, particularly those who hold office, to set about to do as the Lord has said: to find that lost sheep and bring him back into the fold, so that we will find joy with him when we meet our Heavenly Father. (52.)

When we try to judge people, which we should not do, we have a great tendency to look for and take pride in finding weaknesses and faults, such as vanity, dishonesty, immorality, and intrigue. As a result, we see only the worst side of those being judged.

Our news media today also seem to be interested mainly in controversial subjects or someone who is being attacked; and regardless of the ninety-nine good things one may do, it is the one weakness or error that alone is emphasized and heralded to the world.

We are too prone to listen to, accept, and repeat such adverse criticism, such maliciously spoken or printed words, without stopping to realize the harm we may be doing to some noble person; and, as is done so often, we excuse and justify ourselves by saying, "Well, where there is so much smoke, there must be some fire," whereas in reality we are adding to the smoke, when the fire referred to may be only the fire of malice started by some envious person.

Sometimes even when our friends are accused of wrongdoing or gossip is started about them, we disloyally accept and repeat what we hear without knowing the facts. It is sad indeed that sometimes friendships are destroyed and enmity created on the basis of misinformation.

If there be one place in life where the attitude of the agnostic is acceptable, it is in this matter of judging. It is the courage to say, "I don't know. I am waiting for further evidence. I must hear both sides of the question."

Only by suspending judgment do we exhibit real charity. (56-57.)

Are we truly interested in and concerned with the well-being of our neighbors? Do we visit the widows and fatherless, and feed, clothe, and comfort the poor and needy? The prophet Alma in his day "saw great inequality among the people, some lifting themselves up with their pride, despising others, turning their backs upon the needy and the naked and those who were hungry, and those who were athirst, and those who were sick and afflicted."

We read: "Now this was a great cause for lamentations among the people, while others were . . . succoring those who stood in need of their succor, such as imparting their substance to the poor and the needy, feeding the hungry. . . ." (Alma 4:12-13).

Recent changes in their structure and program now enable our Relief Society sisters to devote more of their time and energy to the main purposes for which they were organized—namely, to look after the spiritual, mental, and moral welfare of the mothers and daughters in Zion. They should be teaching the gospel, preparing our women of all ages to be better homemakers, and giving compassionate service, yet there are still many who are sick or lonely or in need of comfort who are not reached. We all should be seeking for opportunities to give aid and comfort to the needy among us. (67.)

Because I believe that Christ is born and is really the begotten Son of God in the flesh, and others do not, is no cause for ill feelings, hate, or lack of brotherhood. Because I believe, as a Mormon, or you as a Catholic, you as a Protestant, or you as a Jew, we should not shun or criticize or have ill feelings, but should respect each other in his views, realizing that everyone's belief in God makes him a better man, a better citizen, to the extent that he follows God's teachings—particularly, as the Savior said, "Love one another, as I have loved you." (76.)

My philosophy has been: Don't be afraid to accept responsibilities if others think you have the ability to do a job and have confidence in you. When you set to work, dedicate yourself to the thing at hand. All you can do are the things you are expected to do, putting first things first, and realizing that anything that is worth doing is worth doing well. (16.)

The most difficult thing for us seems to be to give of ourselves, to do away with selfishness. If we really love someone, nothing is a hardship. Nothing is hard for us to do for that individual. There is no real happiness in having or getting, but only in giving. Half the world seems to be following the wrong scent in the pursuit of happiness. They think it consists in having and getting, and in having others serve them, but really it consists in giving and serving others. (41-42.)

President David O. McKay

My first association with President David O. McKay was when he was a counselor to President Heber J. Grant in the First Presidency and I was bishop of the Cardston First Ward in Canada. I met with him at stake conference and then at an outing at Waterton Lakes, where I was able to observe him in a capacity other than in church administration and saw how he enjoyed nature and fishing with the boys. He was a real sport.

When I went to Edmonton as a member of the Alberta government, I realized that there was very little missionary work being done in western Canada, and since President McKay was in charge of the missionary work of the Church, I began to correspond with him regarding the need for a mission being established in the western provinces.

My correspondence with him at that time helped me realize how keenly interested he was in mankind and their welfare and, as anyone would expect, in the building of the kingdom of God. A mission was finally established with headquarters in Edmonton, and I continued to correspond with him and talk to him as it was getting established.

My call as a General Authority, and then particularly as a counselor in the First Presidency, gave me an exceptional opportunity for close association with him, to partake of his spirit, and to see how the Lord worked and directed the Church through him as his mouthpiece. This was a privilege and honor extended to few men, and one for which I am most humbly grateful and appreciative. (254-55.)

A leading official of the General Motors Corporation once made a courtesy call on President McKay. As he left the building, he turned to the gentleman who accompanied him to the office and said, "There is the most Godlike man I have ever met. If you wanted to make a man in the image of God, there is the pattern." (259.)

It has been a signal honor, privilege, and blessing, and a most rewarding experience for me to have been called by the President of the Church and to act as one of his counselors, and for six glorious years to sit in counsel with him, to feel of his great spirit, and to have been taught and inspired by the Lord's anointed, his mouthpiece here upon the earth. The messages that he asked me to take to the members of the Church wherever I went, and that meant so much to me, were, "Remember who you are and act accordingly," and "Remember that you have an individual responsibility." (262.)

President David O. McKay was a prophet of God through whom the Lord spoke. He knew and bore testimony that God lives and that Jesus is the Christ and gave his life for us. He believed it and he knew it and I know it, and I bear testimony to this effect. This is the Church of Jesus Christ, and if we follow our leaders and live the gospel as given to us in these, the latter days, we will enjoy immortality and eternal life, and while we are preparing ourselves, we will enjoy mortal life more nearly to the full and have greater success and happiness along the way. (263-64.)

Missionary Service

It was thrilling to see in the stake and missions in the Orient how missionaries were able to bring people into the Church, people who were regarded very highly. One convert was a university professor; another, a successful businessman; two, outstanding doctors, one of whom was a heart surgeon. It was most humbling to see how these men praised the work of the young men who had brought them into the Church and influenced their lives, and they bore testimony of the great things that the gospel has done for them since they joined the Church.

I appeal to the bishops and stake presidents to see that these young men, when they return from their tours of duty, have an opportunity to serve.

And to the young men: Your study and your devotion and experience have prepared you for real service in the work of the Lord. Thank the Lord for the privilege you have had of testing in your lives and improving your testimony. Never feel that you have finished or completed your tour of duty in church service. You have only prepared yourself to be of further service in the work of the Lord. Seek and accept opportunities to serve. Never return to the old gang. Be an example. Let the young girls and boys see what a mission will do for a young man, and never let them down. These youth in the wards and stakes, when you return, will look up to you and expect great things of you; and if you live as you should, you will influence their lives for good, as much as you have the lives of those with whom you have come in contact when you were in the service—the service of your country or the service of the Lord.

Encourage these young men with whom you meet when you come home to prepare themselves for missions, temple marriage, and the blessings that are available to faithful members of the Church. Help them to overcome evil and temptations, to appreciate the priesthood that they hold, and to sustain their leaders. (199-200.)

Some Keys to Successful Service

When I was president of the Trans-Canada Pipelines, we had a messenger boy but needed a second one. The new boy, a widow's son, was a bright young fellow who was interested in all that was going on and always had his eyes open to see how he could be helpful. He wanted to serve and assist others and learn what he could about the business. He was not trying to be president of the company, but he was trying to be the best messenger boy it was possible to be and attended night school to be better educated. Everybody liked him. He had only been there a few months when one of the supervisors who had observed him wanted him to come with him, so he was advanced to a more responsible position. Before the end of the year he had another advancement, and he will continue to advance because of his attitude. He was prepared to go the extra mile. He was interested in his company and wanted to be of service and was dependable in every way. The other messenger boy was still there as a messenger boy when I left. Of course, he felt that the company didn't appreciate him and his ability. This type of individual usually complains and asks why he is treated so shabbily and why the management doesn't appreciate him and treat him more fairly. (236-37.)

I should like to give you an example of . . an experience I had when I was Minister of Mines in the Province of Alberta. One afternoon during a session of the legislature, I called in the head accountant of the department and asked him to prepare some information for me so I might answer questions that had been asked in the legislature. I told him I needed the information by three o'clock the next afternoon. He said, "It will take some doing, but we will do what we can."

The next morning when I arrived at the office he was standing at my door with the information in his hand. I said, "I thought you said this would take some doing." He replied, "The three of us stayed here all night to get this material for you."

I had noted before how devoted he was and how anxious he was to be of service, but this was proof without doubt of his integrity and devotion and of his willingness to go the extra mile. It was not long before he was made Assistant Deputy Minister of the department, then Deputy Minister, then chairman of the Conservation Board of the Province, and then chairman of the Energy Board for all of Canada. All this because he was prepared to do his work and then some. Men and things automatically find their places according to their size. A change in size and qualifications will automatically result in a change of place. (235-36.)

To be successful and happy in this life and to gain eternal life, one must prepare himself through training for his chosen vocation. He must be competent, honest, truthful, willing, and the good citizen. (238.)

I would like to suggest to all young people everywhere that if you prepare yourselves to stand against and meet opposition, any temptation, anything serious, you can face it and overcome it. You know, it isn't the mountain you climb that gets you down; it's the sand in your shoes. The little things that come into your life have to be watched—that is where we have to be careful. If we really want to be successful, we have to see that the little things are taken care of. (12.)

Let us not forget that a young man or a young woman of character, industry, faith, intelligence, and loyalty will always be at a premium, and will always be able to find a good place or make one when he can truthfully say: "As for me and my house, we will serve the Lord," and truly seek first the kingdom of God and his righteousness, knowing that all things for his good will be added unto him. (213.)

Public Service: The Example of Ernest C. Manning

As one assumes or accepts public service, he must be prepared to discipline himself and keep himself above reproach. I had the good fortune of working very closely with the premier of Alberta, who is an excellent example of the miracle of personality. This was the Honorable E. C. Manning. He was born and raised on a farm in a rural area of Saskatchewan in a very humble home. In fact, he worked on the farm with his overalls being held together by a nail. However, he had high ideals. He became interested in religion and his fellowmen. He set out to learn all he could about the Bible and how to improve conditions in the country. He worked and studied and prepared until the public became aware of the kind of person he was. He was elected to the Alberta Legislature when he was only twenty-seven years old and appointed to the Cabinet the same year as the youngest minister ever to hold a cabinet position in the British Empire. He later became leader of the political party and Premier of the Province. He was a man of great integrity. People from all political parties respected and trusted him to the extent they crossed party lines and voted for him. As a result, his party remained in power for thirty-five years with him as Premier until he voluntarily resigned. Even while he was Premier, with all the heavy responsibilities of his position, he preached from the Bible every Sunday over radio throughout Canada. He was 100 percent trustworthy and sincere, with no hypocrisy of any kind. When he resigned as Premier of the Province, the Federal Government, of a different political party, showed its confidence in him by appointing him as Senator of Canada. This is an honorary lifetime position. (114-15.)

Woman: A Special Being

From the beginning God has made it clear that woman is very special, and he has also very clearly defined her position, her duties, and her destiny in the divine plan. Paul said that man is the image and glory of God; that woman is the glory of man; and that the man is not without the woman, neither the woman without the man in the Lord. You will note that significantly God is mentioned in connection with this great partnership, and we must never forget that one of woman's greatest privileges, blessings, and opportunities is to be a co-partner with God in bringing his spirit children into the world. (215.)

The girls of today will be the women of tomorrow, and it is necessary that they prepare for that role. Can you imagine the kind of world we will have in the future if the girls of today are weakened morally to the extent that virtue will not be taught in their homes, and if their children, if any, are not nurtured within the walls of homes sanctified by the holy laws of matrimony? (216.)

Women, you are of great strength and support to the men in your lives, and they sometimes need your help most when they are least deserving. A man can have no greater incentive, no greater hope, no greater strength than to know that his mother, his sweetheart, or his wife has confidence in him and loves him. And men should strive every day to live worthy of that love and confidence. (218.)

A mother has far greater influence on her children than anyone else, and she must realize that every word she speaks, every act, every response, her attitude, even her appearance and manner of dress affect the lives of her children and the whole family. It is while the child is in the home that he gains from his mother the attitudes, hopes, and beliefs that will determine the kind of life he will live and the contribution he will make to society. (217.)

And girls, don't underestimate your influence on your brothers and your sweethearts. As you live worthy of their love and respect, you can help greatly to determine that they will be clean and virtuous, successful and happy. Always remember that you can go much further on respect than on popularity. (218-19.)

To mothers, daughters, and women everywhere, let me stress the fact that because of your great potential and influence for good in the lives of all of us, Satan is determined to destroy you. You cannot compromise with him. You must have the courage, the strength, desire, and determination to live as the Lord would have you live—good, clean lives. Girls, keep yourselves virtuous and worthy of a fine young man who has likewise kept himself clean, so that together you can go to the house of the Lord to be sealed in the holy bonds of matrimony for time and all eternity, and prepare a home where God will be pleased to send his spirit children. Then you will be able to face your children secure in the knowledge that your own example is the way to happiness and eternal progression. They are entitled to this heritage. I humbly pray that you will so live as to give it to them. (219.)

Satan and his cohorts are using scientific arguments and nefarious propaganda to lure women away from their primary responsibilities as wives, mothers, and homemakers. We hear so much about emancipation, independence, sexual liberation, birth control, abortion, and other insidious propaganda belittling the role of motherhood, all of which is Satan's way of destroying woman, the home, and the family—the basic unit of society.

Some effective tools include the use of radio, television, and magazines, where pornography abounds and where women are being debased and disgracefully used as sex symbols—"sex-ploited," some call it. Immodest dress, drugs, and alcohol daily take a tremendous toll through the destruction of virtue and chastity and even lives. With modern electronic devices of communication and speedy transportation, much more is being heard throughout the world and by many more people than would be possible otherwise, and it is having its degrading influence and effect. (215.)

The whole purpose of the creation of the earth was to provide a dwelling place where the spirit children of God might come and be clothed in mortal bodies and, by keeping their second estate, prepare themselves for salvation and exaltation. The whole purpose of the mission of Jesus Christ was to make possible the immortality and eternal life of man. The whole purpose of mothers and fathers should be to live worthy of this blessing and to assist God the Father and his Son Jesus Christ in their work. No greater honor could be given to women than to assist in this divine plan, and I wish to say without equivocation that a woman will find greater satisfaction and joy and make a greater contribution to mankind by being a wise and worthy mother raising good children than she could make in any other vocation. (219-20.)

Girls, prepare yourselves to assume the role of mother by gaining knowledge and wisdom through a good education. We teach that the glory of God is intelligence, and so we must all be aware of what is going on around us and prepared to thwart Satan in his attempts to divert us from our divine destiny. With knowledge, wisdom, determination, and the Spirit of the Lord to help us, we can succeed.

We also believe that women should involve themselves in community affairs and in the auxiliary organizations of the Church, but always remembering that home and children come first and must not be neglected. Children must be made to feel that mother loves them and is keenly interested in their welfare and everything they do. This cannot be turned over to someone else. Many experiments have been made and studies carried out which prove beyond doubt that a child who enjoys his mother's love and care progresses in every way much more rapidly than one who is left in an institution or with others where mother's love is not available or expressed.

Fathers too must assume their proper role and responsibility. Children need both parents. While they are at home fathers should assume with mothers the duties attendant upon the young children, the discipline and training of the older ones, and be a listening ear for those who need to discuss their problems or who want guidance and counseling. Through love, establish a good relationship and line of communication with your children. (221-22.)

As women realize the importance of the home and family, and with their husbands keep the commandments of God to multiply and replenish the earth, to love the Lord and their neighbors as themselves, to teach their children to pray and to walk uprightly before him, then will their joy be increased and their blessings multiplied to the extent that they will hardly be able to contain them. (223.)

A Happy Marriage

A happy marriage is never handed to a couple on a silver platter, but it is something we have to build continually. If each will think of the other's convenience, comfort, needs, and happiness, and determine to see the best in each other, try to understand and express love for each other, there will be true love and harmony in the home.

Yes, the only slogan we need in order to be happy in our home is: Love Each Other—three simple words. Apply the ingredients of love. Sacrifice for each other. Make each other happy. If this were always uppermost in our minds, we would have very little trouble indeed. If there is love between the father and the mother, there will be love between the parents and the children and among the children. One cannot overemphasize the importance and value of being courteous, kind, considerate, and polite in the home. (41.)

Education

In our fast-growing industrial society and scientific world, education has become a necessity. In order to obtain dignified and profitable employment, one must be well trained. It is becoming more and more difficult for the common laborer to find employment, and it is becoming more and more important that one be well trained in some field. We strongly urge all of our young people to continue in some form of study after leaving high school. (229.)

Today we find industry searching for well-trained technical students, while in many other professions it is most difficult to find employment. Let us remember and emphasize that attending a technical school is no reflection on anyone and that those who do so train are in very great demand. Brigham Young, who was himself a painter and glazier, reportedly said: "I believe in education, but I want to see the boys and girls come out with an education at their fingers' end as well as in their brains." (230.)

Today our technical colleges provide training in drafting, electronics, farm technology, secretarial and office skills, technical and mechanical skills, medical assistance, photography, computer programming, and many other subjects. Then we have specialized schools offering training in art, music, drama, electronics, and business. In order to choose wisely the best academic program for the future, one should seek guidance from his parents and from a qualified counselor if one is available. He can also get good advice from talking to those who are engaged in the occupation that appeals to him. Having chosen, he should then select a good school that is recognized as such by industry. (231.)

I was interested to read of an occasion when a university professor addressed a group of students who had just closed their college life, and at a final dinner before separating to go their various ways, he said, referring to the furnishings and services which graced the banquet table, "Take this tablecloth. It is of most exquisite workmanship. It involved weaving, bleaching, smoothing, designing. It is damask linen. Is there anyone here who knows from personal experience anything about the labor involved? Have any of you ever contributed any labor to the manufacturing of table linen? Let me draw your attention to the samples of pottery here. Surely the men and women who produce such beautiful things are artists. What a joy it must be for a man to hold a thing in his hand—complete—and say, "I made it." Many forms of labor are involved here, also—digging the clay, carting, fashioning, painting, burning, baking, and finishing."

He then called attention to the cut glass, the silver, the rugs, the carpet, the curtains and drapery, and the mural decorations. He continued, "Here we are, then, a group of men on whom a university has set its stamp. We produce nothing to eat; we could not even lend a hand in the making of anything we see around us; and truth compels me to venture the suggestion that, in ninety-nine cases out of a hundred, the chief motive of a college education is to escape actual participation in just such work as gives, or ought to give, joy to the worker.

"I do not believe that a smattering of languages, of mathematics, and of history is education. I believe the system of cramming these things to pass an examination is pernicious." Then he said, "Why should men consider it degrading to handle tools and make useful and beautiful things?"

He concluded his remarks to his spellbound audience with these words: "Gentlemen, as one example, I wish it were possible for me to introduce to you a young Galilean carpenter, the master builder—Jesus of Nazareth." (231-32.)

Tributes to Father and Mother

As I look back over my life, I should like to pay tribute to and thank my father and my bishop—who was the same man—for the direction and help and guidance and example he gave me all the time I was growing up. He continually taught me: ". . . seek ye first the kingdom of

341

God, and his righteousness; and all these things shall be added unto you." (Matthew 6:33.) He explained to me that "all these things" meant everything that would be for my good, and I am very grateful for learning in my youth that it is not always good for us to have everything we want or think we want. Disciplining ourselves to want only those things that are right for us to have and discerning between the right and the wrong things are part of the training that every young person should experience. My father guided me along these lines. . . .

As I think back over the experiences I had with that wonderful man, and my home training given by my father and mother, I can't help giving them practically all the credit for directing me and teaching me to believe that if I would seek first the kingdom of God and his righteousness, all other things for my good would be added unto me. That was a great lesson for me to learn. (1-2.)

Father taught me many lessons. He used to say, "It is better to aim at the moon and miss it, than aim at nothing and hit it." In other words, set up your goals and strive to get there. If you just barely miss them or if you miss by quite a bit, it is better than aiming at nothing and hitting it.

Another thing he used to say was, "Now, if you want your dreams to come true, you'd better wake up." (11.)

His Mayflower Ancestry

My people came to this, the American continent, in the Mayflower: three of them were on that boat. They came because of their convictions, because they were prepared to sacrifice anything they had—their lives, if necessary—to gain the freedom to live and worship God according to the dictates of their own consciences. I am so thankful that I can trace my genealogy back to them and know that they were that kind of people. (7.)

Counsel for Parents

Great doubt is raised in the mind of a child whose parents profess one thing and do another; where they profess to be Christians and believe in God, but do nothing about it. Elijah came unto the people and said, "How long halt ye between two opinions? If the Lord be God, follow him: but if Baal, then follow him." (1 Kings 18:21.) The Lord has said, "If ye love me, keep my commandments."

Appendix III: Gems of Thought

Children should be taught and trained to honor their father and their mother. Their parents gave them life and cared for them when they could not care for themselves. Every child of every age should love and honor his parents. It is much easier, however, for children to do this if the parents live worthy of the honor of their children and are always an example to them, and wield a real influence for good in their lives. (212.)

It would be most helpful if parents would sit down and discuss with the whole family what they want out of life; what they want to accomplish; and how they can help one another in doing it. After this decision is made, it will be necessary for all of them to answer the questions: Is it worth the effort, or am I prepared to do my part? Can I discipline myself, or have I the will power? Then, each and every one must make up his mind, accept his obligations, and go forward with determination, realizing that it will bring the greatest joy and satisfaction and success in life. (211.)

Parents have no responsibility greater than that of teaching and training their children to be honest, honorable, and righteous citizens; and there is no stronger, more effective way of doing it than for the parent to be what he would like his son or daughter to be. What a great day it will be for the world and the Church when every father and son will do and be what he would like the other to think he is. In other words, father should always try to put himself in the position where he would be glad to have his son say, "I do nothing save that which I have seen my father do." The same applies to mothers and daughters. (212.)

There would be no need of forcing our children to attend Sunday School and church if we as parents attend regularly, because that would be just a part of their lives, and children like to be with their parents. It is difficult for children to understand why they should go to Sunday School or church when their parents feel it is more important or interesting for them to go fishing or golfing. Our Lord and Master has said, "Thou shalt go the house of prayer and offer up thy sacraments upon my holy day." (D&C 59:9.) (208.)

We never gain anything or improve our own character by trying to tear down another. We have seen close friendships destroyed through words spoken and accusations made in the heat of a campaign. Tirades against men in office or against one's opponent tend to cause our youth and others to lose faith in the individual and others in government and often even our form of government itself. As parents, we have the responsibility in our homes to guard against any of these things. (60.)

It is the manner of our living and not the words we use to explain it that makes up the moral fiber of the children God has given us. We should never be surprised if our children grow up to be like us. Therefore, we must take the time to be the kind of people we would like our children to be. (212.)

As members of a family we should be bound together and loyal to one another. In the family we should be taught respect for the feelings of one another and for the feelings and ideals and beliefs of people in other families. What a great strength to the community, the state, and the nation if we would act as brothers. (73.)

Don't let us be fooled or misled by the claim extant in the world today that restraints and conventions are damaging to the psyche of a child. In promoting a permissive and unrestricted society, they would have a child undisciplined for misbehavior. This is a false premise, and we are better advised to heed the counsel of the Lord when he said:

"And again, inasmuch as parents have children in Zion, or in any of her stakes which are organized, that teach them not to understand the doctrine of repentance, faith in Christ the Son of the living God, and of baptism and the gift of the Holy Ghost by the laying on of the hands, when eight years old, the sin be upon the heads of the parents.

"And they shall also teach their children to pray, and to walk uprightly before the Lord." (D&C 68:25, 28.)

Children do not learn by themselves how to distinguish right from wrong. Parents have to determine the child's readiness to assume responsibility and his capacity to make sound decisions, to evaluate alternatives, and the results of doing so. (86-87.)

Though we hear much of the juvenile deliquent, I have every confidence in our youth, and I often wish that I could live long enough to see how much better they administer public affairs than they are being administered today. However, they need guidance, example, courage, and discipline. (105-6.)

Children who are taught obedience, to honor and obey the law, to have faith in God, and to keep his commandments, will, as they grow up, honor their parents and be a credit to them; and they will be able to meet and solve their problems, find greater success and joy in life, and contribute greatly to the solution of the problems now causing the world such great concern. It is up to the parents to see to it that their children are prepared through obedience to law for the positions of leadership they will occupy in the future, where their responsibility will be to bring peace and righteousness to the world. (123.)

Family Prayer

Family prayer in any home will draw the family closer together and result in better feelings between father and mother, between parents and children, and between one child and another. (162.)

I shall never be able to express fully my appreciation to my parents for teaching me to pray secretly and to participate with them in family prayer. My mother taught me at her knee. She made me feel and know that I was talking to the Lord, to our Maker, our Father in heaven, and that he was conscious of my acts and my wishes and my needs. I was taught that I should express my sincere thanks, ask for forgiveness, and ask for strength to do the right. This has always been a great strength to me throughout my life, and today I pray even more diligently than I ever did before that the Lord will guide and direct me in my activities, that whatever I do will be acceptable to him. (161.)

I remember very well a father coming to me one day regarding his oldest son, with whom he was having some difficulty. The boy was a good boy, but he was getting out of hand. I asked the father if they had regular family prayers in their home. He answered, "Well, no, but sometimes. You know, we are too busy and we go to work at different times, and therefore it is most difficult for our family to get together for family prayer."
I asked, "If you knew that your boy was sick nigh unto death, would you be able to get your family together each night and morning for a week to pray that his life might be spared?"
"Why, of course," he said.
I tried then to explain to him that there are other ways of losing a boy than by death. I also explained that where families pray together, they usually stay together, and their ideals are higher, they feel more secure, and they have a greater love for one another. (162-63.)

Family Home Evening

One of the finest programs the Church has instituted is what we call family home evening, where all members of the family are called together once a week. It is quite thrilling to me when I contemplate that each Monday evening, all over the Church throughout the world, our families are gathered together in their homes, and the father, where possible, as head of the house, is directing his family in a discussion of problems pertaining to their spiritual and temporal welfare, using a manual that has been carefully prepared and distributed to each family in the Church. Where these gatherings are held regularly and properly, they are of inestimable value to the family unit, as is evidenced by the many testimonies we receive. I wish to urge every family to follow this program, and I can promise you that as you do so, you will be greatly blessed in unity, love, and devotion and will be delighted with the outcome. Of course, family prayer should be a significant part of this evening, as well as regular family and individual prayer every day. (220-21.)

The Meaning of Christmas

The real meaning and spirit of Christmas is to commemorate the birth of Christ and to remind ourselves of the great message of joy and peace on earth, goodwill toward men, which Jesus brought to all mankind. It is a time when families get together and enjoy one another's companionship and a happy family reunion. Love is demonstrated at Christmas more than at any other time of the year. We forget our differences with one another and endeavor to follow the example of Christ and his teachings, and in so doing we find real joy and happiness and can truly have a merry Christmas. (35.)

Ancestry Chart

Nathan Eldon Tanner
b. 9 May 1898
Salt Lake City, Utah
md. 20 Dec. 1919
Sara Isabelle Merrill

Parents

Nathan William Tanner
b. 19 Oct. 1870
Summit (Wanship), Utah
md. 28 Apr. 1897
d. 12 June 1948

Sarah Edna Brown
b. 20 Sep. 1878
Salt Lake City, Utah
d. 24 Nov. 1959

Grandparents

John William Tanner
b. 6 Nov. 1841
Montrose, Iowa
md. 19 Mar. 1864
d. 13 Jan. 1893

(Roena) Lucy Rhona Snyder
b. 28 Aug. 1848
St. Joseph, Mo.
d. 22 Dec. 1917

Homer Manley Brown
b. 10 June 1854
Salt Lake City, Utah
md. 22 Nov. 1875
d. 2 Feb. 1936

Lydia Jane Brown
b. 10 Aug. 1855
Ogden, Utah
d. 3 June 1935

Great-grandparents

Nathan Tanner Sr.
b. 14 May 1815
d. 17 Dec. 1910

Rachel Winter Smith
b. 1 May 1818
d. 7 Nov. 1896

George Gideon Snyder
b. 19 June 1819
d. 11 Mar. 1887

Sarah Wilder Hatch
b. 2 Nov. 1821
d. 12 Oct. 1861

Homer Brown
b. 9 Aug. 1830
d. 12 June 1905

Sarah Ann Woolf
b. 2 July 1833
d. 14 Oct. 1911

James Stephens Brown
b. 4 July 1828
d. 25 Mar. 1902

Lydia Jane Tanner
b. 27 Jan. 1838
d. 3 Nov. 1872

Great-great-grandparents

John Tanner
b. 15 Aug. 1778

Lydia Stewart (or Stuart)

William Smith
b. 8 Nov. 1779

Lydia Jane Corkin (or Calkins)

Isaac Snyder
b. 17 Apr. 1840

Lovisa Comstock

Wilder Hatch
b. 10 Aug. 1799

Mehitable Barker

Benjamin Brown
b. 30 Sep. 1794

Sarah Mumford

John A. Woolf Jr.
b. 31 July 1805

Sarah Ann Devoe

Daniel Brown
b. 30 June 1804

Elizabeth Stephens

Nathan Tanner Sr.
b. 14 May 1815

Rachel Winter Smith

Selected Bibliography

Books and Monographs

Alberta Legislative Assembly. *Journals of the Legislative Assembly.* Edmonton, 1936-52.

Barr, John J. *The Dynasty: The Rise and Fall of Social Credit in Alberta.* Toronto: McClelland and Stewart, 1974.

Brown, James S. *Giant of the Lord: Life of a Pioneer.* Salt Lake City: George Q. Cannon & Sons, 1900; reprint ed., Salt Lake City: Bookcraft, 1960.

Campbell, Eugene E., and Poll, Richard D. *Hugh B. Brown: His Life and Thought.* Salt Lake City: Bookcraft, 1975.

Gould, Edwin O. *Oil: The History of Canada's Oil and Gas Industry.* Seattle: Hancock House, 1976.

Gray, Earl. *The Great Canadian Oil Patch.* Toronto: MacLean-Hunter, Ltd., 1970.

Irving, John A. *The Social Credit Movement in Alberta.* Toronto: University of Toronto Press, 1959.

Johnson, L. P. V., and MacNutt, Ola J. *Aberhart of Alberta.* Edmonton: Institute of Applied Art, 1970.

Kilbourne, William. *Pipeline: Trans-Canada and the Great Debate, A History of Business and Politics.* Toronto and Vancouver: Clarke, Irwin & Company, Ltd., 1970.

Macpherson, C. B. *Democracy in Alberta: The Theory and Practice of a Quasi Party System.* Toronto: University of Toronto Press, 1953.

Mallory, J. R. *Social Credit and the Federal Power in Canada.* Toronto: University of Toronto Press, 1954.

Mann, W. E. *Sect, Cult and Church in Alberta.* Toronto: University of Toronto Press, 1955.

Tagg, Melvin S. "A History of The Church of Jesus Christ of Latter-day Saints in Canada, 1830-1963." Ph.D. dissertation, Brigham Young University, 1963.

Tanner, George S. *John Tanner and His Family.* Salt Lake City: John Tanner Family Association, 1974.

Tanner, Maurice. *Descendants of John Tanner.* Phoenix: Tanner Family Association, 1942.

Tanner, N. Eldon. *Seek Ye First the Kingdom of God.* Compiled by LaRue Sneff. Salt Lake City: Deseret Book Company, 1973.

Thomas, Lewis H., ed. *William Aberhart and Social Credit in Alberta.* Vancouver: Copp Clark Publishing, 1977.

Articles in Periodicals

"Ancient Sea: High-Grade Iron Ore in the U.S. Is Running Out but Canada Has Great Deposits." *Colliers* 130 (August 9, 1952): 68-73.

Arrington, Leonard J., "The John Tanner Family." *Ensign* 9 (March 1979): 46-51.

"At 82, President Tanner Looks Back Over an Eventful Lifetime of Service to Church and Nation." *Salt Lake Tribune,* July 27, 1980, p. 16B.

Brown, Hugh B. "President N. Eldon Tanner, A Man of Integrity." *Ensign* 2 (November 1972): 12-19.

——————. "The Fight Between Good and Evil." *Improvement Era* 66 (December 1963): 1058-59.

"Canada Seeks Policy on Exporting Energy." *Business Week,* January 25, 1958, pp. 158-59.

Esplin, Fred C. "The Church as Broadcaster." *Dialogue: A Journal of Mormon Thought* 10 (Spring 1977): 25-45.

Evans, Richard L., and Green, Doyle L. "Nathan Eldon Tanner of the Council of the Twelve." *Improvement Era* 66 (January 1963): 17-21, 39-40.

Lyon, T. Edgar. "The Current Restoration of Nauvoo, Illinois." *Dialogue: A Journal of Mormon Thought* 5 (Spring 1970): 12-25.

McMurrin, Sterling M. "A Note on the 1963 Civil Rights Statement." *Dialogue: A Journal of Mormon Thought* (Summer 1979): 60-63.

"Mormons: The Negro Question." *Time,* October 18, 1963, pp. 40-41.

Murray, Herbert F. "A Half Century of Broadcasting in the Church." *Ensign* 2 (August 1972): 48-51.

"N. Eldon Tanner of the First Presidency." *Improvement Era* 69 (November 1966): 984.

"Pipeline Gamble." *Time,* June 18, 1956, p. 40.

Schultz, Harold J. "Aberhart: The Organization Man." *Alberta Historical Review* 7 (Spring 1959): 19-26.

Selected Bibliography

——————. "Portrait of a Premier: William Aberhart." *Canadian Historical Review* 45 (September 1964): 185-211.

——————. "A Second Term: 1940." *Alberta Historical Review* 10 (Winter 1962): 17-26.

Tanner, N. Eldon. "Administration of the Restored Church." *1977 Devotional Speeches of the Year* (Provo: Brigham Young University Press, 1978), pp. 201-9. See also *Ensign* 8 (April 1978): 71-76. This message was also given in general conference in October 1979: Conference Report, October 1979, pp. 60-70.

——————. Conference Report, October 1962, pp. 68-69.

——————. Conference Report, October 1963, pp. 12-14.

——————. Conference Report, April 1965, pp. 93-96. See also the same series April and October, subsequent years through 1981.

——————. "My Experiences and Observations." *BYU Speeches of the Year* (Provo: Brigham Young University Press, 1966). The BYU speeches in 1966 were published separately as pamphlets.

"Toronto Contract Points to Completion of Financing for Trans-Canada Pipeline." *Business Week*, October 27, 1956, p. 194.

Wright, Paul. "Nathan Eldon Tanner Facing Major Hurdle in His Career." *Western Business and Industry*, May 1956, pp. 16-18.

Note on Additional Periodical and Newspaper Sources

President Tanner's public career in Canada is reported and reflected in hundreds of newspaper, magazine, and related sources. *New York Times Index* for the years 1951-60 alone contains nearly four hundred entries indexed under such headings as "Tanner, N. Eldon" (e.g., "Minister Tanner Reports Five Companies to Begin Exploration of Athabasca Tar Sands, March 16, 1959"), "Manning, Ernest C.," "Oil and Gas Development—Canada" (some 265 items, 1951-60), "Trans-Canada Pipeline" (over eighty items, 1951-60). *Reader's Guide to Periodical Literature*, 1930-60, has some two hundred entries. Several of these articles from *Time, Newsweek, Business Week,* and other magazines are listed in the footnotes and bibliography accompanying the present study. The two hundred entries refer to Premiers Aberhart and Manning as well as to N. Eldon Tanner, oil and gas development, the Social Credit Party, and Trans-Canada Pipeline. A profile of President Tanner appeared in *Fortune* 54 (July 1956): 41.

Newspapers containing broad coverage and editorial comment relating to President Tanner's activities, besides the Salt Lake *Tribune, Deseret News,* and *Church News,* include, especially for the period 1935 to 1960, the Calgary *Herald,* the Calgary *Albertan,* the Cardston *News,* the Edmonton *Bulletin,* and the Edmonton *Journal.* For the period 1952-1960, reference may also be made to the Toronto *Star, Saturday Night,* and the Ottawa *Citizen* for journalistic reports of President Tanner's activities. Clippings of many newspaper articles relating to President Tanner's career are found in his personal scrapbooks. Other material was examined and abstracted by Steven L. Olsen of the Historical Department staff during a June 1981 visit to Calgary and Edmonton.

Oral Histories

The following are typescripts relating to President N. Eldon Tanner in the James Moyle Oral History Program, Archives, Historical Department of The Church of Jesus Christ of Latter-day Saints, Salt Lake City, Utah.

Blodgett, J. Alan. Oral History. Interviewed by Gordon Irving. Salt Lake City, Utah, 1981.

Brooks, Willard M. Oral History. Interviewed by Charles Ursenbach. Cardston and Calgary, Alberta, 1974-75.

Bullock, D. Bruce. Oral History. Interviewed by Charles Ursenbach. Calgary, Alberta, 1979.

Dunn, J. Howard. Oral History. Interviewed by Gordon Irving. Salt Lake City, Utah, 1981.

Hanson, Wallace R. Oral History. Interviewed by Charles Ursenbach. Calgary, Alberta, 1973.

Irving, Gordon. Dictation regarding conversation with W. Irwin Tanner. Salt Lake City, Utah, 1981.

Jensen, Isabelle Tanner. Oral History. Interviewed by Gordon Irving. Salt Lake City, Utah, 1981.

astler, Bernard Z. Oral History. Interviewed by Gordon Irving. Salt Lake City, Utah, 1981.

Kirton, Wilford W., Jr. Oral History. Interviewed by Gordon Irving. Salt Lake City, Utah, 1981.

Manning, Ernest C. Oral History. Interviewed by Steven L. Olsen. Edmonton, Alberta, 1981.

Pilling, Doral William. Oral History. Interviewed by Charles Ursenbach. Calgary, Alberta, 1975.

Saks, James C. Dictation. Calgary, Alberta, 1979.

Smith, Douglas H. Oral History. Interviewed by Gordon Irving. Salt Lake City, Utah, 1981.

Sneff, M. LaRue. Oral History. Interviewed by Gordon Irving. Salt Lake City, Utah, 1981.

Spackman, Beth Tanner. Oral History. Interviewed by Charles Ursenbach. Calgary, Alberta, 1979.

Tanner, N. Eldon. Oral History. Interviewed by Davis Bitton. Salt Lake City, Utah, 1972.

————————. Oral History. Interviewed by Charles Ursenbach. Waterton, Alberta, and Salt Lake City, Utah, 1973.

Tanner, Violet H. Oral History. Interviewed by Charles Ursenbach. Cardston, Alberta, 1974.

Ursenbach, Charles. Oral History. Interviewed by William G. Hartley. Salt Lake City, Utah, 1973.

————————. Oral History. Interviewed by Gordon Irving. Salt Lake City, Utah, 1981.

Wood, Vi A. Oral History. Interviewed by Charles Ursenbach. Edmonton, Alberta, 1973.

Unpublished Materials on File in Church Archives

Calgary Stake. Manuscript History.
Cardston Ward. Manuscript History.
Edmonton Branch. Manuscript History.
Lethbridge Stake. Manuscript History.
Western Canadian Mission. Manuscript History.

Manuscripts and Other Unpublished Materials

Beaton, Helen T. "My Father: Nathan Eldon Tanner." Transcript of talk given in Phoenix, Arizona, 1979.

Brown, Victor L. "Tribute to President Tanner." Remarks at presentation of "Executive of the Year" award to N. Eldon Tanner. Brigham Young University, January 29, 1980.

Lee, Harold B. Diary, November 14, 1953. Copy of entry provided by L. Brent Goates from diary in his possession.

Livingstone, Mary C. "N. E. Tanner."

Salt Lake City Area Chamber of Commerce. "Giant in Our City" program. March 29, 1978. Tape recording.

Tanner, Ida C. "Life Sketch of Nathan W. Tanner."

Tanner, N. Eldon. Address at organization of London Stake, February 26, 1961. Tape recording.

————————. Life Story. Dictated to Ruth T. Walker. Leatherhead, England, 1962.

————————. "Tannerisms." Sayings compiled by Northeast British Mission staff, 1965. Edited by Doris D. Smith.

Tanner, Sara M. Life Story. Dictated to Ruth T. Walker. Leatherhead, England, 1962.

Walker, John. "The Political Life of Nathan Eldon Tanner." Term paper written at Brigham Young University, 1980.

Walker, Ruth Tanner. "My Father." Transcript of talk given at Brigham Young University, June 12, 1980.

Wolsey, Heber G. Memorandum, March 1981.

Zion's Cooperative Mercantile Institution. "A Century of Service." Salt Lake City, Utah, 1968. Tape recording.

Index

Index

Index

Index

365

Index

Index

Index

Walker, Cliff (son-in-law of NET), 100, 122, 127, 135-36, 141
Walker, Ruth Tanner (daughter of NET): on grandparents, 16; on dependability of NET, 17; birth and babysitting of, 27-28; discipline of, 38; in family milk business, 40; goes to New York with NET, 100; activity of, in Edmonton Branch, 115; on responsibility of daughters, 125; education of, 126; marriage of, 127; sends Beth money, 127; tends sisters, 130; and husband move to Calgary, 133; on integrity of NET, 135; on dependability, 136; on call of NET to First Presidency, 202; on humor of NET, 302-3; on testimony of NET, 306
Washington National Symphony, 245
Waterton National Park, 43
Welch, Jay, 243
Western Canadian Mission, 116-17, 131
Western European Mission, 186-87, 189-93, 195, 220
Western Pipe Lines, Ltd., 143-45
Westminster College, 280-81, 284
Wheat production in Alberta, 51
"White Hayes" house, 187

White House, 245-47
Widtsoe, John A., 96, 116, 119
Widtsoe, Leah D., 96
Wildlife resources of Alberta, 88-89, 101
Wilkinson, Ernest L., 233-34, 259
Williams, Lowell L., 127
Williams, Ora, 134
Williams, Stirling, 6
Wirthlin, Joseph B., 293
Wolsey, Heber, 29-31
Woman, NET quotations on, 337-39
Wood, A. L., 34
Wood, Vi A., 107, 114, 116-17
Woolf, John A., 6
Woolf, Ken, 21
Woolley, Grant, 48, 121-22
World War II, 79, 82, 116-17, 131, 136
Wright, H. E., 57

Young, Brigham, 214, 233, 274
Young, Clifford E., 117
Young, George Cannon, 233
Young, Gladys Pratt, 132
Young, S. Dilworth, 132

ZCMI, 207-8, 244, 271, 285
Zundell, Isaac E. D., 6